What in the World is God Doing?

What in the World is God Doing?

Is There Any Rhyme or Reason?

Roger E. Tuinstra

What in the World is God Doing?

Copyright © 2020 by Roger E. Tuinstra

Image Rights: Maxim Evdokimov, © 123rf.com

Unless otherwise noted, Scripture quotations are from the ESV® Bible (The Holy Bible, English Standard Version®), copyright © 2001 by Crossway, a publishing ministry of Good News Publishers. Used by permission. All rights reserved.

Scripture quotations marked NKJV are from the New King James Version. Copyright © 1982 by Thomas Nelson, Inc. Used by permission. All rights reserved.

ISBN-13: 978-1-6982-7995-4

Dedication

To my wife, Ruth, who with great patience, support and partnership, has made it possible for me to study, think, and teach the Bible for over fifty years. This book is the fruit of all that study as well as our joint efforts to raise our children and to teach them the ways of God as revealed in his Word. God has given Ruth a tremendous amount of practical wisdom in the application of the Word to everyday living. Those practical insights have helped give life to the academic aspects of my Bible teaching so that, Lord willing, the results can bless the lives of all who read and think about what I've written here.

I also want to dedicate this book to the rest of my family: Tim, Kelly, Iain, Owen, Eben, Aldrin, Mike, Reneé, Nathaniel, Hannah, Lydia, Sarah, Elisabeth, Jonathan, Miriam, Jason, Erin, Drew, Adam, and Ellie. It is my prayer that the things that I have learned in over 65 years of Christian growth, and that I have summarized in this work, will help strengthen your faith, and help equip you to live in, and be a witness to, a culture that does not understand that there is Rhyme and Reason in the universe and a purpose to it all. I love you all very much!

One last dedication is in order. I owe a great debt of gratitude to my dad, Rev. Gerald Tuinstra, for his deliberate and steadfast Bible teaching. It was his faithful teaching that captured the attention of my heart and pointed it to the inerrant and infallible Word of God.

Table of Contents

Preface

This book has been in the works for some forty years. The concepts I've tried to express here began to come together at the beginning, but because of personal growth and continued study, they've become clearer as time has gone by. As I have read, studied, and taught the Bible, it has become obvious to me that God has an overarching purpose in what he is doing. Sometimes, however, it is hard to figure out what that purpose is because the Bible covers such a large span of time and includes several different genres of literature. Why is God so often portrayed in the Old Testament as harsh, but Jesus seems gentle and loving? How is God's plan revealed in such diverse literary forms as narrative and poetry, or letters and prophecy? The Bible contains stories of warriors and kings, prophets and priests, nomads and city-dwellers, but God's eternal purpose is woven through it all. I believe that in order to live a life that is both fulfilling and pleasing to God, we need to know and understand that purpose, and live according to it.

My wife, Ruth, and I have three children with their spouses and fourteen grandchildren. As we have progressed along in life, the burden to share with the rest of the family what we have learned in life has grown steadily. Given our age, we have a sense of urgency in completing this project. I want them all, but especially the grandchildren, to understand what God is up to. Why is life so beautiful and yet so often a struggle? Is history going anywhere? I want my family to have a good understanding of these things.

Because our grandchildren are the primary audience for this book, I have written it so that a teenager ought to be able to understand it. But I also want anyone who happens upon this work to be able to understand it without needing a college education. So if you're looking for a theologically rigorous, highly technical book that might pass for a Master of Divinity thesis, you're looking in the wrong place.

If you are one of those people asking the question, "What in the world is God doing?", I am hoping and praying that the biblical teaching that I've explained here will encourage your heart, increase your faith, and give glory to God, who does, in fact, have an eternal purpose for it all.

Acknowledgements

I would like to use this space to acknowledge the tireless efforts of our friends, Doug and Jami Bond, and to thank them for their editorial and personal advice throughout the final stages of rereading and editing this book. This husband and wife team volunteered many, many hours to help edit my grammar and to help clarify the more ambiguous portions of this work. Their knowledge of the English language as well as their deep understanding of the message that God has given us in His Word were invaluable to me during the editing phase. They faithfully prayed over their efforts, asking for God's guidance and wisdom as they tried to faithfully maintain my voice and message as they edited my work. Thank you very much, my good friends!

I would also like to acknowledge the efforts of my sister-in-law, Wendy Balzer, who, while struggling in her fight against cancer, volunteered to use her skill and experience to help in the editing process as well. Thank you, Wendy!

Introductory
Philosophy and Foundation

*[**Important Introductory Note**: The tone of this introductory section is different from that of the rest of the book. Therefore, if you find that it is hard to understand, or doesn't connect with the way you think, feel free to skip to Chapter 1. But I hope you won't do that, because I believe these ideas are important to wrestle with as we search for truth. This first section provides what I call the philosophy and foundation for the rest of the book. It is introductory, but it is more than that. Everyone builds his or her worldview on some underlying philosophy. Even if that philosophy is not structured or clearly articulated, we each build a worldview on what we have heard, or read, or experienced. In this section, I talk about logic, truth, and how we come to know what we know. So, let's get started! Remember, if you get bogged down, move on to Chapter 1.]*

This book is about the question, "What is God doing?" and "Why?" Another way to phrase it is, "What is the plan or overall purpose for this life – the world, human beings, my life?" Is there a purpose? I believe there is. Throughout our discussion of this question, I am going to be talking a lot about truth, reason, creation, the Bible, and God. Just like everyone else who thinks about these things, I make assumptions that cannot be proven. No one knows firsthand how things began because none of us was there. We all see the same world, investigate the same fossils and have the same books available to us. But we have different interpretations because of what we assume. So, before we begin our journey into God's purposes for mankind, I'd like to explain some of the underlying principles upon which I base my thinking. This is especially important for younger readers. This is, after all, a book which I hope will be read by my grandchildren during their teen years.

As we move about in our culture, we are bombarded with many different viewpoints and philosophies. These may come through school, social interactions, TV, and social media. Some of these ideas appear to have a great deal of wisdom, and sometimes they will present ideas that seem to make more sense than what we learned at home or church. This chapter is meant to help you put these philosophies into proper perspective as you consider what God presents in the Bible as his eternal plan.

The first thing that I would have you think about is the concept of truth. What does it mean that a statement is true? It means that the statement matches what exists. If someone says, "The grass is green," the statement is true if the grass is actually there and it's green. That seems obvious enough, but there are those who would try to confuse you by saying that "green" is a word and not a color. It's just a description of a color. Or, they might say that your idea of green may be different from someone else's. Don't get all tangled up in those kinds of arguments. If you do, you will suddenly find that it is impossible to communicate at all because no one could or would know what anyone means. But in the normal flow of daily life, we communicate successfully all the time. We all know what we mean when we say, "The grass is green."

Take another statement. If someone says, "God exists," that statement is also either true or false. It is a proposition. He is either there or he is not. When the Bible quotes Jesus as having said something, it means the Bible is claiming that on some particular day in history Jesus actually said those things. We use the same kind of true and false statements when we are talking about religious events as when we are talking about anything else.

All of this may seem obvious, but there are those who say that something can be true for you but not necessarily true for me. Someone will say that if you believe in God, that might be true for you, but if someone else doesn't believe, then for them there is no God. But that is not what true or false means. If God is actually there, then denying his existence is a false belief. But it works the other way around as well. If there is no God, then when someone says, "There is no God," he is speaking the truth. It's important for us as Christians to think it through and ask ourselves if we really believe our religious statements are true. We sometimes get carried away with religious jargon and forget that what we are claiming is actually true and that we are living in that reality. It's not a myth or fairy tale.

This leads us to the next important idea and that is that there are logical truths. For example, a thing and its opposite cannot both be true. Four can't be four and five at the same time. In fact, four can never be five! Hopefully your reaction is, "Of course!" It can't be light and dark at the same time in the same place. A statement can't be both true and false at the same time.

There are many rules of logic that could be studied, but for now I will share one family of rules that I think is rather important. The best way to describe this is to use an example. I will make several statements, not all of which are true, but I want to define a couple of words for you so that we can discuss them.

Let's start with the following statement:
If the animal is a dog, then it has four legs.

This is obviously a true statement for normal healthy dogs.

But what about this statement:

If the animal is not a dog, then it does not have four legs.

This is called the *inverse* of the original. The inverse is constructed by leaving the sentence in the same order and adding the word "not." You can see in this example that this inverse is false. Just because an animal is not a dog, doesn't mean it doesn't have four legs. So, if you hear an original statement and then reword it as an inverse, the new statement is not necessarily true. It might be, but it doesn't have to be.

3

What about this one: *If the animal has four legs, then it is a dog.*

This is called the *converse* of the original statement. The converse is constructed by switching the first and last part of the sentence. We moved "legs" to the beginning and "dog" to the end. And, of course, this is false also. So what we've seen is that if a statement is true, both the inverse and the converse might be false. You can't know for sure unless you learn it from some other statement.

Then there's this one: *If the animal does not have four legs, then it is not a dog.*

This is called the *contrapositive* of the original. For this one we switched the two ends of the statement and inserted "not." We moved "legs" to the beginning and "dog" to the end and put the word "not" in the sentence. This statement is true.

Now here's the principle: If the original statement is true, the contrapositive statement will always be true. The inverse and converse will not necessarily be true as you could see from the previous examples.

Why is this important? It's important because people misuse these rules all the time and in so doing become illogical and make false statements without knowing it. Sometimes they do it on purpose to deceive. Sometimes they do it by accident and draw false conclusions. It's very easy to draw false conclusions if you're not careful. Suppose John says, "If it's raining Saturday, I'll come help you." On Saturday he shows up. What can you conclude? Did you assume it must be raining, at least where John was? Let's check it out.

Our four statements are as follows:

Original:	If it's raining, I'll come.	True
Inverse:	If it's not raining, I won't come.	Possibly False
Converse:	If I come, it's raining.	Possibly False
Contrapositive:	If I don't come, it's not raining.	True

4

Since he showed up on Saturday, can you assume it's raining? No, because this situation is represented by the converse and is not necessarily true. The converse is, "If I come help you, then it's raining." The original statement and the converse are not necessarily both true. The statement that would have been true is, "If I don't come on Saturday, it's not raining."

I'm sorry if this seems complicated, but it is an important concept to understand. Here's an example from the Bible:

Jesus said, "*If you love me you will keep my commandments.*" If you see that someone keeps Jesus' commandments, does that mean he loves Jesus? No, not necessarily. That again is using the converse which is not necessarily true. The inverse, which is also not necessarily true is, "*If you don't love me, you won't keep my commandments.*" Some people work really hard at keeping Jesus' commands for some other completely different motive than love. If an original statement is true, the only other statement that <u>must</u> be true is the contrapositive. In the case of Jesus' statement, the contrapositive would be, "*If you don't keep my commandments then you don't love me.*"

Sometimes people will try to argue the inverse which basically puts a "not" in each part of the original statement. Let's look at another Biblical example. "*If we confess our sins, God will forgive.*" The inverse is, "*If we don't confess our sins, God won't forgive us.*" This isn't logically true. I say not "logically true" because you can't draw that conclusion from the original statement. It might be true if Scripture verifies it somewhere else. Sometimes the Bible will make a statement that is true and then will also give you the inverse which it says is also true. In that kind of situation, the original, the inverse, the converse and the contrapositive will all be true. Here's an example of that:

Mark 11:25, 26 And whenever you stand praying, if you have anything against anyone, forgive him, that your Father in heaven may also forgive you your trespasses. [26] But if you do not forgive, neither will your Father in heaven forgive your trespasses.

Notice the two parts:

If you forgive, then your Father will forgive you. This statement alone doesn't tell us whether the inverse, *"If you don't forgive, then your Father won't forgive,"* is true. But the Scripture specifically tells you in verse 26 that the inverse is also true.

I don't mean to belabor this, but it's important in life, and it's important in interpreting what the Bible says in order to be sure you don't draw conclusions that aren't logically consistent. God is a logical being and he created us in his image so that we can communicate with others and hear the communication which he has given us in his Word.

There are those who believe that logic is something that was invented in the western world, i.e., Europe and the United States, by white men, and that other kinds of logic which don't follow these "rules" are just as true and valid. But the use of logic in science and mathematics has produced tremendous results and benefits for mankind throughout the world. Logic works because it's true. And in spite of what many people think, the Bible uses this kind of logic all of the time; the Bible is not a "western" book nor a modern one. It seems to me that God thinks this way.

There are those who say that what is true depends on your perspective, your viewpoint, the angle at which you are looking at something. Since everyone's perspective is different, they say, truth for everyone is different. People who think like this often are of the opinion that there are no foundational truths at all. But what they don't realize or don't want to admit is that a perspective from one angle does not falsify or negate the reality of that object. The object is there, and although it appears differently when looked at from various angles, it nevertheless has its own existence. Philosophers say we have nowhere to stand where we can get the right perspective on truth. That might be the case for us, but it is not the case for God. God certainly is in that position and he can explain things from his perspective. Some say that since we as humans can't find the neutral point, we can't know anything for sure. If this were the case, we wouldn't be able to make progress in any area at all. Knowledge as we know it would come to a screeching halt. I take the position that truth exists and that we can know things *truly*, even if we cannot know them *completely*. We may not be able to find a place to stand where we have the right perspective on everything. But God certainly is in that position. And he can explain things from his perspective.

The next important thing we need to look at is the question of how we know what we know. In philosophy this is called *epistemology*. There are three basic ways we know anything. We know first of all from firsthand observation. That is one of the first ways we begin to learn as children. We observe what is going on around us, and we gain knowledge from what we see, touch, feel, smell, and hear. The second way we gain knowledge is from what someone else tells us. The someone we learn from can be a living person right there with us such as a parent or teacher. Or the person we learn from could be an author through a book we are reading. The final method is through scientific experiment which is really a variation of the first method of observation. Scientists perform carefully controlled experiments and then observe either directly or through instruments what happens. From repeated observations and experiments, we gain knowledge. Most often then, these observers report what they have discovered by passing along that information to others in a classroom or in writing.

As we discussed earlier, there are those who deny that we can know anything for sure. They believe that we will always have some bias or prejudice in what we observe, and therefore our observations are distorted. They also believe it is not possible to communicate clearly and without bias, and therefore we end up not really knowing what we think we know. Their arguments sound smooth, intellectual and enticing, but do not give in to them. If they do not believe they know anything or that they can communicate anything, why do they write so many books and try to convince you that knowledge of truth does not exist? If what they say is true, then it is false. Why? Because if we can't know anything and can't communicate anything, then they don't know what they are trying to communicate, and they can't be sure any of us will hear the message they are sending. But we know from our day to day experience that we do know things and we can communicate information. We may not know everything perfectly, and we may not communicate perfectly, but we are able to know and communicate at a level that allows us to understand each other, and that enables culture to develop, knowledge to increase, and both of these to spread.

In the case of the topic we are studying in this book – the subject of God and his plan – we have to be humble enough to realize and admit that we don't know everything about God. But just because we can't know everything doesn't mean we can't know anything for sure.

When it comes to gaining knowledge, one of our most important methods is reading. Of course, this is just another form of gaining knowledge from someone else, in this case the author of the book or article. It's interesting to note that the God of the Bible is focused on words. God spoke the worlds into existence with the words, "Let there be...." The Ten Commandments were written down by God himself. The Bible claims that all Scripture is given by inspiration of God and is profitable (2 Timothy 3:16). In the Old Testament period, prophets gathered the people together and read to them (Nehemiah 8). In the New Testament Jesus asks, "Have you not read?" at least six times. So we see that words and reading are central to God's way of communicating.

Hebrews 1:1, 2 tells us:

> God, who at various times and in various ways spoke in time past to the fathers by the prophets, has in these last days spoken to us by His Son, whom He has appointed heir of all things, through whom also He made the worlds (NKJV).

John tells us in his Gospel, "*In the beginning was the Word, and the Word was with God, and the Word was God*" (John 1:1). And then in verse 14 he writes, "*And the Word became flesh and dwelt among us.*" Jesus Christ is The Word, and he is God's essential message of communication to us. God is a God of words!

As we proceed through this study, we will be relying on reading what the Bible tells us about God and his plan for the ages. This is how we come to know what happened in the past and what is in the mind of the creator as he continues to work in history.

The next thing we need to understand is that much of what we believe to be true is based upon our *presuppositions*. Notice I said, "believe to be true." Presuppositions are statements or ideas we believe are true without being able to prove them. We assume them. Even in math and science there are things we believe are true, and we build our logic on top of them. I once had a class where we assumed that the number 1 existed and that the next counting number could be found by adding 1 to a previous number. From there we had to build our mathematics using very careful logic. But the interesting thing is that we had to assume some things. The important thing to understand is that everyone does this! When someone comes to you with an argument that contradicts a deeply held belief of yours, remember that that person has some assumptions that he has not and cannot prove. It's helpful to try to find out what those are. You can continually press the question, "How do you know that?" But remember, you have presuppositions too, and need to ask yourself that same question.

Sometimes we are led to believe that an atheist is arguing from a more objective position because he does not start out believing in some god or supreme being. He's supposedly going to just look at the factual evidence and base his decisions on what he discovers. But the atheist is starting from the presupposition that he's an independent observer, standing alone in the world, and that there is no God who created him or the universe. He cannot prove any of that, but it is his starting position. Similarly, when some scientists are investigating the origin of the universe or life, they assume that there is no God. But isn't that really a closed-minded approach? Information and evidence may be missed because they have ruled out certain information in advance. They have presuppositions. But we do, too. It cannot be avoided. Everyone has them.

The concept of presuppositions is important when we go back to think about how we learn what we know. I'm intrigued by what people believe when confronted with a news article. For example, during the George W. Bush administration, the President asserted that Sadam Hussein had weapons of mass destruction. My purpose here is not to get into the politics of this but just to observe that a large segment of the population believed this was a false statement. Another large group believed it was true. I know I'm oversimplifying a more complex situation, but it seems to me it all comes down to the presuppositions someone has about the truthfulness of the President. Those who believe he is a liar believed he lied about the weapons. Those who believe he was honest believed that the weapons existed. None of us regular people knew the president personally or had any inside knowledge about weapons. We learned from news reports and then we evaluated those reports based on our presuppositions. But the important thing to remember is that what we believed didn't change whether those weapons existed or not. We believe certain things are true, but how hard we believe them or how long we have held that belief does not change the truth of whether something exists or not. The goal is to find what is actually true and base our beliefs on those truths and keep our presuppositions to a minimum.

The same principle is true when we consider how we learn about history. We weren't around to observe events in history. So, how do we know Lincoln was really assassinated? How do we know men really set foot on the moon? When we are reading a book on history, we may take the writer's perspective at face value. If we have some presuppositions about the events, we will apply those. Maybe we've had some negative experiences with the author, and so we will distrust what the author writes. If it is a subject we are very interested in, we will read many books covering the same events and will draw our conclusions based on what we have read filtered through our presuppositions. The more we investigate and read, the more some of our initial presuppositions may change to fit the truth that begins to become clear as the learning continues.

In the same way, that is how I want us to read the Bible. Remove as many presuppositions as you can and read it for what it actually says. It needs to be treated the same way we treat other texts, testing its ideas against what we already know about life and history. The more these match up, the more sure we are that what we are reading is the truth.

The last thing I want us to think about in this introductory chapter is the question of origins. When we begin to talk about God's plan for the world, we need to include the creation event because that's where history begins. How do we know what happened? How do we get at the truth? The problem is that no one was there in the beginning except God. The only way to "know" what happened is through one of the three methods I've already explained. We either had to be there to observe what happened, and that approach is obviously out of the question. We need someone who was there to tell us what happened. And no one alive today can do that. Or we need to read an account of what happened written by someone who was there. If we don't have any of these options, our only other option is to investigate traces of evidence of past events that may still linger in archeological or geological digs or in astronomical evidence. People who believe a Creator made all of this, and people who believe it all evolved by natural processes both have the same evidence to examine. The difference is how it is interpreted, and the interpretation they bring to the evidence is based on their presuppositions. In the case of origins, it is not possible to do an experiment to repeat the event because those initial conditions cannot be replicated. We would need to have a universe at our disposal and billions of years to carry out our experiment. Obviously, that's not possible.

The crucial question is whether there is a God that did the creating or whether it all happened by random, unguided chance. The Bible says that God was there in the beginning, but the theory of evolution presumes that he was not. The Christian's starting presupposition is that God exists. One of the two views is wrong. There either is a God or there is not. Believing or not believing does not change whether God is there or not. If he's there, all the disbelief in the world is not going to change that. If he's not there, all the faith in the world is not going to create him!

The naturalistic theory of evolution makes our existence on the earth nothing but the result of blind and random chance. That is, at some time in the past there was a big bang which propelled all the matter of the universe out from one point. There was no plan involved and no one caused it; it just happened. Over time, pieces cooled to form planets. Some of the material coalesced and became stars. Over millions of years, various atoms collided with other atoms and gradually, accidentally, without any intelligent guidance, life came into being and eventually evolved into the forms of life we see today, and among those, you and me.

But there are some troublesome presuppositions in the naturalistic view. Where did the matter and energy come from which caused the big bang? Had they always existed, or did they appear from nothing? You will have a very difficult time finding a scientist who believes that once there was absolutely nothing – no energy, no matter, nothing – and then -poof- there was something. There has always been something or someone. Christians claim that God has always been here. Naturalists believe that matter or energy or both have always been here. The interesting thing is that we can't prove it one way or the other. Either view has to be taken on faith. Why does one person choose one belief and another person the other? It's a matter of deeply held presuppositions and it's a matter of faith. There isn't place in this book to go into all of the evidence, but it seems ludicrous to me that all of what we see around us including all of the existing life forms have arisen by chance through random genetic mutations. The DNA is of such complexity that multiple functions would have had to evolve at the same time to create life. Moreover, most mutations result in the death of the organism, not improvement of the species. If you believe in the creation account in the Bible, you don't need to be intimidated by the thought that your faith is unfounded and superstitious. Everyone has faith, and it seems to me that the faith it takes to believe in evolution is a much more unsupported and illogical faith than believing in an intelligent creator.

If we are here because of indeterminate random events as evolutionists claim, then there is no pattern or plan, no right or wrong, no meaning to life and no purpose other than the purpose we individually bring to our lives. And that really is the worldview of this age, isn't it? We are told we are autonomous self-defined beings. We are merely a higher form of animal. The plants and animals and we humans have resulted from random, purposeless, mindless chance events. How we live and what we consider good or bad, moral or immoral, beautiful or ugly are a result of our own personal choices or the rules of society as a whole as we evolved over time. Ultimately, according to evolutionists, these feelings and thoughts are merely electrical and chemical impulses running on neurons in our nervous system. Determining whether a particular course of action is right or wrong depends then on whether it is good for mankind or the world in general or ourselves in particular. But then, who makes the decision as to what good is? Who is going to decide? And all of these decisions are claimed to be the result of electronic impulses traveling down neurons in our brains that were put together randomly!

If there is no God, we can do anything which we believe will serve our best interests. Our best interests might be interpreted as personal best interests or whatever is best for the human race as a whole. If there is no God and we are just highly developed animals, then experimentation on fetal tissue could well be defended as providing some benefits for the human race. If God did not create us in his image, then we could justify hiring women to carry fetuses to a certain stage of development and then abort them so that experiments can be conducted. There would be nothing wrong with that. If there is no God caring for his creation, there is nothing wrong with injecting our elderly with death-inducing drugs so that they don't have to suffer through Alzheimer's disease or other ailments which afflict them. If we are indeed on our own, what is "right" for one period of time, may be "wrong" at some other time. There is no ultimate authority to which we can go to determine the right thing to do in any circumstance. And this is exactly what some people profess. And this is where our entire culture is going: life on our own terms, life without God.

You will often hear the argument that what's right or wrong is a personal matter until it affects someone else. This is because individual human autonomy is the key value in our culture. What you do is only wrong when it harms someone else. But how do we know that this is an absolute rule? Who is the author of that rule? We just invented that idea. Is that the majority opinion? Some people and cultures don't believe this. What makes us think that this is true? And why do we even think there is such a thing as right or wrong? Where did that idea come from? Why would such an idea even enter our heads?

Some will say that throughout the course of human history there has been a core set of values that most cultures acknowledge as being right. Things such as not stealing from one another and not killing one another are almost universal values. But if you try to use the same argument to show that marriage is the union of a man and a woman because it is almost universally true, your argument will be immediately demolished as archaic and invalid. But if the idea of universal values holds true for murder, it holds true for marriage as well. One can't have it both ways.

The questions and conclusions I've just described are not an argument for God. His existence doesn't depend on them. Just because I've raised these questions doesn't prove there must be a God. They are simply conclusions that we are forced to come to if he's not there. The problem is that no one can live this way. We can't live as though there is no such thing as right or wrong. We can't live as though there is no real meaning or purpose in our existence. Even though someone doesn't believe God exists, he almost always lives as though he does exist. In other words, he lives like there is some fundamental standard that everyone ought to live by and some ultimate purpose behind our existence. We don't all agree what that standard is, but everyone acts like there is a standard. Any time you hear someone say, "He *ought* to have done this or that," you know he is appealing to some absolute standard he believes exists somewhere. If we don't live like this, our only alternative is despair.

In this view, even normal human emotions lose their meaning. What exactly is the beauty of a sunset? Is our experience merely a physical phenomenon, as naturalists would claim or is there something deeper going on? When we "enjoy" a sunset, the various colors of light enter the lens of our eye. The light hitting our retina stimulates chemical and electrical signals that travel to our brain. Our brain responds by sending signals to other places in our body releasing various chemicals that we interpret as awe. We say, "Wow! Look at that." "Beautiful!" Are those just sounds produced by vocal cords that were stimulated by electrical and chemical signals? Is there is no real beauty there? Not according to naturalistic theory. Naturalists, of course, appreciate beauty, but they have to make a giant irrational leap to get beauty and awe out of their belief that we are just electro-chemical machines. Nobody can actually live in a way that is consistent with the naturalistic worldview.

Now what does all of this discussion have to do with our topic? In the succeeding chapters, I hope to show what God is doing and why. How could I or anyone else possibly know this? I don't have any firsthand knowledge of it. I don't claim that God has spoken audibly to me. However, we have the Bible that claims that it is the word of God. Anyone can write a book and have it claim that it is the true word of God. So, the Bible isn't true because it says it is. If it's true, it must be for some other reason.

There is not time nor space to go through all of the evidence, but let it suffice to say that throughout the centuries, the Bible has been accepted and believed by more people than any other book. That doesn't make it true either. But when the Bible is examined historically for accuracy, consistency and reliability in what it claims, it comes across as authentic and believable. It is logically consistent. And ultimately, I work from the presupposition that it is true and see what happens. Usually when you assume something is true and work out all of the consequences, you eventually find out whether your original assumption was correct. It's the kind of indirect proof that we use in mathematics all the time. If you run into contradiction after contradiction, you begin to realize your assumptions are wrong. However, if life, experience, personal testimony, historical facts, and other indicators corroborate your assumptions, then you know you are on the right track.

So what I do is assume the Bible is the truth. Then I assume that it can be understood in the same way we can understand anything else we read. That is how we learn things from books. We read for comprehension. We assume that communication between the author and reader through the written word is possible. We assume that when the Bible claims something is true, that it really is true. When it says Jesus died, that means that on some particular day at some specific time his heart stopped beating and he died. When it says that no one seeks for God, we assume that means that there is not one person who seeks for God on his own initiative. Some Biblical writers use poetic imagery. So, when the Bible says that the trees clapped their hands, we know we are reading poetry. We know intuitively that the Bible is not saying that trees have hands.

As you read this book you will notice that I will bring these concepts back time and time again. We need to understand what "true" means; we need to understand that logic is reliable; we need to understand that the way we "know" what is true is through the common everyday means of our senses and the testimony of

16

others, and finally that everyone, including ourselves, bases his or her beliefs on presuppositions.

With all of this introduction and philosophical foundation out of the way, let's get into the real goal here – to discover the rhyme and reason for our existence. What in the world is God doing, and why is he doing it?

Chapter 1
God Calls a People

What in the world is God doing?! This is the question that underlies the content of this book. If you have read the introductory philosophical chapter, you know that I believe the Bible reveals the truth about the world, about God, and about ourselves. That is our starting point. In this chapter, we take a look at the big picture and then gradually bring it down to where we fit in that picture. The simplified "boiled down" answer to the question, "What in the World is God doing?" can be answered in one short sentence: **He is calling out or gathering together a people for himself from among all the peoples of the earth so that they might be for the praise of his glory.** In Romans 9:23, 24, God says that he is working *"in order to make known the riches of his glory for vessels of mercy, which <u>he has prepared beforehand for glory</u> –even <u>us whom he has called</u>, not from the Jews only but also from the Gentiles"* (emphasis added).

And in Titus 2:13, 14 *"Jesus Christ … gave himself for us to redeem us from all lawlessness and to <u>purify for himself a people for his own possession</u> who are zealous for good works"* (emphasis added).

We will be fleshing out the meaning and implications of this statement as we work our way through this study. Even though the answer is short, the implications are far reaching. We'll need to examine the answers to questions such as "Why is God doing this?"; "What precipitated the necessity for this calling?"; and "How is he going about it?" We will never totally know or understand God's ways. We can only know what he reveals to us through his Word. God says, "*For my thoughts are not your thoughts, neither are your ways my ways, declares the* LORD. *For as the heavens are higher than the earth, so are my ways higher than your ways and my thoughts than your thoughts*" (Isaiah 55:8–9). Let us never forget that. In all of our efforts to understand and describe what God is doing, we must not forget who he is and who we are.

The Bible begins with the fact that God exists and is the creator of everything else. *"In the beginning God created the heavens and the earth"* (Genesis 1:1). Nothing would exist if God had not made it. There would be no earth, no moon, no stars. There would be no oceans and prairies. There would be no fish, no dogs or cats, no birds or animals of any kind. In fact, there would be no atoms, molecules or chemicals. God is the creator of everything, but he himself has always existed. God is what holds everything together (Colossians 1:17). God is totally self-existent. That is, he was not created, and he has no needs. He is totally content and happy. God has never changed. He has never increased or decreased in knowledge or wisdom. Nothing has ever occurred to God because he has always known all there was to know.

Look at these portions of Scripture that describe the power of God and his creative ability:

> Who has measured the waters in the hollow of his hand and marked off the heavens with a span, enclosed the dust of the earth in a measure and weighed the mountains in scales and the hills in a balance? (Isaiah 40:12)

And this passage in Job:

> Where were you when I laid the foundations of the earth? Tell me, if you have understanding. (Job 38:4)

God goes on to describe many of the wonders of creation and to challenge Job to admit that he, a man, cannot do the things God can do; neither can he reason the way God reasons. God is not a man that he should change his mind (Numbers 23:19). Isaiah 40:28 tells us that *"The Lord is the everlasting God, the Creator of the ends of the earth. He does not faint or grow weary; his understanding is unsearchable."*

He is always there and always alert. He understands everything perfectly. He knows how all of our modern inventions work. He knows how our minds function. He knows everything you think and the motivation behind everything you do.

As difficult as this is for us humans to understand, this is the way it is. This is the nature of the universe we live in. The Bible is claiming that this is the truth, the way things really are. These claims require a response. Are they true or false? Will we believe them or not?

What was there before creation? Before anything else existed, God was there. The Bible teaches us that God is spirit, but he is also triune in his nature. That means that he is three persons who are all one God. Each person of the trinity is fully God. He is God the Father, God the Son, and God the Holy Spirit. Knowing this helps us to understand there were personality, love, fellowship, and communication before the world existed. For billions of years, God the Father, God the Son, and God the Holy Spirit were loving, communicating, and sharing their common life together. There is meaning in the universe!

Personality, love, communication, and fellowship are not figments of our imagination. They are not just electronic brain waves as some would have us believe. On the contrary, personality is part of the fundamental nature of God, and hence the fundamental nature of the universe. And since we are created in his image, our personalities are real and not just electrochemical impulses. In John 17:24, Jesus says, "*you* [speaking of God the Father] *loved me before the foundation of the world.*" In that same prayer he asks the Father to glorify him with the same glory that he had with the Father before the world began (17:5). When God created the world, he said, "*Let us make man in our image*" (Genesis 1:26, emphasis added). So in the beginning, the triune God, communicating in love and glory, was all there was.

We also learn from Scripture that before time began, God's plans and decisions had been made. For example, look at the following passages:

The counsel of the LORD stands forever, the plans of his heart to all generations. (Psalm 33:11)

Many are the plans in the mind of a man, but it is the purpose of the Lord that will stand. (Proverbs 19:21)

Remember the former things of old; for I am God, and there is no other; I am God, and there is none like me, declaring the end from the beginning, and from ancient times things not yet done, saying, "My counsel shall stand, and I will accomplish all my purpose." (Isaiah 46:9–10)

And he made from one man every nation of mankind to live on all the face of the earth, having determined allotted periods and the boundaries of their dwelling place. (Acts 17:26)

Even as he chose us in him before the foundation of the world, that we should be holy and blameless before him. (Ephesians 1:4)

In him we have obtained an inheritance, having been predestined according to the purpose of him who works all things according to the counsel of his will. (Ephesians 1:11)

Who saved us and called us to a holy calling, not because of our works but because of his own purpose and grace, which he gave us in Christ Jesus before the ages began. (2 Timothy 1:9)

There was agreement and covenant among the members of the trinity before time began as to how our redemption would be accomplished. The Son agreed to be a participant along with the Father and the Holy Spirit in creating the world and mankind. John 1 tells us that all things were made by the Word. He agreed to become a man and assume human nature (John 1:14; Gal. 4:4-5; Heb. 2:10-15). He agreed to be placed under the law, obey it perfectly, and in spite of perfect obedience, to die to pay the penalty for sin (Ps. 40:8; Matt. 5:17,18; John 8:28, 29; John 10:18; John 17:4; Gal. 4:4,5; Phil. 2:6-8; Heb. 10:7-9). He agreed to provide believers with forgiveness and renewal of their lives through the New Covenant (Luke 22:20; John 17:12, 19-22; Heb. 2:10-13; 7:25). He agreed to give his people eternal life (John 17:2).

And he agreed that he would be a representative of his people (1 Cor. 15:45; Heb. 9:24; Rom. 5:14).

The Father promised that he would prepare a body for him (Luke 1:35; Heb. 10:5). He promised to give the Son everything he needed for his task, including the Spirit, and would support him and deliver him from the power of death (Isa. 42:1-7; 49:8; Ps. 16:8-11; Matt. 12:18; John 3:34; Acts 2:25-28). He promised that he would make the Son the surety or guarantor of the New Covenant (Hebrews 7:22). As a reward for his work, he promised to make him head of the church, his spiritual body (Acts 2:33; 1 Cor. 12:13; Eph. 1:22). He also promised to give him a numerous seed in reward for his work (Ps. 72:17 John 6:37; Romans 5:18-19; Col. 2:9; Heb. 2:13; Isa. 53:10, 11). And finally, he would commit to him all power in heaven and on earth for the government of the world and the church (Matt. 28:18; Eph. 1:20-22; Phil. 2:9-11; Heb. 2:5-9; John 17:4; Col. 1:18).

The Holy Spirit's role was to empower Christ for his ministry (Luke 4:1, 14, 18; John 3:34), and to apply the benefits of Christ's redemptive work to God's people after Jesus left (John 14:16-17, 26; John 15:26; John 16:13-15; Acts 1:8; 2:17-18, 33).[1]

The entirety of this plan and agreement is eternal, meaning wherever you go in eternity past and drop in at that point, you would find the plan already in existence. Nothing that has happened in history is a surprise to God requiring a "Plan B"!

If we shift our gaze from the time before the beginning all the way to the end of time and beyond, what will we see? Of course, the triune God is still there. But if we take a closer look at God, we find that God the Son has become a man. He has a glorified human body. According to his own testimony he has flesh and bones (Luke 24:39). If we look closely, we can see that this man has been wounded. He has wounds in his hands, feet, and side. How is it possible for God to have a body, and more than that, a body that is wounded? And as a man, how did he survive these wounds? Or

---

[1] L. Berkhof, *Systematic Theology,* Wm. B. Eerdmans Publishing Co., 1939, 1941, pp. 269-270.

did he? He is sitting on a throne and is ruling the universe, a universe that wasn't there in the beginning.

But since the beginning, other things have changed as well. There is a heaven and an earth and other objects in the created universe. There are spirit beings such as angels and demons. Also, we see many men and women going about their daily routines worshiping God and involving themselves in a variety of activities, and they look genuinely happy doing so. There doesn't seem to be any sign of anger or frustration on their faces. Here is how the apostle John describes what he saw:

> Then the angel showed me the river of the water of life, bright as crystal, flowing from the throne of God and of the Lamb through the middle of the street of the city; also, on either side of the river, the tree of life with its twelve kinds of fruit, yielding its fruit each month. The leaves of the tree were for the healing of the nations. No longer will there be anything accursed, but the throne of God and of the Lamb will be in it, and his servants will worship him. They will see his face, and his name will be on their foreheads. And night will be no more. They will need no light of lamp or sun, for the Lord God will be their light, and they will reign forever and ever. (Revelation 22:1–5)

In another scene, John describes a song he heard:

> And they sang a new song, saying, "Worthy are you to take the scroll and to open its seals, for you were slain, and by your blood you ransomed people for God from every tribe and language and people and nation, and you have made them a kingdom and priests to our God, and they shall reign on the earth." (Revelation 5:9–10)

We'll come back to this passage later, but for now notice that there are people who have been redeemed to God from every tribe, nation and language on the earth. These are the people who are the object of God's plan for the ages. These are people of all nationalities who are serving both as priests and kings reigning on the earth. Some of these are even serving as judges of angels (1 Corinthians 6:3). Who are these people? That is the question!

As we continue to look and listen to events unfolding toward the end of time, we detect a relationship among all of these people and God the Son. We hear him say that he is not ashamed to call them his brothers (Hebrews 2:11). And then it dawns on us that if these people are brothers of the Son of God, then they also are the sons of God and stand to inherit all the blessings that God gives to his Son (Romans 8:17). We find the people rejoicing that they have been glorified together with him (Colossians 3:4). We hear some of them reminiscing about the day that the Son of God returned to earth in glory and took on the reins of power. Some are testifying to the astounding privilege they were given to appear with him in glory (Colossians 3:4, See also 2 Thess. 1:10, 1 Thess. 2:12). And we even hear the Son of God speaking to his Father referring to himself and the brothers that his Father had given him (Hebrews 2:13).

And finally, as we continue to watch and listen, we learn that all of these people were given to the Son of God by the Father as an inheritance (Ephesians 1:18). This is an amazing thing! A three-person Godhead at the beginning has become God surrounded by a whole host of adopted human beings, beings who were made of dust, now sharing in the glory of the Son of God and partaking of the divine nature (2 Peter 1:4), described as being of one spirit with him (1 Cor. 6:16-17), and being a member of his flesh and bones (Eph. 5:30). God had said many centuries earlier that there would be a people of his planting in whom he would be glorified (Isaiah 60:21). God calls this group *the fullness of him who fills all in all* (Ephesians 1:23). Who fills all in all? God! This group is the fullness of God?!

As we continue to observe what is going on, we realize that all these events are taking place not in heaven alone, but also upon an earth that is bustling with activity. And these men and women who were adopted by God and claimed as brothers to the Son of God are reigning and governing the affairs of the earth. Some are the mayors of cities. Some are the governors of states. There seems to be a great overflowing praise toward God and the extreme love that he has shown to beings who are basically creatures made of dirt. What is going on here?

As we look at this future time more carefully, we also notice a place of punishment and torment. People are crying and wailing in some kind of suffering. There appears to be a fire burning, and people are in unbelievable torment (Rev. 21:8). Why are they there, and what did they do to deserve this? They must certainly have rebelled or offended God in some dramatic way to be suffering in this way. Did the kind and loving Son whom we know as Jesus agree with the punishment they are suffering? Jesus himself told us about this when he was on earth when he said: *"Then he will say to those on his left, 'Depart from me, you cursed, into the eternal fire prepared for the devil and his angels'"* (Matthew 25:41). Something wonderful and something awful have obviously happened between the beginning, when there was only the triune God, and now. What has happened and why?

As we begin to sort out the narrative given to us in the Scripture, we must understand that we could not have invented a God like the one revealed in the Bible. The revealed character of God is so different from our own that we could never have invented a being like him. The character of God is what it is, not because we want him to be that way, but because that is the way he has described himself in the Bible. We're "stuck" with the God we have, not with the god of our own imagination. Most of us are not comfortable with a God who knows everything and who owns everything, including us. Such a God can do with us what he wills, and that is not a comfortable position to be in for most men and women. If God had not created us, we wouldn't be here. We owe our existence to him. Man is not the center of the universe.

The Scripture is very clear as to why God created the universe. Colossians 1:16 tells us that all things were created by him and for him. Psalm 19:1 tells us: *"The heavens declare the glory of God; the sky above proclaims his handiwork."* Paul the apostle, when preaching to the philosophers in Athens, explained it this way:

> The God who made the world and everything in it, being Lord of heaven and earth, does not live in temples made by man, nor is he served by human hands, as though he needed anything, since he himself gives to all mankind life and breath and everything. And he made from one man every nation of mankind to live on all the face of the earth, having *determined* allotted periods and the boundaries of their dwelling place, that they should seek God, and perhaps feel their way toward him and find him. Yet he is actually not far from each one of us, for "In him we live and move and have our being"; as even some of your own poets have said, "For we are indeed his offspring." (Acts 17:24–28, emphasis added.)

God created everything for himself, for his own pleasure and for his own glory. In fact, that is what Proverbs 16:4 says directly: "*The Lord has made all for himself.*" There was no one to impress with his creation at the beginning. You and I often create something with the intention of impressing others. But not so for God. Nothing else existed besides God. He simply wanted to create for his own enjoyment. (For a beautiful description of creation and God's enjoyment of it, read Psalm 104.) If we are the product of God's creative ability, we must recognize that he owns us. We are his. We belong to him. He can do with us as he sees fit.

Some people stumble over the fact that God created everything for his own glory and enjoyment. God doesn't want us to seek our own glory, so why should God be like that? When we do things for our own glory, we are trying to elevate ourselves above our peers. We are saying we are better than they are. But God actually is far superior to his own creation. He has no peers. He is the origin, center, and focus of all that is. There is nothing wrong with God doing whatever he wants for his own enjoyment and glory. When you create something, a painting, a piece of music, a backyard patio, do you have any problem suggesting to your creation that you own it? You made it, and so you can change it, take it apart, get rid of it altogether, or whatever you want. It's your creation. If we were to ask God to value someone else's glory more than his own, whose glory would that be? Some human's? Some angel's? Wouldn't that make God an idolater to bow in submission to the glory of someone else? He wouldn't really be God then, because whoever he was bowing to, or whoever he was praising, would be greater than he is.

God wanted creation to be a perfect expression of his creative ability. He wanted the creation to express his character, ideas, and perfection. He wanted the people he created to have a relationship with him, and to enjoy his goodness and bounty. He wanted his people to enjoy the rest of creation as much as he was enjoying it. He wanted to communicate with them and share his love with them just as the three persons of the trinity were enjoying fellowship and community among themselves. This is an important concept to understand. When God created life, he created human beings in a totally different category from the rest of the animal world. We are created in the image of God. Therefore, we have the ability to create, communicate, love, and understand. We are rational creatures. As such, we can look at the creation God made, and the way he interacts with it, and evaluate it. We have the ability to bring glory to God by our grateful appreciation and thankfulness and praise for what he has accomplished.

In the book of Ephesians. we find this astounding statement: *"So that through the church the manifold wisdom of God might <u>now</u> be made known to the rulers and authorities in the heavenly places. This was according to the <u>eternal purpose</u> that he has realized in Christ Jesus our Lord"* (Ephesians 3:10–11, emphasis added). We also read, *"So that <u>in the coming ages</u> he might show the immeasurable riches of his grace in kindness toward us in Christ Jesus"* (Ephesians 2:7, emphasis added). The people that we saw praising God earlier were told as they were welcomed into the kingdom, *"Come, you who are blessed by my father, inherit the kingdom prepared for you <u>from the foundation of the world</u>"* (Matthew 25:34, emphasis added). These statements show that there is an eternal purpose. God, in eternity past, had a plan and purpose in all that he intended to accomplish through the succeeding ages. And what is that broad purpose? He is going to make known his multifaceted wisdom, and he is going to demonstrate the riches of his grace for all the ages to come. He is going to demonstrate these things to the principalities and powers in the heavenly places. Who are these principalities and powers? They are all of the created spirit beings we now call angels and demons. And what will these principalities and powers see? They will see that God has extended his grace and kindness to a group of beings he had created from dust but who had rebelled against his rule and authority. This is the group he calls his church. The word *church* itself means *the called-out* assembly. We'll be developing all of this throughout this book, but I just want you to picture the broad scheme we have in view.

At the beginning there is the triune God. At the end there is the triune God, along with a group of people who have been showered with grace and kindness, even though they had rebelled against their creator and refused to submit to his authority. This group is now called out to be joined to the second member of the trinity, is heir of all God's kingdom, and will rule and reign with him. And throughout eternity, intense and unending praise will come from the lips of these who could very easily have been subjected to punishment for their rebellion. And when the Son of God returns in all his glory, his people will be glorified with him. He is bringing many sons to glory (Hebrews 2:10). The Son will be glorified in his saints (2 Thessalonians 1:10). Jesus the Son will rejoice because of the glory of the inheritance that he has received in his people (Ephesians 1:18). And the promise is given that when the Son returns, his people will be with him in glory (Colossians 3:4). These people, created from the dust of the ground, now are heirs of God, partakers of the divine nature, and in fellowship with the triune God. Mankind was created by God so that he could live among them. Right now he is in the process of calling and preparing that group of people for himself! And forever, the goal of eternity will be to demonstrate his grace toward these people and to live among them himself.

If you have a Bible handy, turn to Acts 15:14, where you will find a description of an early church council being held in Jerusalem. James is speaking and he says:

> Simon has related how God first visited the Gentiles, to take from them a people for his name. (Acts 15:14)

There you have the purpose. God had focused on the Jewish nation in the Old Testament. But now God is calling out a people from among the Gentiles as well.

All people belong to God in one sense because he made them. But not everyone acknowledges God, is thankful to him, or desires to have a relationship with him. God wants to have a people for his very own prized possession. He desires to have a people upon whom he can lavish his love and favor.

Ever since the fall, God has had a special people. You may recall that the nation of Israel was called of God to be his chosen people. Deuteronomy 7:6-8 tells us:

> For you are a people holy to the LORD your God. The LORD your God has chosen you to be a people for his treasured possession, out of all the peoples who are on the face of the earth. It was not because you were more in number than any other people that the LORD set his love on you and chose you, for you were the fewest of all peoples, but it is because the LORD loves you and is keeping the oath that he swore to your fathers, that the LORD has brought you out with a mighty hand and redeemed you from the house of slavery, from the hand of Pharaoh king of Egypt.

But now God is calling out Gentiles as well. In Romans 9:23 and 24 Paul tells us that God has prepared vessels of mercy to whom he will make known the riches of his glory. Then he quotes from the prophet Hosea:

> Those who were not my people I will call "my people," and her who was not beloved I will call "beloved." And in the very place where it was said to them, "You are not my people," there they will be called "sons of the living God." (Romans 9:25, 26)

During Old Testament days, God's love and favor were extended in a special relationship with the nation of Israel. In using the passage from Hosea, Paul is telling us that God also has a people among the Gentiles. The Gentiles were not God's people, but now he is revealing that there would be a group of people called from the nations of the world. In Hosea's day it was in the future tense: *"I* **will** *call them 'my people.'"* In Romans, Paul states that this call to the Gentiles is a present reality.

Peter describes the calling of these people in 1 Peter 2:9:

> But you are a chosen race, a royal priesthood, a holy nation, a people for his own possession, that you may proclaim the excellencies of him who called you out of darkness into his marvelous light.

In the same way that God did not have to create the world or anything in it, he did not have to call out a people for himself. He could have been content living in heaven with the angels and watching over the universe that he had created. He could have simply continued the loving relationship he had within the trinity. But he chose not to. He decided instead to establish a relationship with his creation. He wanted to have communication with those he had created. The persons of the trinity were in a loving, communicating relationship, and since he had made us in his image, he not only wanted his creatures to communicate with and love each other, but he wanted to involve himself with them as well. He actually wanted to dwell with them.

Looking at verse 9 of 1 Peter 2, you will find the word "chosen." He says, *"You are a chosen people."* The word "chosen" implies that there is a special relationship between God and these people. They are chosen by God. They are selected by him for the particular privilege, pleasure, and responsibility of having a relationship with God as his special possession. The selection process was not a random drawing of some sort or a lottery. Neither was it a beauty contest, talent contest, or intelligence contest. The people to be included in God's possession were selected by God for reasons known only to him.

We do know what God did *not* consider in choosing his people:

> For consider your calling, brothers: not many of you were wise according to worldly standards, not many were powerful, not many were of noble birth. But God chose what is foolish in the world to shame the wise; God chose what is weak in the world to shame the strong; God chose what is low and despised in the world, even things that are not, to bring to nothing things that are, so that no human being might boast in the presence of God. (1 Corinthians 1:26–29)

The people whom God has chosen are weak and lowly people. They are the people without talent. They are the unattractive, the despised. They are not necessarily the wisest or the strongest. There will be no boasting. They will not be able to claim that God chose them because of their good looks or special abilities. They were chosen so that God might shower them with his blessing, his righteousness, his holiness and redemption, in order that he might display them as a testimony of his grace forever!

In addition to being chosen, 1 Peter 2:9 tells us that these people are a **royal** priesthood. We understand what royalty is. Royalty refers to a king or queen, a prince or princess. The royal family is the family of the ruler of the country. The people being discussed here are royalty. That is, they belong to the family of the king. Which king? Romans 9:26 says that they will be called *"sons of the living God."* God is the supreme monarch of the universe. Anyone in his family would be the royalty of all royalty because God is the King of kings. We see then that these people whom God is calling to be his very own are going to be his sons and daughters and therefore they will be of royal blood.

In his first letter, John describes the joy of being a son of God:

> See what kind of love the Father has given to us, that we should be called children of God; and so we are. The reason why the world does not know us is that it did not know him. Beloved, we are God's children now, and what we will be has not yet appeared; but we know that when he appears we shall be like him, because we shall see him as he is. (1 John 3:1–2)

Not everyone in the world is a child of God. This title only goes to those whom he has called. God's children will be strangers here on the earth because in the same way that the world did not know Christ when he came, the world will not know his children. But God's children have the assurance that when Jesus appears, they will be like him. The family resemblance will be made complete. As you let your mind meditate on these things, try to keep yourself from thinking of this as religion and try to grasp the significance of this as a reality. Instead of being simply another creature inhabiting the earth, man was created with special capabilities by God, and then is offered a place in God's family as a child of God.

In Ephesians 1:4, Paul writes: *"Even as he chose us in him before the foundation of the world, that we should be holy and blameless before him."* We'll look more at this Ephesians passage later, but for now simply notice that God's choosing took place before the creation of the world! How would you feel if you knew that God had his eye on you before you were even born? God, of course, knows everything. He knows what you are going to say before you say it. He knows what you are thinking right now as you read this. Before you were born, he knew what you would be like. He knew what your strengths and weaknesses would be. He knew which sins you would commit. He knew who your parents were going to be and the kind of home environment you would have. And just as he knows this about you, he knows this about everyone.

Wouldn't it make you praise God and rejoice with thanksgiving if you knew that God, knowing all about you, still chose you before the foundation of the world? What an amazing thing! The God of the universe is calling out a people for his name, the same ones on whom he's had his eye for all these millions of years. They would become a son or daughter of God! That's why Peter could say that they are part of the royal family, and Paul could write in Romans 8:15-17 that they are co-heirs with Jesus Christ:

> For you did not receive the spirit of slavery to fall back into fear, but you have received the Spirit of adoption as sons, by whom we cry, "Abba! Father!" The Spirit himself bears witness

with our spirit that we are children of God, and if children, then heirs—heirs of God and fellow heirs with Christ, provided we suffer with him in order that we may also be glorified with him.

We as mere human beings would be presumptuous to declare that we are the children of God and that we would share in the same inheritance that God's only son Jesus Christ would receive. But the Bible states this as a fact. God's people will be his children, and as such would be part of the royal family and would be joint-heirs with Jesus Christ himself. So think about this. There was God the Father, God the Son, and God the Holy Spirit at the beginning. God planned to create a being from the dust of the ground. He made them in his own image, breathing into them spiritual life. And then made plans to adopt them as his own sons and daughters, giving them the same inheritance that he had planned for his Son. They will share equally with him in all that God has given to him. Hebrews 2:11 tells us that Jesus will not be ashamed to call them brothers. And Romans 8:29 tells us that Jesus is the firstborn among many brothers. They will be placed in the family with all the rights as adult sons.

Going back now to 1 Peter 2:9, he writes that there would be a royal **priesthood.** A priest is a go-between for man and God. All these children of God will have the responsibility of communicating with God on behalf of people and people on behalf of God. Anyone would certainly consider it a privilege if he or she were asked to be the go-between for some citizens' group and the President of the United States. What a far greater privilege it would be to be the representatives of God who would serve as a go-between for man and God! As part of the family, God's people will be able to go to God to discuss the needs of their families, friends, and neighbors. They can then go back to their friends and tell them how God wants to work mightily in their lives. This is what Paul means in 2 Corinthians 5:20 where he says, "*Therefore, we are ambassadors for Christ, God making his appeal through us. We implore you on behalf of Christ, be reconciled to God.*"

There are many people with great needs, worries, and fears. Many of these people have lost their way and do not seem to know where the answers are to be found. The people of God, God's children and priests, will go to God on behalf of lost mankind. They will pray for them and ask God to meet their needs in a very powerful way. They will also go to the people and introduce them to the God of heaven. They will encourage them to be reconciled to God so that they too might have a close personal relationship with him and be a part of his family. This is a very special and humbling responsibility. God's people have that responsibility.

God has given specific promises to his people regarding prayer:

Jesus tells us in Matthew 7:7, "Ask and it will be given to you; seek and you will find; knock and it will be opened to you."

John 16:24 says, "Until now you have asked nothing in my name. Ask, and you will receive, that your joy may be full."

John 15:7 says, "If you abide in me, and my words abide in you, ask whatever you wish, and it will be done for you."

1 John 3:21,22 says, "Beloved, if our heart does not condemn us, we have confidence before God. And whatever we ask we receive from him, because we keep his commandments and do what pleases him."

These are just a few of the promises which God has given to his children regarding what they can expect in answer to prayer. He has given these promises because his children are priests. They intercede on behalf of others. God has not made these promises to everybody. Are you a member of God's family? Are you part of the royal priesthood? If so, how is your priestly ministry going? Are you effectively communicating God's love to those around you, and are you sharing the burdens of your family and friends with God?

The third description given in 1 Peter 2:9 is that God's people will be a **holy nation**. Holiness is a term that many people misunderstand. It simply means being set-aside for some particular or exclusive use. Instruments used in the tabernacle or temple of the Old Testament were holy because they were not to be used for regular home purposes. They were reserved for temple sacrifices and worship. A clay pot used to hold water for temple use might look like the clay pots used in people's homes. However, it was a dedicated pot. That is, it was reserved for use in the temple and was not to be taken home to be used in the regular dish washing. In the same way, the people whom God is gathering for himself will be a people reserved for God's exclusive use. They are not to be shared with anyone else, nor are they to view their work as ordinary or mundane. They have been set aside to carry out particular responsibilities for God. They will not dedicate their lives to the typical routines of life, but they will be dedicated to the service of God. Even the day-to-day chores and employment responsibilities which have to be done will be carried out from a different perspective and purpose because they are being done from the viewpoint of service to their God. For this reason, these people are told, *"Whether you eat or drink, or whatever you do, do all to the glory of God"* (1 Corinthian 10:31). So you see, even eating and drinking in the daily course of life are to be done for the glory and praise of God.

You might be wondering what good it is to talk about a special people when you don't feel like it applies to you. God promises that if you come to Christ in faith and receive him as your savior, you too will be a member of the family. John 1:12 says, *"But to all who did receive him, who believed in his name, he gave the right to become children of God."*

Jesus said, *"For God so loved the world that he gave his only begotten son, that whosoever believes in him will not perish, but will have everlasting life"* (John 3:16).

Jesus also said, *"Come unto me all ye that labor and are heavy laden and I will give you rest"* (Matthew 11:28). If you have received Christ in this way and have believed on him, then God has claimed you for special service as his royal child and priest. The ones whom God has chosen are those who come to him in faith, taking God at his word and applying his word to their lives.

As we continue to study the passage before us (1 Peter 2:9), we see that one of the specific responsibilities of this special people is to **declare the praises of God**. God is all knowing, all powerful, perfectly righteous, just and fair. God is creator of everything. He rules everything perfectly. He knows what the best course of action is for any situation. Because God is so great, he deserves our praise. All of God's creation perfectly fulfills its obligation to praise God as he ought to be praised, with exception of mankind. Before God calls us, we do not even think to give him the credit that is his due. In Romans 1:21, Paul explains that this lack of praise and thankfulness is the central core of sin: *"For although they knew God, they did not honor him as God or give thanks to him, but they became futile in their thinking, and their foolish hearts were darkened."* God's people, however, will give him praise because that is their privilege and responsibility. This characteristic, along with faith, will set God's children apart from the rest of humanity.

Paul explains the very same thing in Ephesians 1:11 and 12:

> In him we have obtained an inheritance, having been predestined according to the purpose of him who works all things according to the counsel of his will, so that we who were the first to hope in Christ might be to the praise of his glory.

The one essential calling and purpose of the people of God is to praise God and bring glory to him. They will do so as they do their daily work. They will do it through their family life. They will bring him glory in the way they keep their house or mow their lawn. They will bring him praise and glory in their worship. Ultimately, in the ages to come, they will praise him forever. This is the reason for their existence. God is already full of glory, but his people will give expression to that glory in their lives. People all over the world will have a better idea of what God is like when they see his children, holy and dedicated to God, living lives of praise and glory to him.

1 Peter 2:9 tells us that God is the one who called these people out of darkness into his wonderful light. We will discuss the nature of this darkness and light in a later chapter. We can see from the context however, that God did several things which imply the helpless and hopeless situation in which these people were found before they had been called. They were in darkness, they were not a people, and they had not received mercy. God rescues them from the darkness, he calls them a people, and he shows them mercy.

Mercy is defined as "a refraining from harming or punishing offenders, enemies, or persons in one's power." Before they were called, these people were described as not having received mercy (1 Peter 2:10). That is, they were under God's condemnation. God's punishment is on the unbelieving world. God is angry with the wicked every day (Psalm 7:11). John 3:36 tells us that whoever does not believe on the Son will not see life, but the wrath of God remains on him. God removes his children from that wrath by showing mercy. The threat of punishment has been removed for them.

Before being called by God, these people were also in darkness and they were not a people. They did not belong to God as a special possession. God made a special point of calling them out of darkness. It is almost as though God were out in the sunshine, and these people were way back in a dark cave. I can just picture God outside calling, inviting people to give up living in the darkness and to come out to join him in the sunlight.

Paul explains this same thing to the Ephesian Christians this way: *"For you were once darkness, but now you are light in the Lord"* (Ephesians 5:8). He wrote this to the Colossian Christians, *"He has delivered us from the power of darkness and conveyed us into the kingdom of the Son of His love"* (Colossians 1:13). You see, the ones whom God calls are in darkness. Every one of his children had been in darkness and were blinded by the darkness (1 John 2:11). There aren't any naturally good and radiant people for God to call. All are in that darkness. Psalm 107:10-12 reads this way:

> Some sat in darkness and in the shadow of death, prisoners in affliction and in irons, for they had rebelled against the words of God, and spurned the counsel of the Most High. So he bowed their hearts down with hard labor; they fell down, with none to help.

But even though they were in this condition, God called them. God doesn't want us to wander around in the darkness, groping and searching for the meaning to life. The next verse in Psalm 107 says this: *"Then they cried to the Lord in their trouble, and he delivered them from their distress."* When we are desperate enough in our helpless and hopeless condition, we cry out to the Lord and he rescues us!

Why were they in a position where they needed God's mercy? Why does God say people are in darkness? How did they get into that cave? We will examine these questions in the next chapter. For now, we simply need to understand that before God rescued them, they were in a hopeless situation. They were not able to help themselves. They were without hope and without God before he rescued them (Ephesians 2:12). Isn't it amazing that God would take a group of people who were apparently subject to punishment and make them a special people with such privilege and responsibility?

We have just begun our investigation into the question of the "Rhyme and Reason" of it all. We have found that he is calling out of the world a people to be his very own, to have a relationship with him and to serve him. We have seen that his purpose for calling together a group like this is to demonstrate his mercy and grace to the principalities and powers for ages to come. And we have seen that the calling of this group has been his purpose from before time began. It's always been his plan. To be a part of that group would be a privilege beyond what any of us could imagine. Are you part of that group? Have you been rescued from darkness and brought into the light of God? Or are you still wandering around in the dark? Have you been adopted into the family of God so that God's mercy instead of his wrath is upon you? Or do you feel as though you and God are still strangers to one another? Are you a royal priest, or do you feel like an outcast and a nobody when it comes to your relationship with God? Are you a member of this holy nation? Would you like to be? Do you know anyone who is a member of this group? Read on!

Chapter 2
Our Predicament

In the last chapter, I introduced you to the concept that God is calling out a people for himself. We examined the Scriptures that teach us that God made us for his glory and pleasure, and that he is preparing a people for himself to be a royal priesthood to worship and serve him forever.

In this chapter, we want to discuss <u>why</u> God is calling a people <u>out</u> from the mass of humanity. What's wrong with us that God would be calling people away from the norm into some kind of special relationship? Why would 1 Peter 2:10 say that God had called them out of darkness into his light? What kind of darkness were they in and how did they get there? Are you and I in that darkness too?

In Genesis 1:26, God says,

> Let us make man in our image, after our likeness. And let them have dominion over the fish of the sea and over the birds of the heavens and over the livestock and over all the earth and over every creeping thing that creeps on the earth.

God gave Adam and Eve, the first man and woman, certain responsibilities. He told Adam and his wife that they were to have dominion over the entire creation. They were given special charge to take care of the garden where they lived.

Adam and Eve were created in the image of God. That means that although they were similar to animals in body structure and function, they were different from animals in that they could be creative and communicate; they could love, appreciate beauty, use their mind to reason, and so on. This difference between man and animals is so significant that there is not a scientist on the face of the earth who does not recognize it. The question that should be asked when investigating these things is, not how much man and higher animals are similar to each other (as evolutionists do), but how and why they are so different. The gap is enormous!

The Bible teaches us that the nature of man is threefold: body, soul, and spirit. In 1 Thessalonians 5:23b Paul writes, *"May your whole spirit, soul and body be kept blameless at the coming of our Lord Jesus Christ."* Therefore, in addition to the visible physical body, we also have a soul and spirit. The author of Hebrews tells us that the Word of God is able to divide between soul and spirit (Hebrews 4:12). On the day when Adam was created, God created him from the dust of the ground (Genesis 2:7) and then breathed into him the breath of life, and Adam became a living soul. The word for breath and the word for spirit come from the same root. So God gave Adam spiritual life, and as a result, Adam became a living soul. (When Paul quotes this passage in 1 Corinthians 15:45, he uses the Greek word *psyche* for soul. This is the same root from which we get the word *psychology*. When someone studies psychology, he is studying the attitudes, actions, and feelings of the soul.) God then created Eve from Adam's body such that Adam would say, *"This at last is bone of my bones and flesh of my flesh; she shall be called Woman because she was taken out of Man"* (Genesis 2:23).

With the body, a person is able to communicate and maintain contact with the outside physical world. He sees with his eyes and hears with his ears. He can talk and make gestures, all of which allow him to communicate with others and to detect what is going on around him.

With the spirit, a person is able to communicate with God. God is a spirit, and those who worship him must do so in spirit (John 4:24). God's spirit bears witness with our spirit (Romans 8:16). Adam, having been created in the image of God, had a spirit that was just as much in communication with God as his body was in communication with the world around him. He was an incarnated spirit. In other words, he was essentially a spirit-being enclosed in a body. The soul communicates with God through the spirit, and with the world through the senses of the body.

The soul is the part of man which is really him. It is what makes up his mind, will, and emotions. When you make a decision to do something, your decision is made in your mind and will. When you appreciate a beautiful sunset, it is your soul which is experiencing the sight. Your soul communicates with the outside world through the body, and it communicates with God through the spirit. While you are reading this page, your eyes are picking up the lettering, but it is your mind which is paying attention to its meaning. Your mind is part of your soul. If God were to communicate with you, he would reach your soul through your spirit. Jesus said, *"The words that I have spoken to you are spirit, and life"* (John 6:63).

Those who have a totally secular view of the world believe that there is no such thing as mind separate from the chemical and electrical activity in the brain. They also don't believe that there is any such thing as spirit or soul. In their view, man is basically a very elaborate machine and nothing else. All of our thoughts, feelings, and emotions are the result of chemical and electrical reactions throughout the nervous system and the other systems of the body. Remember, in the secular view there is no designer. There is just the accidental development of different kinds of organisms among which man is of the highest order.

When God created people, he gave them dominion over the rest of creation. That means he put them in charge of it. It is important to note that God has never removed that responsibility from us. We are still responsible before God to have dominion over creation. This means we are to take care of it and manage it for the glory of God. Adam was given the responsibility of naming the animals. Developing a nomenclature is a means of bringing objects within our grasp for understanding and organization. When a young child begins to give names to things and identifies their shape or color, he begins to have dominion over that part of his world because he begins to understand it and use it for his further growth and learning. In a similar way, Adam began to analyze and notice differences and similarities among the animals and began to get a grasp of the structure and organization of his world. We continue that process as we discover more about our world, and then name these newly discovered things and processes.

Another thing we should observe is that God placed Adam in the garden *"to work it and keep it"* (Genesis 2:15). So we see that even before the fall, God gave man responsibility and work to do. The work was not beset with the difficulties that came after the fall, but nevertheless, man did not just wander around with nothing to do. This tells us that work at its very core is good. We were made for good, wholesome, satisfying work.

Because of our superior abilities and the sinful results of the fall, our dominion has sometimes turned into exploitation. Many people are concerned about what we are doing to our environment, and rightfully so. We need to take care of our environment. Sometimes, however, they blame the exploitation of the environment on our Christian heritage. They say that our literal interpretation of the statement of Genesis, where God has given us dominion over the rest of creation, produced an exploitative attitude. Let me suggest that exploitation and mismanagement of our resources are the result of the selfishness and greed that came from the fall. True Christian obedience results in thoughtful and careful use of the resources which God has given us.

On the other hand, we must make sure that we recognize the distinction God has made between ourselves and everything else in creation. We are not one with all other creatures as though we had evolved from them and share the same life. We are a distinct creation and are responsible for caring for all the rest of it. God has given us food, medicine, shelter, as well as the many various living creatures on earth. He gave them to us to use wisely and to manage carefully. And he gave us vegetation and meat for food. In order for us to eat meat, animals need to be killed. And God, in his covenant with Noah, gave him every animal as a food source, just as he had given him green plants (Genesis 9:3). God never gave us permission to exploit and destroy. But he also does not want us to worship our environment. It is there for us to use wisely.

Population growth, as well as our increasing ability to use natural resources, will make changes in our environment. These changes cannot be avoided. There will be more CO_2 in the environment because there are more people. God's amazing design of the natural order will handle this very well. Naturalists who believe the world and life are evolving should be the last ones to claim that the world and balance that exist today are the ideal and final state. Things change. As mankind multiplies, and as he learns to use the resources of the earth in different ways, there will be readjustments in the variety and distribution of life on the planet.

Attempts to prevent the expansion of a species' range or the domination of one organism over another are really expressions of the idea that the given order we see today is optimal and should not change. This is a logical inconsistency and seems to me to be more of a creationist argument than an evolutionary one. Evolutionists say that everything is constantly changing, so I ask why should the current condition not continue to change? Why should the current distribution of species be maintained? In saying that, however, I am not suggesting that we should wantonly disrupt and mismanage the entire ecosystem that God has wondrously given us. I'm just suggesting that their argument does not seem to fit their worldview. Evolution, by definition, implies change.

So, there they were, Adam and Eve, two embodied spirits, living in the garden which God had created. They took care of it. They enjoyed fellowship and companionship with one another. They also enjoyed fellowship and companionship with God. They were God's creation and they were perfect just like God was in the sense that there was no evil in them. God would come to the garden and visit them, and they would have fellowship with him. God enjoyed love and fellowship among the persons of the trinity before he made man, and after man had been created, God invited them to participate in that same kind of relationship with himself. It was spiritual beings in real communication with each other. It was the beginning of a theme we see all the way through Scripture: God wants to dwell with his creation, his people.

God's intention was that all of man's needs would be met by his gracious provision. He planted a garden with them in mind, and then caused the trees to grow for their food. He provided Adam with a wife who loved him and with whom he could communicate on the human level. Adam's spiritual needs for communication with God were met by God himself. Adam's soul-needs – love, beauty, peace, creativity – were all met in his surroundings, including his wife, which God had provided. God had created Adam and Eve perfectly human. They were not gods. They were not angels. They had needs, but those needs were met through God's provision. They enjoyed good food. There was nothing wrong with that. They enjoyed the physical relationship they had with each other. There was nothing wrong with that either. Being "only human" was not synonymous with being sinful. God is not against our humanness. He is not against our physical bodies and the enjoyment of the world that he has made. He is not opposed to earthly things. He was the one who had made them after all.

Adam and Eve were emotionally whole. They did not get on each other's nerves. They tried to do things which would encourage each other. They enjoyed the discussions they could have together, and they looked forward to the times when God came to visit with them. They enjoyed their work in the garden. The vegetation grew naturally, responding to their care. They did not know what it was to be in want, for God was there to provide for their needs.

Adam and Eve were undoubtedly creative people. After all, they were created in the image of God. God is creative and so are we. God probably enjoyed watching them learn about their surroundings. As days went by, they discovered new ways of doing things. They discovered some of the secrets which God had built into nature. God expected that to happen. He designed the earth to respond to man's investigative interests. Human beings would go on to invent wheels, chariots, steam engines, automobiles, and computers, all from the resources of the earth.

Adam and Eve were given one negative commandment. They were told not to eat from one particular tree that was in the garden. This tree was called the tree of the knowledge of good and evil. God told them that they would die if they ate from it. Sometimes people chafe against the commandments of God as though they were limiting. But look at the freedom Adam and Eve had! God told them that they may freely eat of every tree in the garden, except one. The whole variety of fruit and their varied flavors was open to them, except one. Our lives are like that too. There are lots of legitimate things for us to do and very few restrictions in comparison.

Many of you are familiar with the way the serpent tempted Eve (Genesis 3:1-7). The serpent's plan was simple enough. He put doubts in Eve's mind as to God's intentions by asking, "*Did God say, 'You shall not eat of every tree in the garden'?*" He accused God of deception. He told Eve that the reason that God didn't want them to eat of the tree was because he knew that when they ate of it, they would be like God, knowing good and evil (Genesis 3:5). He was basically accusing God of being selfish, wanting this knowledge only for himself. He blatantly accused God of lying when God had said that they would die on the day they ate the fruit of that tree.

Eve began to take a second look at the tree and its fruit. She saw first of all that it was good for food. The process of self-justification had begun. She presumed God must not have meant what he had said since the fruit looked delicious and was good for her health. She saw that it was pleasing to the eye. It looked good! She also began to believe what the serpent had told her about how it could make her wise. She must have reasoned that it would be a good thing to have more wisdom. Perhaps she could be a bigger help managing the garden.

Immediately after they had eaten from the tree, they knew what evil was. They knew what it was to disobey the God who had created them. They had rejected all God had provided, and rather than giving thanks for it, they went after the one thing they were told they couldn't have. They were no longer innocent. They tried to avoid God when he came to visit them that evening (Gen. 3:8). You know what that is like, don't you? Every time you are around the person you deceived, you feel like looking the other way. You hope that they won't discover what you've done, or if they already know about it, you hope that they won't mention it. Through the entire time you are together, your relationship and communication are strained. It just isn't right. That's the way it was with Adam and Eve and God.

God had told Adam and Eve that they would die when they ate of the forbidden fruit. It is obvious from the text that Adam and Eve continued to live quite a while afterward. Had the serpent been right after all? He had told them that they would not die if they ate of the tree. Adam and Eve actually did die the day they disobeyed God. They died spiritually and they began to die physically. They died spiritually in that their spirit died and they were separated from God. The ability to communicate with their creator at that spiritual level had been destroyed. Their sin had separated them from God (Isaiah 59:2). The love and worship they should have felt for their creator were gone. It was now replaced by fear and guilt.

Spiritual death is as fatal to communication with God as death of the body is for communication with other people. Adam and Eve could continue to say prayers, but there would be no communication. A child playing with a toy phone can pick up the receiver and talk into it, but there's no one listening. Or a parent might pick up the receiver and pretend to carry on a conversation that from all outward appearances looks and sounds like the real thing. But there is no one on the other end. The same thing happened to Adam and Eve. The capability of carrying on a spiritual conversation with their creator had been severed. Isaiah 59:1,2 tells us, *"Behold, the LORD's hand is not shortened, that it cannot save, or his ear dull, that it cannot hear; but your iniquities have made a separation between you and your God, and your sins have hidden his face from you so that he does not hear."* And David writes in Psalm 66:18, *"If I regard iniquity in my heart, the Lord will not hear."*

But their reaction to their sin also changed their relationship with each other. What had been a wonderful experience of perfect married bliss turned sour. They immediately became self-conscious of their nakedness and made attempts to cover themselves (v. 7). What had been a perfectly open relationship now involved hiding – hiding from God and hiding from each other. When Eve heard Adam asking her something, she probably wondered if he had an ulterior motive. Was he being critical in a subtle way? Could she trust him to be telling her the truth? When he said he loved her, was it really love, or did he just want what he could get? When Eve asked Adam to go out to get some fruit for supper, was she just asking him to get some supper, or was she implying that what he had brought in last night was not good enough? Was she trying to boss him around? Distrust and discord were undoubtedly the rule.

They began to make excuses and to blame one another for what had happened. Instead of taking responsibility for their actions, Adam blamed Eve, and Eve turned around and blamed the serpent. Communication and love had gone. At the same time that spiritual death came, their souls were damaged as well. It was as if removing the spiritual interaction left the soul without governance. Jealousy and strife were now a part of their make-up. Selfishness had become dominant in their character where once there had been love and selflessness. Their ability to make wise decisions had been hampered. Their will to do what was right had become marred so that their will was governed by a concern for physical and emotional self-preservation. Their motivations were impaired.

Their bodies also were affected. From that moment on, they began to die. Each succeeding generation died at an earlier age. Sickness became part of life. The Bible teaches us that even the rest of creation was affected (Romans 8:19-22). God caused weeds to grow, and Adam was required to work hard to make the ground produce the food which once he had been able to gather effortlessly.

God loved Adam and Eve, but he brought a curse upon them and the ground. Many people today incorrectly reason that if God loves someone, he won't do anything that they perceive is negative. God in love often disciplines his children. When we love those for whom we are responsible, we will discipline lovingly, fairly, and consistently to bring about the characteristics that we know they are capable of. That is why God disciplines those he loves. God is also a God of justice and righteousness, and he could not allow rebellion to exist. Therefore, he brought a curse upon them.

No longer would things grow effortlessly for them. God told them that it would require sweat and effort to grow their food. Often, we wonder why we have to work so hard. If you have a garden, you know how hard it is to get things to grow. Even those who don't garden know how hard it is to earn a living, keep the house and car in good repair, and do all the other chores that need to be done. It is a constant effort. God intends that we work hard. He has never revoked this curse. God is opposed to laziness. I believe it is for a very good purpose. Now that mankind has fallen into sin, God knows that the best thing would be for us all to keep busy. That way we would have less time to get into trouble. In 2 Thessalonians 3:6-12 we read:

> Now we command you, brothers, in the name of our Lord Jesus Christ, that you keep away from any brother who is walking in idleness and not in accord with the tradition that you received from us. For you yourselves know how you ought to imitate us, because we were not idle when we were with you, nor did we eat anyone's bread without paying for it, but with toil and labor we worked night and day, that we might not be a burden to any of you. It was not because we do not have that right, but to give you in ourselves an example to imitate. For even when we were with you, we would give you this command: If anyone is not willing to work, let him not eat. For we hear that some among you walk in idleness, not busy at work, but busybodies. Now such persons we command and

encourage in the Lord Jesus Christ to do their work quietly and to earn their own living.

Many of the problems we have today result from our trying to circumvent this curse. We don't like to work. We want lots of time to relax and do nothing. God's intention is for us to work hard to make ends meet. The rule that Paul gave us in the above passage makes it clear that if someone does not work, he should not eat. There are many social programs today which violate this principle. People are given money because of their poverty, but many are not required to work even though they are able-bodied. This is a circumvention of the curse which God brought upon us, and it will result in damage to the character and self-esteem of every person who receives such hand-outs.

For her punishment, Eve was told that she would suffer pain in childbearing, and she would be under the leadership of her husband. Instead of being in subjection to God alone, Eve would now be responsible to her husband. He would have to answer for her actions. Nothing had been said to her in the past about her responsibilities to her husband. There was mutual caring and a desire to support one another. Now that had all changed. With sin in the picture, there would be selfishness on both sides and a desire to manipulate and control. God told Eve that her desire would be toward her husband. I believe this means that as part of the disruption in the original order, Eve would seek to usurp authority from her husband. She would desire to be in charge. In my observation in life, it seems to me that many men, maybe most men, seek to avoid being decision-makers. In most cases, women gladly step into that role, but this is a reversal of God's good purposes for both men and women.

Eve apparently hadn't consulted with Adam before eating the forbidden fruit. Now Adam would have the final say. Nothing has happened since the fall to change this curse. In fact, it carries over into the church. In 1 Timothy 2:11, God tells us that his design for men and women in the church is rooted in creation: "*Let a woman learn quietly with all submissiveness. I do not permit a woman to teach or to exercise authority over a man; rather, she is to remain quiet. For Adam was formed first, then Eve."*

People today are continuing in the rebellion of Adam and Eve. God has given the order for the church and the home and yet many are trying to change that order so that it is more palatable. When we husbands or men in the church refuse to take the leadership, God's specific commandments are being violated and we can expect confusion and frustration to result. When wives or women in the church usurp the position God has given to the man, God's blessing is withdrawn and his discipline is applied.

All of this sounds strange to the modern and post-modern ear. The idea of male leadership is ridiculed as a vestige of a previous time, a time when men were seeking to dominate women. It is all viewed as a power struggle. And it has become a power struggle, but not for the reasons most assume. It's a struggle because Adam and Eve sinned and God's punishment in the form of a curse has been applied. When we chafe against it, our struggle is really with God. Many claim that these old-fashioned notions must be overcome if we are to make progress. My challenge to each of my readers is to determine in your own mind if you are going to believe the Bible or not. Many are choosing the "or not." If you are a Christian, you need to sort this out. You can't be in two worlds at the same time. It doesn't work.

Notwithstanding the curses, and with his merciful purposes in view, God sacrificed an innocent animal and provided skins to clothe Adam and Eve. As far as we know, that is the first animal to have died. Prior to Adam's sin, people ate plants for their food. Death in the animal kingdom was nonexistent. The Bible tells us that without the shedding of blood there is no forgiveness (Hebrews 9:22), and so an animal died in order to cover Adam and Eve's nakedness and to forgive their sin.

Few people today realize the implications of what happened that day so long ago. Adam and Eve sinned against God. They disobeyed him, and he was justly offended by their rebellion. This is not a fable or religious jargon. We believe this is an event that actually took place on this earth in history. That is the way the Bible describes it. The Bible says that the God who is actually there created mankind for a particular reason, and those he created turned against him and rejected his authority over them. God had created them to praise and honor him. He had created them so that he could live with them and fellowship with them and so that they would bring him glory. He had provided everything for them and now they had taken it upon themselves to look for satisfaction elsewhere. By choosing to eat of the forbidden tree, they were stating that they no longer trusted God to provide everything. Instead, they had chosen to investigate what he had withheld from them. How serious an offense this is!

If there is no God, and man has just evolved through random processes by chance, then sin is nonexistent, and man is responsible for his own fate and for deciding what is right and wrong. But this is not the Bible's view. The Bible says that we are here by the decision of an almighty, righteous, and personal God. The very creation that he had made defied him and took steps to become independent. He had not created robots. His creatures had the ability to choose freely, and they did. The results of that fatal choice are still felt today in ways you may not have realized. The first consequence is that when Adam sinned, the rest of humanity was included in that sin. Let me explain.

When the President of the United States declares war on another country, he is not the only one impacted. He is one man, but in making the declaration of war, he involves everyone in the country in that decision. In lesser ways, our congressmen and representatives make decisions on our behalf. They have been given the right, by virtue of their election to the office, to make decisions for you, even if their decisions are not the ones you would have made.

When Adam sinned, he was doing the same thing. He sinned for all of us. He made the decision as our representative. Turn to Romans 5:12-19.

> Therefore, just as sin came into the world through one man, and death through sin, and so death spread to all men because all sinned.

This verse shows us that sin entered the world through one man. Adam's choice was not just an isolated incident. It was the doorway through which sin entered. The verse says that in this way, through one man, *"death came to all men."* The last part of the verse closes the argument by saying that all sinned. This does not simply mean that just as Adam sinned, so everyone else in the world has also sinned. That is true, but the verse is saying that when Adam sinned, we all sinned. Adam sinned as our representative, and therefore, his sin is our sin, and we are guilty because of our connection with Adam. The Bible doesn't explain how it can be, it just says that it is so. Verse 13 explains what verse 12 means:

> For sin indeed was in the world before the law was given, but sin is not counted where there is no law. Yet death reigned from Adam to Moses, even over those whose sinning was not like the transgression of Adam, who was a type of the one who was to come.

Notice in these verses how the writer makes two especially important points. First, sin is not taken into account if there is no law. Between the time of Adam and the time of Moses, there was no law. The only law had been the one Adam and Eve violated. The ten commandments were not given until Moses' day. If there is no law, a person can't break the law, and therefore sin is not counted against them. That sounds reasonable and fair, doesn't it? The second point is related to the first. Even though sin was not counted against the people in those days, they died anyway. Death is the consequence for sin. The argument in this passage is clear. The sin of Adam counted as the sin of everyone in the human race and therefore death has come upon all men because of it. Adam had broken a specific command of God. We know from Scripture that God is perfectly righteous, and so we know that God would not have declared everyone guilty if they were not really guilty.

Further portions in this same section confirm this teaching.

Verse 15 - *"For if many died through one man's trespass...."*

Verse 16 - *"The judgment following one trespass brought condemnation...."*

Verse 17 - *"For if, because of one man's trespass, death reigned through that one man...."*

Verse 18 - *"Therefore, as one trespass led to condemnation for all men...."*

Verse 19 - *"For as by one man's disobedience many were made sinners...."*

1 Corinthians 15:22 - *"For as in Adam all die...."*

Because Adam acted on our behalf, each one of us was born a sinner. Let's make this personal. Before you had a chance to do anything right or wrong, you were already counted by God as a sinner. Just as the penalty for Adam and Eve was immediate spiritual death and eventual physical death, the same is true of you and me. We were born into this world spiritually dead. The Bible speaks of it as spiritual darkness. In addition, our physical bodies are prone to sickness and eventually will die. Our spiritual death and ultimate physical death have nothing to do with how we live our lives. We are already sinners the moment we are born.

Look at the following verses with me:

> Ephesians 2:1 And you He made alive, who were dead in trespasses and sins. (NKJV)

> Colossians 2:13 And you, who were dead in your trespasses and the uncircumcision of your flesh....

People in this position are described as being without hope and without God (Ephesians 2:12). They are also described as darkened in their understanding and separated from the life of God (Ephesians 4:18). Scripture states, *"But whoever hates his brother is in the darkness and walks in the darkness, and does not know where he is going because the darkness has blinded his eyes"* (1 John 2:11). Since this is true of everyone, God is going to have to act to bring his people to life out of spiritual death, and to light out of their darkness if he is to have a people. Every single person is in darkness. There is no one in the light that God can call. That's why Peter told us that God's chosen people were those he had called out of darkness into his marvelous light (1 Peter 2:9). That is the focus of our discussion in this chapter.

As we come into the world, then, we are already sinners. The punishment that came upon Adam and Eve is upon all of us. Our spirits are dead, and there is no communication with God. Our spirits are dead, and there is NO communication with God. Isaiah the prophet wrote, *"Your iniquities have made a separation between you and your God, and your sins have hidden his face from you <u>so that he does not hear</u>"* (Isaiah 59:2, emphasis added).

Even though our spirit is dead and our bodies are dying, our souls are alive, but sin has taken its toll there as well. As children we begin to look out for the interests of "Number One." We don't need to be taught how to lie, or to throw a temper tantrum when we don't get our way. Our sinful desires turn our affections to things other than God. Our wills are self-centered. Our emotions are devastated by the events in our lives. You know in your own life the emotional scars that you bear because of circumstances you have gone through. People are depressed and lonely. We know down deep that this is not right. This is not what is best for us as people. God agrees with that. He did not make us to be depressed and sorrowing people. He made us to be joyful, thankful people. Sin has hurt our souls by turning our focus away from God and onto ourselves, our feelings, and circumstances.

Sin has also done damage to our physical bodies. We see so much sickness around us. We see people suffering physically from diseases. We see people getting old and becoming more and more helpless. Do you think that this is the way God originally created it to be? No. All this suffering is a result of sin. God, knowing how sin and its consequences would affect mankind, could have rejected his plan from the outset. God knows all possible scenarios and all the "What ifs?" of his plans. Why did he proceed with this plan? The only reason I can think of is that it was the best one for our good and his glory out of all the potential plans available. Why? I believe that God purposed to accomplish an amazing miracle so that through all the misery and pain sin has caused, ultimate victory would be achieved, and he would show himself to be a merciful God, thus revealing a side of his character that would otherwise have remained hidden.

People who think in secular terms say, "That is just the problem with you Christians. You blame everything on sin. You look to God to help you and then to heaven for ultimate release. If you would just face the reality of our plight, maybe you could work to help solve the problems of the world instead of just blaming it on sin." God intends his children to be of help in as many ways as possible. He has called them the "light of the world" and "the salt of the earth." He provides them with the compassion necessary to help those who are poor and afflicted. By giving wisdom to medical researchers, he provides help for the sick. Nowhere in the Bible do we get the idea that we should all sit back and blame sin for our problems, think about heaven, and ignore the problems of the world. Problems can only be attacked with real solutions when we know the actual cause of the problem. As long as we look to sociology and psychology to solve what is basically a moral and spiritual problem, there will be no lasting solutions.

In addition to being sinners because of Adam's sin, every one of us has "seconded the motion." In other words, each one of us has demonstrated that we agree with Adam's decision by making similar decisions ourselves. There is not one individual on the face of this earth who has not disobeyed the commandments of God in one way or another. As the Bible says in Ecclesiastes 7:20, "*Surely there is not a righteous man on earth who does good and never sins.*" We will never be able to say that we should not carry the punishment of Adam's sin because it wasn't our fault that he disobeyed. We demonstrate every day that we agree with Adam's decision. We hear God's commandments and the dictates of our conscience and we still do the wrong thing.

During the history of mankind, God has dealt with us in a variety of ways. We have already seen how God has dealt with the disobedience in the garden of Eden. Many today would claim that they would be able to be good if it weren't for the environment in which they were raised. If they had just had a better home life, or more understanding parents, or had lived in a better neighborhood, they would have done much better at living an obedient life. The environment in which Adam and Eve found themselves was as perfect as it can get. There were no parents and no ungodly neighbors. There was no one to give them a bad example. Yet they disobeyed God's one command.

Following their ejection from the garden and the birth of their children, something else happened which confirmed their failure to submit to God's way. Cain and Abel, Adam and Eve's sons, both brought sacrifices to the Lord. Cain brought a sacrifice of the fruit of the ground, and Abel brought a sacrifice from his flock. God did not accept Cain's sacrifice because a blood sacrifice was required. Cain was angry. God told him, "If you do what is right, will you not be accepted?" God had given man a conscience. Since the fall, he now knew the difference between right and wrong. He knew when he was acting responsibly and when he was not. Cain could have brought the proper sacrifice, but he chose not to. He believed that as long as he was sincere, God would accept him. God did not accept him. It is possible to be sincere but wrong. Cain had done the wrong thing. Even after Cain brought the wrong sacrifice, God gave him the chance to change his mind and bring the appropriate sacrifice. But Cain would not do it. Instead, he was stubborn, and became angry, and killed his brother.

How did other men fare during this time after the fall but prior to the law? Were the results better than they had been in the garden? In Genesis 6:5 we read, *"The Lord saw that the wickedness of man was great in the earth, and that every intention of the thoughts of his heart was only evil continually."* This was God's assessment of the situation, and he dealt with it by sending a flood. God observed that EVERY inclination of man's heart was evil ALL THE TIME. What an indictment! Only one family in the entire earth received grace from God. That was Noah and his household. Out of the millions of people on earth at that time, God saved eight people! Eight people!!

After the flood, God told Noah and his sons to *"Be fruitful and increase in number and fill the earth"* (Genesis 9:1). He went on to tell Noah to govern the earth in a responsible way. He told him that if someone takes another person's life, then the murderer should pay with his life. He says in verse 6, *"Whoever sheds the blood of man, by man shall his blood be shed; for God made man in his own image."* Notice the sanctity God puts on human life even though man had sinned. God gave the government the responsibility of taking the life of murderers as expressed to Noah long before God gave the law to Moses. It is a principle that God has never revoked. God expects individuals to turn the other cheek and not to seek revenge. But God has also ordained that murderers be executed by governmental authorities. He is the source of the rules for governing. It doesn't change with the times. We can argue back and forth for centuries about whether capital punishment is a deterrent to crime or not. Whether it is or isn't, God has commanded that the government take the lives of those it has convicted of murder.

How did this episode end? It ended in the building of a tower to avoid the commandment to spread throughout the earth. There is nothing essentially wrong with building a tower. But there was more to this construction project than appears on the surface. The people wanted to make a name for themselves (Genesis 11:4). God had told them to disperse and fill the earth. They were not interested in being obedient to God. The pride of their heart was such that making a name and building a tower were more important than spreading out and filling the earth as God had commanded. God punished them and forced them to disperse by changing their languages. Human beings had failed this test also.

The next episode finds God calling Abraham in Genesis chapter 12. Abraham was an idolater. He too lived in darkness, but

God called him out of that darkness. God just showed up one day and freely promised him that he would make a great nation out of him, and that all the nations of the earth would be blessed through his descendants. Paul describes the promise as one which makes Abraham heir of the world (Romans 4:13). God promised him a land. God told Abraham's son Isaac,

> Do not go down to Egypt; dwell in the land of which I shall tell you. Sojourn in this land, and I will be with you and will bless you, for to you and to your offspring I will give all these lands, and I will establish the oath that I swore to Abraham your father. (Genesis 26:2–3)

God's promise was made to Abraham and his seed (Genesis 22:18). This is important because in this book we are showing that God is gathering a people for his name. We will discover that this promise to Abraham includes a multitude of people who will be heirs with Abraham of the promise of God. This is an unconditional promise made to Abraham and to his heirs, and includes great blessings including the forgiveness of sin and the gift of the Spirit of God within them.

If you follow the story of Abraham and his children, you will find that they became less and less an influence for God. Jacob's children became involved with the Canaanite people in many ways, including marriage with them. God intended his people to be a blessing. In order to do that, they needed to stay separate and distinct from the pagan culture around them. They would not be a blessing while living in disobedience to God and while blending themselves in with the God-dishonoring practices of the pagan peoples.

What happened? As a result of a famine, the descendants of Abraham ended up in Egypt. The religion of the Egyptians forbade them to intermingle with the Israelites and so God used the time in Egypt to segregate his people in such a way that they could develop into a large nation. But they stayed on, even after the famine had ended. They did not follow the simple directive of God to return to the land which God had promised to give them. God had used Joseph and the wealth of the Egyptian people to save the Israelites, but he didn't want them to stay there. God wanted the nation of Israel to be a special people – different from all the other peoples on the face of the earth. He didn't want them copying the lifestyles of the other nations. He loved them and had great plans for them. He had given them a land, and he wanted them to live in it and enjoy it. If they had been obedient, and if they had been living in faith, they would have gone back. But the luxuries of Egypt were too attractive. The desire of their heart was toward the food, the entertainment, and the culture in general. Leaving would have meant giving up too much.

What was the result? They came under the bondage of Pharaoh. Even there, though, God was with them. Psalm 105:24 tells us that God made his people very fruitful; he made them too numerous for their foes. But then God turned the hearts of the Egyptians to hate his people so that he could force a confrontation (v. 25). He raised up Moses to be a leader for them and showed many signs and miracles to demonstrate his power. He even destroyed the firstborn of every Egyptian family to get their attention. The Egyptians finally let the people go free.

Following their release from the captivity of Egypt, God gave the Israelites his law, the Law of Moses. God tells them in Exodus 19:5, *"Now therefore, if you will indeed obey my voice and keep my covenant, you shall be my treasured possession among all peoples, for all the earth is mine."*

It's interesting to observe that this is the same expression Peter uses to describe the people God is calling out for himself, as we discussed in the previous chapter. How did the Israelites respond? The people responded in verse 8: *"We will do everything the Lord has said."*

As the Israelites prepared to enter the land God had promised them, Moses reviewed what had taken place in Egypt and during forty years of wandering in the wilderness. He chastised them for the fact that they were a stiff-necked and rebellious people. He wondered about how they would manage in the years after he was gone if they were behaving this way while he was their leader (Deuteronomy 31:27).

But they did enter the promised land under the leadership of Joshua. They were fairly successful at first, but then began to demand a king so that they could be like all of the nations around them. God reluctantly allowed them to have a king, but it wasn't long before the kingdom became divided and eventually both the northern and southern kingdoms were taken captive by foreign powers. Why had this happened? Because they disobeyed God and followed the sinful practices of the neighboring countries.

How does this portion of the story end? In 2 Kings 17 we find that Israel is going into captivity. In verse 7 we are given the reason: *"And this occurred because the people of Israel had sinned against the Lord their God."* How had they sinned? They had disobeyed the commands God had given. They had worshiped other gods. They had taken wives for themselves from among the heathen nations. They had failed to remove all the pagan influences from the land the way God had told them to. Because of their disobedience, the nation was plundered, and the people were carried away into captivity, dispersed among the nations of the world.

Ezekiel 10 tells the sad and tragic account of the glory of God leaving the temple. The Shekinah glory, as it is called, had been displayed in the earliest days of the tabernacle, and then in the temple in Jerusalem, but now was leaving. As the Spirit leaves, he pauses on the threshold and then pauses again as he gets ready to depart. He seems reluctant to leave, but he does. As this happens, Ezekiel asks God if he is going to make a complete end of the people of God. It is at this point that God promises what is called the New Covenant in which he will make a complete transformation of human hearts rather than just imposing laws from the outside. We'll discuss this more as we go along.

So far, each period of history has demonstrated the utter failure of the human heart to live a life pleasing to God. In every situation, from walking with God in a perfect garden to becoming a nation directed by a miracle-working God, human beings could not be faithful.

The next period of time involves the coming of Jesus Christ. His coming brought an end to the law and introduced the day of grace. First, John the Baptist and then Jesus himself announced that the Kingdom was at hand. The Jewish nation knew what he meant. For many centuries, the people had been waiting for the Messiah to come to set up his kingdom. The people of Jesus' day were especially interested in the appearance of the Messiah because they believed he would give relief from Roman oppression. What a surprise it was when Jesus announced that he was the promised one. It was surprising that he had come from a poor family and an insignificant village. In addition, they were dismayed that Jesus was not in favor of a violent overthrow of the government which was what the more zealous factions wanted.

Then there was the message which Jesus was preaching. It was a message of internal righteousness as compared to the outward ceremonial righteousness of the Scribes and Pharisees. It was a message whose standard was actually higher than they were used to. In response to all of this, the religious leaders rejected Jesus as their Messiah. Once again, mankind had proved that it was not particularly interested in doing things God's way. The people through their leaders said "No!" to God. The second person of the Trinity had taken on human flesh and was rejected by the people!

Peter, in a tremendous message on the day of Pentecost, rebuked the people for having turned their Messiah over for crucifixion. He said, *"Let all the house of Israel therefore know for certain that God has made him both Lord and Christ, this Jesus whom you crucified"* *(Acts 2:36).*

The people responded, apparently sincerely, with the question, *"Brothers, what shall we do?"* Peter told them to repent and be baptized to show that their repentance was genuine. In a similar speech in Acts 3, Peter tells his hearers that if they would repent and turn to God, their sins would be wiped out and the times of refreshing would come from the Lord. He explains that God would send the Christ to them as all the prophets had foretold. What was the official response of the leaders? They arrested Peter and John and commanded them not to preach any more. They were silencing the very messengers that God had provided to announce the good news. In effect, the leaders were telling God to be quiet. They did not want to hear any more about it. Not too many years later, Jerusalem was destroyed, and the people were scattered across the face of the earth. God had judged his people.

Today, the command is to believe on the name of the Lord Jesus Christ. We are told that we can be saved by simply trusting in his name. What will be the result? Does the world run to him in faith? No. On the contrary, there are only a relative few who trust him. Most do not want to be under the leadership of Jesus Christ. Jesus himself said that the way to eternal life is narrow and there are few who find it. The way leading to destruction is broad and there are many who take that road (Matthew 7:14ff.). When he returns, there will again be judgment. The Bible prophesies a future kingdom in which the Lord Jesus Christ himself will rule and reign over the entire earth for a thousand years. All will be peaceful. Righteousness will be the characteristic of that rule. Certainly, under those circumstances, the solution to man's basic problem will have been found. But in spite of this, we read,

> And when the thousand years are ended, Satan will be released from his prison and will come out to deceive the nations that are at the four corners of the earth, Gog and Magog, to gather them for battle; their number is like the sand of the sea. (Revelation 20:7–8)

Can you imagine that? After a thousand years of the rule and reign of Christ, after a thousand years of peace and prosperity, there are thousands who are willing to go into battle against their king!

God describes his conclusions about our situation in Romans 1:29-32:

They were filled with all manner of unrighteousness, evil, covetousness, malice. They are full of envy, murder, strife, deceit, maliciousness. They are gossips, slanderers, haters of God, insolent, haughty, boastful, inventors of evil, disobedient to parents, foolish, faithless, heartless, ruthless. Though they know God's righteous decree that those who practice such things deserve to die, they not only do them but give approval to those who practice them.

Thus, we can see that the history of mankind is one of sinful failure. Whether in a perfect garden or in the presence of God in human form performing miracles, man has disobeyed God and rejected him in each and every case. It is because of this continual failure that God describes the situation this way:

Now this I say and testify in the Lord, that you must no longer walk as the Gentiles do, in the futility of their minds. They are darkened in their understanding, alienated from the life of God because of the ignorance that is in them, due to their hardness of heart. They have become callous and have given themselves up to sensuality, greedy to practice every kind of impurity.

(Ephesians 4:17–19)

In this description, is God indicting the entire human race or just a particularly evil subset of the whole population? Romans 3:10-12 gives God's verdict:

None is righteous, no, not one; no one understands; no one seeks for God. All have turned aside; together they have become worthless; no one does good, <u>not even one</u>. (Emphasis added.)

All the way through the Bible the description is the same. Way back before the flood, God said: *"The LORD saw that the wickedness of man was great in the earth, and that every intention of the thoughts of his heart was only evil continually"* (Genesis 6:5).

The prophet Jeremiah wrote, *"The heart is deceitful above all things and desperately sick; who can understand it?"* (Jeremiah 17:9).

Solomon, the wisest man who ever lived, wrote, "*Surely there is not a righteous man on earth who does good and never sins*" (Ecclesiastes 7:20).

Jesus said, "*And this is the judgment: the light has come into the world, and people loved the darkness rather than the light because their works were evil*" (John 3:19).

Even though we don't like to hear this verdict, we know that something is not right. You have to admit that even in our "enlightened" age, people are still cruel to other people. In spite of the fact that man has devised "better" and "more up-to-date" methods of dealing with the problems of society, these solutions do not work. There is endless friction in our homes. There is competition between husbands and wives for control of the home. Sexual immorality and the resulting emotional devastation which results continue unabated. All the while, people are claiming that such liberation is actually good for us. Why is there all of this heartache, discouragement, and frustration all around us when things are supposedly so much better?

We usually offer any explanation except the real one. The actual reason kids rebel or get involved in drugs or immoral sex is due to the death of their spirits and their separation from God. It is due ultimately to sin. It is not an educational or social question. It is a moral one. The reason husbands and wives fight each other is a sin problem. The reason nations war against each other is a sin problem. All our man-made attempts to solve the problems are doomed to fail because we face a heart issue. As the prophet Jeremiah wrote, "*For my people have committed two evils: they have forsaken me, the fountain of living waters, and hewed out cisterns for themselves, broken cisterns that can hold no water*" (Jeremiah 2:13). God is like a spring of flowing water. Our solutions are like trying to get a drink from a polluted pond using a broken cup we found in a dump.

Since communication with God has been broken, we no longer look to God to supply all our needs. Because the fellowship is not there, we look to other things and other people to meet our most basic needs. We go into marriage, hoping that our spouse will be able to meet our physical and emotional needs. If he or she can't, we carry grudges and begin looking to other relationships to fill the void we feel. When someone who experiments with drugs finds an experience which seems to fill some deep unfulfilled need, drugs become the god for that individual. But nothing can fill the void but God.

God wants our attention to be focused upon him and the needs of others. He wants to be the one we look to for the supplying of our needs rather than looking to our physical beauty or our enviable toys. He wants to receive the thanksgiving and praise for all of the good gifts he provides for us (Acts 17:25). Not doing so is the root of our sin problem.

The problem is that we have a total misunderstanding of the nature of God. God is holy and righteous. That means he is so pure that evil can have no place in his being or in his presence. In Habakkuk 1:13 the prophet writes concerning God, *"You who are of purer eyes than to see evil."*

In Matthew 5:48 Jesus says, *"You therefore must be perfect, as your heavenly Father is perfect."*

In Galatians 3:10 Paul writes, *"Cursed be everyone who does not abide by all things written in the Book of the Law, and do them."*

James 2:10 states, *"For whoever keeps the whole law but fails in one point has become guilty of all of it."*

Part of the perfection God requires is not only avoiding the usual sins but having the right attitude toward God. Jesus said that the chief commandment was to love God with all our heart and soul and mind. Who can live up to that standard? How well do you love God with all your heart and soul and mind? In the first chapter of Romans where Paul is developing these same points, he says: *"For although they knew God, they neither glorified him as God nor gave thanks to him."* Are you perfect at giving thanks to God and giving him the glory that he deserves? No one is!

God has revealed himself in nature to every human being. In spite of this, we have substituted ourselves or our stuff as the object of our worship. We have misplaced affections. Because God has revealed himself to everyone through the things he has made, we know about his eternal power and Godhead – he gave us life and breath and all things – and yet we do not give him thanks for all he has done on our behalf. Because this is true of all of us, God says that we are without excuse (Romans 1:20). No one can say, "I didn't know that!"

God's ultimate judgment on sin is eternal death. Death essentially means separation. In the day that Adam and Eve sinned, they became separated from God. Their spirits were no longer able to communicate with God the way they used to. This situation is especially serious because the Bible teaches that every person will live forever. Your soul will continue to live even after your body dies. Because God is of too pure eyes to behold evil, and since man's spirit is dead so that fellowship and communication with God have been broken, God cannot permit man in his fallen condition to have a place in his kingdom with him. That's why Jesus told Nicodemus that unless a man is born again, he cannot see the kingdom of God (John 3:3).

God has prepared a place for the devil and his angels, a place called Hell. The Bible and even Jesus warn of Hell. The Bible also clearly teaches that there will be people sent there. In one sense, it should seem obvious to us that a place like Hell must exist if there is to be justice. Most would agree that child abusers and torturers must ultimately be punished if there is to be justice in the universe. In that sense, the good news is that God promises justice. The bad news for us is that that justice will also be applied to us. You should not think of this as a religious teaching. This is how things actually are. It corresponds to reality. Hell actually exists and people are actually there even as you read this. Jesus himself said, *"I don't know you or where you come from. Depart from me, all you workers of evil! In that place there will be weeping and gnashing of teeth..."* (Luke 13:27-28).

2 Thessalonians 1:8-10 says:

> When the Lord Jesus is revealed from heaven with his mighty angels in flaming fire, inflicting vengeance on those who do not

know God and on those who do not obey the gospel of our Lord Jesus. They will suffer the punishment of eternal destruction, away from the presence of the Lord and from the glory of his might, when he comes on that day to be glorified in his saints, and to be marveled at among all who have believed, because our testimony to you was believed.

Is this for the extremely wicked people only? – the murders and robbers? Jesus said:

> Not everyone who says to me, "Lord, Lord," will enter the kingdom of heaven, but the one who does the will of my Father who is in heaven. On that day many will say to me, "Lord, Lord, did we not prophesy in your name, and cast out demons in your name, and do many mighty works in your name?" And then will I declare to them, "I never knew you; depart from me, you workers of lawlessness" (Matthew 7:21–23).

Why would Jesus speak this way to those who prophesied in his name and did many wonderful deeds? The answer is that God, being a just God and a righteous God, cannot permit sin in his presence. He cannot just overlook it as though it didn't exist.

All of us sinned in Adam and all of us have continued along the same path. The penalty which the Judge of the universe has pronounced on sin is death – immediate spiritual death, eventual physical death, and separation from God for all eternity.

What would you think of a human judge who regularly let people off the hook for the crimes they had committed? How would you feel about a judge who consistently released murderers, permitting them to return to their communities? Most of us would accuse such a judge of malpractice and would demand that he be removed from the bench. Yet, thousands of people expect to disobey God's laws and suppose that God is going to overlook it. They suppose that even though God, who cannot lie, said that the soul that sins will die, he will somehow change his mind, and everything will turn out all right. They look at him as a heavenly grandfather who shows love and kindness toward everyone in the world regardless of what they have done. Jesus said, "*Whoever believes in the Son has eternal life; whoever does not obey the Son will not see life, for the wrath of God remains on him*" (John 3:36). James tells us that a friend of the world is an enemy of God (James 4:4). Will God allow his enemies and those upon whom his wrath rests to enter into heaven and fellowship with God for all eternity? Of course not! God is angry with the wicked every day (Psalm 7:11). In any case, why would anyone who doesn't love God here, and doesn't enjoy listening to his word, and stays away from worship here want to spend forever doing those very same things? It doesn't make sense.

God's judgment is not only a future event. The Bible teaches us that God's wrath is being revealed even now. Carefully read Romans 1:18 and following. Portions of the passage are reprinted here:

> For the wrath of God is revealed from heaven against all ungodliness and unrighteousness of men, who by their unrighteousness suppress the truth. For what can be known about God is plain to them, because God has shown it to them. For although they knew God, they did not honor him as God or give thanks to him, but they became futile in their thinking, and their foolish hearts were darkened. Therefore God gave them up in the lusts of their hearts to impurity, to the dishonoring of their bodies among themselves, because they exchanged the truth about God for a lie and worshiped and served the creature rather than the Creator, who is blessed forever! Amen. For this reason God gave them up to dishonorable passions. For their women exchanged natural relations for those that are contrary to nature; and the men likewise gave up natural relations with women and were consumed with passion for one another, men committing shameless acts with men and receiving in themselves the due penalty for their error. And since they did not see fit to acknowledge God, God gave them up to a debased mind to do what ought not to be done. (Romans 1:18–28)

Did you notice in this passage the number of times it says, "God gave them up"? Because we do not glorify God and worship him as God nor give him the honor due to his name, and because we exchanged the glory of God for the creature and suppressed the truth and did not think it worthwhile to retain the knowledge of God, God's wrath is being revealed from heaven at this present time. He isn't sending down fire and brimstone. He is simply giving people up to do those things which their sinful hearts are inclined to do. The sexual perversion and other sins of our day are not merely rebellion against the laws of God; they are in reality the very punishment of God on sinful man. God is under no obligation to prevent it or the suffering that results

In this chapter, we've discussed at length the depravity of man, his inability to live according to God's way. However, one more thing needs to be said. Because of our sin and our having turned our back on God, there is a blindness that prevents us from understanding his word and seeking him.

> Romans 3:11: No one understands, no one seeks for God.

> 1 Corinthians 2:14: The natural person does not accept the things of the Spirit of God, for they are folly to him.

> 2 Corinthians 4:4: The god of this world has blinded the minds of the unbelievers, to keep them from seeing the light of the gospel of the glory of Christ, who is the image of God.

> John 6:43,44: Jesus answered, "No one can come to me unless the Father who sent me draws him."

No man seeks after God? Don't we see a lot of people worshiping God? Aren't the people in every nation and culture developing ideas of God because they are looking for him? It seems like that might be true, but in reality, they are looking for a god of their own invention. The God revealed in the Bible is a God who is all powerful. He expects us to have a personal relationship with him, not just some sort of mystical religious experience. He is a jealous God who does not accept the worship of other gods. God is a one-way God. God is not the one who says, "It doesn't matter what you believe as long as you are sincere." Jesus said, "*I am the way the truth and the life. No man comes to the Father except through me"* (John 14:6).

Buddhists might be able to accept Jesus Christ as one of the many channels of divine light, but Jesus will not accept Buddhism as an acceptable way to God. People don't like the narrowness of that. We find as many excuses as possible to explain why Jesus didn't mean what he said. People aren't searching for a God like that. I've heard of people who have said, "If that is what God is like, I don't want anything to do with him." We all want a god that is to our liking. But that god is an idol and does not exist.

What it all boils down to is this: since we are born dead in trespasses and sins and our spirits by nature are insensitive to communication with God, we are all at the mercy of God and the decisions he makes. If he does nothing, we are lost. Without the intervention of God there is no hope. The only hope for us is that God would make the move necessary to rescue us from the bondage we are in. And that is exactly what we are talking about in this book. What in the world is God doing? Is there any rhyme or reason to it all? He is reaching down into a sea of lost and dying humanity and rescuing a people to be his own possession: a people he will clean up and purify; a people on whom he can shower his love and attention; a people upon whom he will bestow his blessings; a people who will be to the praise of his glory so that in the ages to come they might show forth the riches of his grace. This will be a people who deserve to die, but upon whom God will extend his mercy. This will be a people who have been called out of darkness into his marvelous light. Our only hope is to be included in that group.

Jesus said, *"Come to me, all who labor and are heavy laden, and I will give you rest"* (Matthew 11:28).

John 1:12 says, *"But to all who did receive him, who believed in his name, he gave the right to become children of God."*

Revelation 22:17 reads: *"The Spirit and the Bride say, 'Come.' And let the one who hears say, 'Come.' And let the one who is thirsty come; let the one who desires take the water of life without price."*

Have you come to God through Christ or are you still looking for another way? Has God rescued you from the darkness? If not, why don't you turn to him today and claim his promise to rescue you?

Chapter 3
God's Remedy

If you have followed the discussion so far, you know that the Bible teaches us several things. First, it teaches us that God is calling out a people to be his own possession. These people become the children of God, part of his family; they are to be a royal priesthood, a holy nation, and God's own special people. Secondly, we saw that although mankind had a good relationship with God in the beginning, sin soon broke that relationship and now we have become enemies of God. The communication lines have been severed and we stand in open rebellion against God. Even at our natural best, we don't know how, nor do we desire to have a relationship with the true God. There is none who seeks for God (Romans 3:11), and everyone says, "We will not have this man reign over us" (Luke 19:14). Our desire to be king and our refusing to be in subjection to God are at the root of the sin problem. We are unwilling to glorify God as God, and we are not thankful for all of his provision for us (Romans 1:21). Even a sigh, if coming out of a grumbling and complaining spirit, is a "rebel sigh."

In this chapter, we will look at God's method for dealing with these two truths: the fact that he is gathering a people for himself, and the fact that the pool of people he is calling from is in rebellion against him. How can he call out a people for his own special possession when everyone on the face of the earth is under his condemnation and judgment? Can God really have fellowship with people that don't care about him and don't desire to know him or to have a relationship with him?

In John 3, the Bible records a discussion between a pharisee named Nicodemus and Jesus. Nicodemus came to Jesus at night, because he was fearful of what his Jewish colleagues would say. After Nicodemus had acknowledged Jesus as a teacher who had come from God and praised him for the miracles he had done, Jesus startled him with the following response: *"Truly, truly, I say to you, unless one is born again he cannot see the kingdom of God"* (John 3:3). It's extremely important for us to understand what this means, because we can't see the kingdom of God without this new birth.

Jesus is saying that people will not see (let alone enter) the kingdom of God unless they are "born again." Nicodemus wondered if someone would have to re-enter his mother's womb and be born all over again. Jesus replied that there is a natural birth of the human body and there is a birth of the spirit. In the same way that natural human life is passed on through conception and natural birth, spiritual life is given through spiritual conception and spiritual birth. Flesh gives birth to flesh and it is spirit that gives birth to spirit (John 3:6). This spiritual birth is necessary because all of us enter the world without spiritual life – our spirits are dead because of sin. We must be born again. This is not a religious phrase. It is a reality.

Just as the original source of life was God, spiritual life also has its source in God. We know that God is a spirit. God made Adam's physical body at creation and breathed into him the breath of life, and he became a living soul. The Bible uses the same word for spirit as it does for breath or wind. When God breathed into Adam, he was giving him spiritual life. This made Adam a living soul (*psyche*). After the fall, because of the judgment of God, the spiritual relationship between him and God was severed. God had told him that the day he ate of the forbidden tree, he would die. If spiritual life is to be restored, the initiative is going to have to come from God. He is the only source of spiritual life.

What Jesus was saying to Nicodemus was this: "Nicodemus, you have the wrong idea about eternal life. It has nothing to do with being good because no one is good except God. There is nothing you can do to try to put yourself in a special position spiritually. It is necessary for you to be renewed and regenerated spiritually by the Spirit of God in order to be a part of the kingdom of God. Just as you were born physically into the human family, it is necessary for you to be born spiritually into God's family in order to be a son of God. And just as you had nothing to do with your first birth, you have nothing to do with your second birth. Just like the wind blows here and there and you never know where it is coming from or where it is going, the same is true of those born of the spirit (John 3:8). You never know where or when the next child of God will be born."

Someone who has not been born again is said to be *"dead in trespasses and sins"* (Ephesians 2:1). This is the way we all come into the world. Our bodies are dying, our souls are damaged, and there is a vacuum in our souls because our spirits are dead. Sometimes the Bible speaks of someone in this condition as being "in the flesh" (Romans 7:5; 8:8). This is why, in the Old Testament, God speaks of a future day and a new covenant in which he is going to give people a new heart and a new spirit (Ezekiel 36:26). This is why Jesus chastised Nicodemus a little bit by saying, *"Are you the teacher of Israel, and yet you do not understand these things?"* (John 3:10). He should have been familiar with the Old Testament teaching on this subject.

What Jesus told Nicodemus is still true today. God is in the process of calling out a people for his name. If they are to be in God's family, they must have spiritual life in them. In other words, they need to be born again. If they are going to be a part of God's family, it isn't enough for them just to be human. Many people are religious and go to church regularly. However, if they remain spiritually dead, they are separated from the life of God and there is no communication with God. Paul describes this condition in Ephesians 4:18, *"They are darkened in their understanding, alienated from the life of God because of the ignorance that is in them, due to their hardness of heart."*

As Isaiah writes, *"But your iniquities have separated you from your God"* (Isaiah 59:2). There is no relationship with God. The only hope for anyone is that he be born again.

Just as your physical conception and physical birth did not depend upon your will or desire, your spiritual conception and birth do not depend upon your will or desire either. That is why John 1:13 says: *"who were born, not of blood nor of the will of the flesh nor of the will of man, but of God"* (emphasis added). That which is spiritually dead, having no desire to seek after the true God, cannot generate life in and of itself. Jesus' friend Lazarus was dead and buried in a tomb. Jesus' call to come out of the tomb gave him life and he responded. Similarly, God is calling people by his Spirit to come alive, and they do.

Spiritual life (or the new birth) is essential if we are to be able to see God's kingdom. Jesus did not tell Nicodemus what he was supposed to do to have this life. He was not given a plan to follow to gain eternal life. He was never promised that he himself would ever have eternal life. He was told however, that just as Moses had lifted up a snake in the wilderness, and that as many as looked at it would be healed of their snake bites (Numbers 21:8), so whoever looks to the Son of God and believes in him would not perish (as a result of the sin in his soul), but would have everlasting life. The people who had been bitten by the snakes had no other choice. They knew that they had been bitten and that death was certain. When Moses told them to look at the snake in order to be saved, that is all they had to do. The same is true for receiving eternal life. The problem is that unlike the Israelites, many people don't realize that they have been bitten by the sting of death, and therefore don't know to look to the Son of God for rescue. That's the reason we're told to go and spread the good news. Recognize the lostness of your soul, look believingly to Christ and you will be saved. Paul told the Philippian jailer, *"Believe on the Lord Jesus Christ and you will be saved"* (Acts 16:31). He holds out the same promise to you and me today.

As we look at the teaching of the Bible about this new birth, we'll have to consider several factors. The first is the problem of sin. How does God deal with the fact that every person is under God's condemnation? God operates on the principle of law, and he cannot just overlook this problem. In spite of what many people say, God cannot and will not simply let sin pass by. We have already discussed the fact that a just and holy God must be consistent with his own laws and his own righteous character. He does not intend to simply sweep the law aside and let everyone into heaven no matter how they behave or the attitude they have toward him.

How can God regenerate people and call them his children when they are guilty sinners? In order for God to call out people for himself, they must be rescued from the bondage to sin which they are in, their guilt must be dealt with, they must be righteous in God's sight, and their spirits must be given life. God's intention is to save his people from bondage and death. God has stated very clearly that this is the purpose for which Christ came. In speaking to Joseph before Jesus' birth, the angel of the Lord said, *"She will bear a son, and you shall call his name Jesus, for he will save his people from their sins"* (Matthew 1:21). If you were drowning, you wouldn't be considered saved until you had been rescued from the water. You wouldn't be saved just because the rescue boat had pulled alongside. In the same way, you can't be saved from sin just because you've been in church regularly or have been praying recently. God has planned deliverance from the power and penalty of sin for all who come to him. Someone who is still living under the power of sin and is living a life of sin cannot be described as having been saved <u>from</u> their sins.

Because of the fact that it was a man who brought sin into the world and caused the condemnation of all men, it was necessary that there be another representative who could reverse the process. Every living person can trace his ancestry back to Adam, and therefore each one of us is already under the condemnation of God and continually makes the same choices that Adam made. But God entered the human race himself to be the second Adam. He chose to do so in the person of his only begotten son, Jesus Christ, the second person of the Trinity.

Jesus Christ, although a man, was also God. He was just as much God as though he had never been man, and as much man as though he had never been God. The Bible makes the deity of Christ very clear.

> In the beginning was the Word, and the Word was with God, and the Word was God. He was in the beginning with God. (John 1:1-2)

In this verse, we can see that this thing called the Word existed in the beginning, and furthermore this Word was God Himself. In verse 14, John tells us that

> The Word became flesh and dwelt among us, and we have seen his glory, glory as of the only Son, from the Father, full of grace and truth.

It is obvious from the context therefore, that the Word is none other than Jesus Christ. In John 10:30, Jesus said, "*I and the Father are one.*"

Jesus told Philip in John 14:9, "*Don't you know me, Philip, even after I have been among you such a long time? Anyone who has seen me has seen the Father. How can you say, 'Show us the Father'?*"

In John 17, Jesus prayed, "*And now, Father, glorify me in your own presence with the glory I had with you before the world existed.*"

Colossians 2:9 reads, "*For in [Christ] the fullness of deity dwells bodily.*"

Romans 9:5: "*To them belong the patriarchs, and from their race, according to the flesh, is the Christ, who is God over all, blessed forever. Amen.*"

Hebrews 1:3: "*He is the radiance of the glory of God and the exact imprint of his nature, and he upholds the universe by the word of his power.*"

It is clear from the reaction of the religious leaders of Jesus' day that they thought he was claiming to be God. He was not just a son of God or just a godly example. Jesus Christ is the God of the

Universe. The essential question is, "What did Jesus Christ come here to do?" Did he come to show us how to live and to be a good example for us to follow? He certainly did that, but much more.

The Bible teaches that Jesus came to reverse or undo what Adam did. Jesus, being God, was sinless. Therefore, he was able to be a representative for the human race in the same way that Adam had been our first representative. It not only would take someone who was perfect to accomplish this, it would take a human being. That is why it was essential that Jesus be born into this world as a man. He was the only one who could legally represent us in order to reverse the decision which Adam had made. It is almost as though God is giving humanity a second chance to make the right decision. Jesus is even called the *second man* in 1 Corinthians 15:47. Jesus came, and this time, humanity's response was obedience.

Jesus lived a perfect life. He was tempted in all points just as we are, but he did not sin (Hebrews 4:15). When Jesus was talking to his disciples in John 14, he said in verse 30, *"I will no longer talk much with you, for the ruler of this world is coming. He has no claim on me."* Satan could not find a weak spot in Jesus' spiritual armor. He had no hold or authority in Jesus' life. Jesus perfectly lived the life which Adam did not choose to live. Jesus successfully stood against the temptations of Satan. In standing his ground, Jesus proved that a man could resist and choose not to sin. He proved that there is nothing essentially wrong with human nature in and of itself. God has no quarrel with our humanness. He made us to be human. Adam and Eve were as perfectly human before they sinned as they were afterwards. Sin is something which has come in as a stranger, an invader. It does not belong to our basic human nature. Jesus proved that.

In spite of the fact that Jesus had never sinned either personally or in Adam, he still died. He did not have a natural father and so the guilt of Adam did not transfer to him. In spite of that, he died both physically and spiritually. While Jesus was on the cross, he cried out with the words, *"My God, my God, why have you forsaken me?"* (Matthew 27:46). This was the cry of one who had known intimate and eternal fellowship with the Heavenly Father, but at this moment, there was separation. The Father had turned his back on his own son. Jesus did not call him father at that moment. At that moment, he knew the pain of separation which Adam and Eve had felt after they had sinned. He knew the separation which everyone who is separated from God feels. Even though he had not sinned, he now knew what its effects felt like. Separation from God was hell for Jesus.

An amazing truth is revealed in the Bible concerning Jesus' death as it relates to us. Since Jesus did not die for his own sin, God offers to apply the death of Christ to the record of anyone who will believe him. We'll look at some passages of Scripture in just a minute, but stop and think of what we've just said. If you believe what God is saying and are willing to accept it for yourself, God will reckon Jesus' death as your death, and he will credit your account with the perfect righteousness and obedience of Christ. Does the Scripture really teach this?

> Isaiah 53:4,5: Surely he has borne our griefs and carried our sorrows; yet we esteemed him stricken, smitten by God, and afflicted. But he was pierced for our transgressions; he was crushed for our iniquities. (Emphasis added.)

> 1 Peter 2:24: He himself bore our sins in his body on the tree, so that we might die to sins and live for righteousness; by his wounds you have been healed. (Emphasis added.)

> 2 Corinthians 5:21: For our sake he made him to be sin who knew no sin, so that in him we might become the righteousness of God. (Emphasis added.)

> Galatians 3:13: Christ redeemed us from the curse of the law by becoming a curse for us. (Emphasis added.)

> Hebrews 2:9: But we see him who for a little while was made lower than the angels, namely Jesus, crowned with glory and honor because of the suffering of death, so that by the grace of God he might taste death for everyone. (Emphasis added.)

1 Peter 3:18: For <u>Christ also suffered once for sins</u>, the righteous for the unrighteous, that he might bring us to God, being put to death in the flesh but made alive in the spirit. (Emphasis added.)

Hebrews 9:28: So Christ, having been <u>offered once to bear the sins of many</u>, will appear a second time, not to deal with sin but to save those who are eagerly waiting for him. (Emphasis added.)

1 John 3:5: You know that he appeared <u>in order to take away sins</u>, and in him there is no sin. (Emphasis added.)

1 Corinthians 15:3: For I delivered to you as of first importance what I also received: that <u>Christ died for our sins</u> in accordance with the Scriptures. (Emphasis added.)

When Jesus died on the cross, his death paid the penalty which God's law required of you. God had told Adam and Eve that the day they ate of the forbidden tree, they would die. Everyone who has ever lived has been under the sentence of death because of Adam's sin and because of their own sin. God's law requires death for sin. But, if Jesus died the death that is required of all of us, then the entire issue of punishment for sin has been settled. No further payment for sin is necessary. As far as God is concerned, the issue is finished. When Jesus died on the cross, he said, "It is finished," and that is exactly what he meant. Case closed! For the Christian, the final judgment has already been completed.

Because of Jesus' death on the cross, God is no longer counting people's trespasses against them. In 2 Corinthians 5:19 we read *"that is, in Christ God was reconciling the world to himself, not counting their trespasses against them."*

The sin question has been settled forever because of what Jesus Christ did on the cross. God has demonstrated his love toward us in that Christ died for us while we were still sinners (Romans 5:8). The Bible describes the result of this sacrificial death of Jesus as forgiveness and cleansing.

> In him we have redemption through his blood, the forgiveness of our trespasses, according to the riches of his grace. (Ephesians 1:7)

> And you, who were dead in your trespasses and the uncircumcision of your flesh, God made alive together with him, having forgiven us all our trespasses. (Colossians 2:13)

> And by him everyone who believes is freed from everything from which you could not be freed by the law of Moses. (Acts 13:39)

> As far as the east is from the west, so far has He removed our transgressions from us. (Psalm 103:12)

> And no longer shall each one teach his neighbor and each his brother, saying, 'Know the Lord,' for they shall all know me, from the least of them to the greatest, declares the Lord. For I will forgive their iniquity, and I will remember their sin no more. (Jeremiah 31:34)

> And from Jesus Christ, the faithful witness, the firstborn of the dead, and the ruler over kings on the earth. To Him who loves us and has freed us from our sins by his blood. (Revelation 1:5)

What we have been talking about so far applies mainly to the guilt that results from being sinners ourselves. What about the guilt we still carry from Adam? Even if God forgives us of our personal sins, don't we still carry with us the guilt which is on our account because of Adam's sin as our representative? Scripture gives us a very clear answer to this question as well. In the same way that Adam was our representative and brought death to the entire human race, Jesus Christ also becomes a representative and brings righteousness to those who are related to him.

Look at these words from Romans 5:12, 15b-18:

> Therefore, just as sin came into the world through one man, and death through sin, and so death spread to all men because all sinned. For if many died through one man's trespass, much more have the grace of God and the free gift by the grace of that one man Jesus Christ abounded for many. And the free

gift is not like the result of that one man's sin. For the judgment following one trespass brought condemnation, but the free gift following many trespasses brought justification. For if, because of one man's trespass, death reigned through that one man, much more will those who receive the abundance of grace and the free gift of righteousness reign in life through the one man Jesus Christ. Therefore, as one trespass led to condemnation for all men, so one act of righteousness leads to justification and life for all men.

For as by a man came death, by a man has come also the resurrection of the dead. For as in Adam all die, so also in Christ shall all be made alive. (1 Corinthians 15:21)

In summary, what these passages are saying is that in the same way that Adam's sin brought condemnation to all of those who are related to him, Jesus' righteousness brings life for all those related to him. Some people feel that it was unjust for God to count Adam's sin against all humanity. The truth is that God is applying the same principle both for the condemnation and for the justification. In the same way that Adam's sin is credited to the record of everyone born into Adam's family, God is crediting Christ's righteousness to all those who are born into his family. God is not only the judge, but he is the one who paid the penalty that his own law demanded. He can be both just and the justifier of the one who believes in Jesus (Romans 3:26).

Some of those who belong to Christ are reasonably good people, and others have been involved in the worst kinds of sins. In both cases they were unrighteous because of the condition they were in when they were born. But as bad or good as they may be, God is not going to even look at their own righteousness, but is going to replace their righteousness with Christ's righteousness. "*All our righteous deeds are like a polluted garment*" (Isaiah 64:6). That is why we need a different righteousness applied to our lives. He doesn't add Christ's righteousness to what we already have, but he replaces what we have with the righteousness of Christ. That is what is meant in 2 Corinthians 5:21 where Paul writes, "*God made him who had no sin to be sin for us, so that in him we might become the righteousness of God.*" Therefore, Jesus not only paid the penalty of our sin so we wouldn't be punished, but he has gone further than that. He is willing to apply the very righteous life of Christ to our account so that when God looks at our record to see how we have done, he sees us as perfectly righteous.

This is what Paul was praying for in Philippians 3:9. He wanted to *"be found in him, not having a righteousness of my own that comes from the law, but that which is through faith in Christ--the righteousness from God that depends on faith."* This is the only kind of righteousness that will be worth anything when we stand before God. When it comes to a decision as to whether we belong in heaven with God or are sent to Hell, the decision will not be based on what we have done, good or bad, but whether or not we have been credited with the righteousness that has its source in God himself. When God clothes someone with the righteousness of Christ, God can then declare that person "not guilty."

The gospel, or good news, is called the power of God for salvation to everyone who believes (Romans 1:16). That is because in the gospel, a righteousness from God is revealed. It is a righteousness that is received through faith (v. 17). We would not have known about this except that God has told us about it in the Scriptures. It is certainly not something that we could have invented. It goes against all the other natural religions of the world. All other religions have their participants working to earn their way to heaven. Christianity is completely opposite. Here we find God meeting his own requirements and giving it to his children as a gift.

Paul tells us that the problem that the nation of Israel had in their religious life was that they had a zeal, but that zeal was not according to knowledge (Romans 10:2). We can't just make things up. Our faith and our zeal have to be according to knowledge and that knowledge comes from God through his word. In chapter 10 of Romans, Paul tells us that what they had done wrong was to try to establish their own righteousness rather than accept the righteousness that comes from God (v. 3). They did not submit to

God's righteousness. They tried to do it their own way. In verse 4, he tells us that Christ is the end of the law so that there may be righteousness for everyone who believes. I'm being repetitious so you understand the point. God not only requires that our sins be wiped away, but he requires perfect righteousness. We are incapable of performing at that level. So God, in his grace, gives us credit for the perfect obedience and righteousness of Christ if we'll just accept it and believe it.

The law's authority has been removed, Christ's righteousness is applied, and the Bible speaks of the blood of Christ washing away sins. Read carefully the following verses:

> Matthew 26:28: This is my blood of the covenant, which is poured out for many for the forgiveness of sins.

> Romans 5:9: Since, therefore, we have now been justified by his blood, much more shall we be saved by him from the wrath of God.

> Hebrews 9:14: How much more will the blood of Christ, who through the eternal Spirit offered himself without blemish to God, purify our conscience from dead works to serve the living God.

> 1 John 1:7: But if we walk in the light, as he is in the light, we have fellowship with one another, and the blood of Jesus, his Son, cleanses us from all sin.

God has purposed that Jesus Christ should die as the payment for the sins of the world. He also has purposed that the shedding of Jesus' blood would wash away sins providing cleansing and forgiveness. He has further purposed that Jesus' own righteousness would be applied to the credit of all his children. God's remedy for sin is thorough. It has been dealt with from every angle. What many people do not realize is that God is offering to apply the benefits of the death of Christ to anyone who will receive it as a gift from him. There are no strings attached. There is nothing which we have to do to try to earn what God is offering as a gift. The Bible speaks of receiving this gift by faith. If it is given as a result of our works, then it is no more of faith. It would then be some sort of payback for our efforts, but God is giving a gift (Romans 11:6).

Faith simply means believing God: To believe God's assessment of the human condition and then to believe God concerning the remedy which he himself has provided. Faith means that we not only believe God with our minds, but that we believe it at such a deep level that we accept it as truth for ourselves and our own situation. We believe that God has done and will do what he has said that he would do. Salvation from sin then is received as a gift from God by faith. Salvation is not a reward for faith. Faith is the method by which salvation is received. Look at the following Scripture passages:

> Ephesians 2:8,9: For by grace you have been saved through faith. And this is not your own doing; it is the gift of God, not a result of works, so that no one may boast.

> Titus 3:5: He saved us, not because of works done by us in righteousness, but according to his own mercy.

> Romans 5:17: For if, because of one man's trespass, death reigned through that one man, much more will those who receive the abundance of grace and the free gift of righteousness reign in life through the one man Jesus Christ.

> Romans 4:2-8: For if Abraham was justified by works, he has something to boast about, but not before God. For what does the Scripture say? "Abraham believed God, and it was counted to him as righteousness." Now to the one who works, his wages are not counted as a gift but as his due. And to the one who does not work but believes in him who justifies the ungodly, his faith is counted as righteousness.

> Romans 4:22-25: That is why his faith was "counted to him as righteousness." But the words "it was counted to him" were not written for his sake alone, but for ours also. It will be counted to us who believe in him who raised from the dead Jesus our Lord, who was delivered up for our trespasses and raised for our justification.

Romans 10:9,10: Because, if you confess with your mouth that Jesus is Lord and believe in your heart that God raised him from the dead, you will be saved. For with the heart one believes and is justified, and with the mouth one confesses and is saved.

John 1:12: But to all who did receive him, who believed in his name, he gave the right to become children of God.

Acts 13:38,39: Let it be known to you therefore, brothers, that through this man forgiveness of sins is proclaimed to you, and by him everyone who believes is freed from everything from which you could not be freed by the law of Moses.

1 Corinthians 1:21: It pleased God through the folly of what we preach to save those who believe.

Galatians 2:16: Yet we know that a person is not justified by works of the law but through faith in Jesus Christ, so we also have believed in Christ Jesus, in order to be justified by faith in Christ and not by works of the law.

Romans 6:23: For the wages of sin is death, but the gift of God is eternal life through Jesus Christ our Lord.

God loved the world so much that he sent his son Jesus Christ to die the death that every one of us should have died. He paid the ultimate price of separation from God which should have been ours to pay. He can therefore in justice forgive our sins and declare us righteous in Christ. He offers it all as a gift to anyone who believes him and trusts him to mean what he says. Even in the Old Testament, Abraham was declared righteous because he believed God.

Will everyone believe God? No, not all will believe. But the Bible assures us that all of God's children will believe. Look at what Jesus said to the crowd when he was preaching to them in John 6. They had asked him what works they should do to carry out the works of God. Jesus answered in verse 29: *"The work of God is this: to believe in the one he has sent."*

In the middle of Jesus' teaching, he says something very interesting. He says in verse 37 that all that the Father gives to Jesus will come to him. God has a people which he has called to be his own. We don't know who they are, but he knew them before the foundation of the world, and he has given them to Jesus. This verse tells us that all of those will come to Christ. He goes on to tell them that he will not turn any of them away. In verse 39, he gives the additional promise that he would not lose any of them and will raise them up on the last day.

When the people rebelled against this teaching, Jesus said something amazing to them. Instead of trying to coax them into believing, he says:

> Verse 44: No one can come to me unless the Father who sent me draws him, and I will raise him up at the last day.

> Verse 45: Everyone who has heard and learned from the Father comes to me.

Is God being successful at what he is doing? Is God frustrated because he is trying to accomplish something which is doomed to fail? These verses tell us that he will not lose any. God will be successful in accomplishing his plan. In John 10, Jesus speaks of his people as sheep. He makes the following statements:

> Verse 3: The sheep hear his voice, and he calls his own sheep by name and leads them out. When he has brought out all his own, he goes before them, and the sheep follow him, for they know his voice. A stranger they will not follow, but they will flee from him, for they do not know the voice of strangers.

> Verse 11: I am the good shepherd. The good shepherd lays down his life for the sheep.

> Verses 14-16: I am the good shepherd; I know my own and my own know me. ...I lay down my life for the sheep. I have other sheep that are not of this sheep pen. I must bring them also. They too will listen to my voice, and there shall be one flock and one shepherd.

Verses 25-30: Jesus answered, "I told you and you do not believe. ... but you do not believe because you are not among my sheep. My sheep hear my voice and I know them and they follow me. I give them eternal life, and they will never perish and no one can snatch them out of my hand. My Father, who has given them to me, is greater than all; no one is able to snatch them out of my Father's hand. I and the Father are one."

God has his people all over the world. Many don't know it yet. God encouraged Paul in his endeavors in one particular city with these words: "*Do not be afraid, but go on speaking and do not be silent, for I am with you, and no one will attack you to harm you, **for I have many in this city who are my people**"* (Acts 18:9-10, emphasis added).

Jesus taught the people the truth about his calling his sheep. Some of the people rebelled at the teaching. What is his response to them? Does he try to convince them that they should come to him? Does he rebuke them for not believing? No. He simply tells them that they do not believe because they are not his sheep. He reminds them that his sheep listen to his voice and they follow him. That is a certainty. The sheep know the shepherd's voice. The sheep are secure. No one can snatch them out of Jesus' hand, and no one can snatch them out of the Father's hand.

Is there the possibility that the gospel message will be preached and that some of the sheep will perhaps not believe? Is there some way that they might not recognize the call? The scripture teaches us that his sheep hear his voice and they follow him. Look at Acts 13:48: "*When the Gentiles heard this, they began rejoicing and glorifying the word of the Lord, and as many as were appointed to eternal life believed.*"

What in the world is God doing? Is there any "Rhyme or Reason" to all that is going on in the world? Yes there is. God came and took the penalty of all the sin of the world upon himself. He suffered hell on behalf of his people. And now God is calling together a people to be his own special possession. All around the world he is calling them. They are listening and are following his voice. He is giving them eternal life. He is regenerating their spirits and making them a part of his family. He is giving Christ's righteousness to them as his gift.

How is he doing this? Is there a voice from heaven? No. He is calling through the proclamation of the gospel. This good news of salvation was first announced by the Lord, and then was confirmed by them that heard him, and has since been passed down from generation to generation (Hebrews 2:3).

In Romans 1:16, Paul writes:

> For I am not ashamed of the gospel, for it is the power of God for salvation to everyone who believes, ...For in it the righteousness of God is revealed from faith for faith, as it is written, "The righteous shall live by faith."

In 2 Thessalonians 2:14, he writes, *"To this he called you through our gospel, so that you may obtain the glory of our Lord Jesus Christ."*

In Romans 10:14, the following logical thought progression is given to us: *"How, then, will they call on him in whom they have not believed? And how are they to believe in him of whom they have never heard? And how are they to hear without someone preaching?"*

The answer to each of the questions is that they can't. God is calling out a people for his name through the gospel. Those who are his hear the voice of their God, their shepherd, as they hear the gospel preached to them. They follow the call, believe on him, and have all the benefits of the death of Christ freely applied to them.

God, the shepherd of the sheep, provides all that his children need. Do they need faith to believe? God grants it, for it is written, *"For by grace you are saved through faith, and that, not of works, it is the gift of God."*

Do they need to repent? *"God may perhaps grant them repentance leading to a knowledge of the truth"* (2 Timothy 2:25). *"God exalted him at his right hand as Leader and Savior, to give repentance to Israel and forgiveness of sins"* (Acts 5:31). *"So then, God has even granted the Gentiles repentance unto life"* (Acts 11:18).

Do they need righteousness? *"Those who receive the abundance of grace and the free gift of righteousness [will] reign in life through the one man Jesus Christ"* (Romans 5:17). Do they need to have their heart opened? *"One who heard us was a woman named Lydia, ...who was a worshiper of God. The Lord opened her heart to pay attention to what was said by Paul"* (Acts 16:14).

What a tremendous salvation God supplies. Everything his people need, he freely provides. Before we end this chapter, it is essential that we ask the question of you: where do you stand in relation to the salvation of God? As you read these passages of Scripture, do they ring true to you? Can you hear God calling you to faith in his promise of salvation?

Does the announcement that Jesus has died to pay your sin penalty come as good news to you? Have you accepted it in faith, rejoicing over the fact that God would be willing to enter the world himself to take the penalty that you deserved for the sins you have committed and for the sinner you were at birth? God invites you to trust him for salvation today. He tells us that today is the day of salvation. Do you believe him? Are you trusting him to be your savior? If so, God states very clearly that faith is counted by him as righteousness. He has promised us that those who come to him in faith have everlasting life. If you have come to him in faith and are trusting him to save you, you have that eternal life and will never perish.

He will never turn any away. Perhaps you have come to God in faith, but you wonder whether or not he will receive you. God has promised that if you give up on your own attempts to save yourself through your efforts and if you trust him to save you, he will do so. He will not turn you away. You will never perish. Your sins have been washed away by the blood of Christ, and your account has been credited with the righteousness of Christ!

Can you see now what Scripture means when it says that he has called his people out of darkness and into light? Darkness is a lost, unregenerate, unforgiven condition. Light is the knowledge that God loves you personally and has taken your sins away.

> For God so loved the world, that he gave his only Son, that whoever believes in him should not perish but have eternal life. For God did not send his Son into the world to condemn the world, but in order that the world might be saved through him.

Whoever believes in him is not condemned, but whoever does not believe is condemned already, because he has not believed in the name of the only Son of God. (John 3:16–18)

Whoever believes in the Son has eternal life; whoever does not obey the Son shall not see life, but the wrath of God remains on him. (John 3:36)

Chapter 4
Spiritual Life

We are in the process of discussing God's purposes in the world. What is he doing and why? As I mentioned earlier, God is infinite and there is no way that we, as finite beings can understand everything that God is doing. It would be ludicrous for us to think we could. However, God has revealed in his Word, the Bible, all that we need to know about what he is doing. In the previous chapters, we have seen that, primarily, God is calling out a people to be his own possession so that they would bring him praise and glory forever.

In the last chapter, we discussed the fact that if God is going to gather together a people for himself, something has to be done about the fact that everyone is in rebellion against this King. God, who is perfect, cannot tolerate sin. From eternity past it has been God's plan to redeem a people for himself by paying their sin debt with the death of his own son on the cross.

We also saw that when Christ died on the cross, he took upon himself the penalty for the sins of the whole world. That means that the sin question has been forever settled. Those who receive Christ and belong to God have had their sins forgiven, and the righteousness of Christ is credited to them. We must believe the message of the gospel and receive Christ personally. Those who receive Christ are given the right or authority to become the children of God. They are born again by the Spirit of God. Those who do not receive the Son of God will not see God, and God's wrath and condemnation remain on them. Christ's death does not profit them since they have not received and believed the truth (John 3:36).

Forgiveness, however, is only one part of the solution to the problem. It would be futile for God to forgive our sins and even grant us the righteousness of Christ, and at the same time leave us spiritually dead. The good news of the gospel is that we can have life in Jesus Christ. Jesus said, *"I came that they may have life and have it abundantly"* (John 10:10). We want to turn our attention now in greater detail to the character of that new life. To begin this part of our investigation, we need to turn to the Old Testament to look at several passages dealing with an agreement God calls the New Covenant or new agreement. Look at Jeremiah 31:31:

> Behold, the days are coming, declares the Lord, when I will make a new covenant with the house of Israel and the house of Judah, not like the covenant that I made with their fathers.... For this is the covenant that I will make with the house of Israel after those days, declares the Lord: I will put my law within them, and I will write it on their hearts. And I will be their God, and they shall be my people. (Jeremiah 31:31–33)

> And I will give you a new heart, and a new spirit I will put within you. And I will remove the heart of stone from your flesh and give you a heart of flesh. And I will put my Spirit within you, and cause you to walk in my statutes and be careful to obey my rules. (Ezekiel 36:26-27)

Notice several things about this New Covenant:

1) It is made with Israel.

2) It will not be like the old covenant.

3) God's law will be written on the mind and heart. This is a new heart, a new spirit. The old will have been replaced.

4) God will be their God and they will be his people.

5) God's Spirit will be in them.

6) They will be moved to follow the laws of God.

We are going to investigate each part of this New Covenant one part at a time.

It is made with Israel.

Since the New Covenant was made with Israel, what does it have to do with us Gentiles? After the death of Christ, God revealed that he was going to break down the barrier between Jew and Gentile, and that he was creating one new body. Read for instance Ephesians 2:11-16:

> Therefore, remember that at one time you Gentiles in the flesh … were at that time separated from Christ, alienated from the commonwealth of Israel and strangers to the covenants of promise, having no hope and without God in the world. But now in Christ Jesus you who once were far off have been brought near by the blood of Christ. For he himself is our peace, who has made us both one and has broken down in his flesh the dividing wall of hostility by abolishing the law of commandments expressed in ordinances, that he might create in himself one new man in place of the two, so making peace, and might reconcile us both to God in one body through the cross, thereby killing the hostility.

God's chosen people during the Old Testament was the nation of Israel. He had made certain promises to them about their future glory and the many blessings they would inherit. These promises are still in effect. In the New Testament, God informs us that he is doing something new. He is going to call together a people from among all the nations of the world, not from Israel alone. This people will be included in all of the blessings that God had given to Abraham at the beginning. The Gentiles had basically been locked out of God's blessings. Only a few Gentiles were ever absorbed into the nation of Israel so that they could receive the blessings God provided for that nation. Many more could have enjoyed that privilege, but most did not take advantage of the opportunities God had provided. This was either because they refused to join Israel, or, more likely, because they didn't know anything about the God of Israel.

The New Covenant clearly applies to the new body of people God is putting together today. At the last supper, Jesus said, *"This is my blood of the new covenant, which is poured out for many for the forgiveness of sins"* (Matthew 26:28). The fact that Jesus announced that his blood was the blood of the New Covenant and the fact that his blood has now been shed, means that the New Covenant has begun. The writer of Hebrews says that it is a better covenant because it is based on better promises (Hebrews 8:6).

In Hebrews 8, he goes on to say,

> For if that first covenant had been faultless, there would have been no occasion to look for a second. (Hebrews 8:7)

> In speaking of a new covenant, he makes the first one obsolete. And what is becoming obsolete and growing old is ready to vanish away. (Hebrews 8:13)

A covenant is like a will. In order for the will to go into effect, there must be the death of the person who makes the will. In Hebrews 9 we read:

> For where a will is involved, the death of the one who made it must be established. For a will takes effect only at death, since it is not in force as long as the one who made it is alive. Therefore not even the first covenant was inaugurated without blood. (Hebrews 9:16–18)

The author is pointing out that in dying, Jesus brought in the New Covenant. Just as the old covenant was inaugurated with blood, so too is the New Covenant. In the Old Testament, there were various sacrifices and anointings to consecrate the furniture and utensils of the tabernacle. In the New Covenant, God was demonstrating that it too, like the old, had to be brought into force with the shedding of blood. The effect of the shedding of his blood was to wash away our sins and to cleanse our consciences so that we could serve the Lord effectively. Without that sacrifice, there would be no changing our basic character. Look back at verses 14 and 15 of that same chapter of Hebrews:

> How much more will the blood of Christ, who through the eternal Spirit offered himself without blemish to God, purify our conscience from dead works to serve the living God. Therefore he is the mediator of a new covenant, so that those who are called may receive the promised eternal inheritance, since a death has occurred that redeems them from the transgressions committed under the first covenant.

Empty worship, without the real possibility of a changed life, is a futile activity leading to ultimate death. Many people today are involved in worship experiences, but they possess no life in themselves. When Christ died and brought the New Covenant into effect, he cleansed our consciences from such dead works. We no longer have to wonder whether our worship is acceptable. We don't need to try to appease an angry, offended God. We are now free to serve the living God. We are free to have a relationship with him. As this passage tells us, those who are called will now receive the promised eternal inheritance. Jew and Gentile alike have that kind of access to God now under the New Covenant.

Paul explains in the book of Romans that all those who are of faith are part of the new man that God is calling together.

In Romans 4 we read:

> For the promise to Abraham and his offspring that he would be heir of the world did not come through the law but through the righteousness of faith. For if it is the adherents of the law who are to be the heirs, faith is null and the promise is void. For the law brings wrath, but where there is no law there is no transgression. That is why it depends on faith, in order that the promise may rest on grace and be guaranteed to all his offspring—not only to the adherent of the law but also to the

one who shares the faith of Abraham, who is the father of us all. (Romans 4:13–16)

Therefore, the promises are not only for those who are Abraham's physical offspring, the Jews, but for those who are Abraham's spiritual offspring, the offspring of faith. God had made certain unconditional promises to Abraham. The law with its commandments came 430 years later, but the Bible says that those requirements cannot nullify the unconditional promises God had given to Abraham and his offspring (Galatians 3:17).

All of this does not mean that God's interest in Israel no longer exists. I am not saying that God's future plans for Israel are being absorbed in the church. I am simply saying that during this current period of time in God's plan, God is applying the spiritual benefits of the New Covenant to those he is calling to be his people. Those he is calling come both from Israel and the Gentile nations. Although the promise of the New Covenant was originally made with Israel, its spiritual blessings are in force now for everyone who believes. That's why we have to spend some time investigating it.

It will not be like the old covenant.

The second point to be made regarding the New Covenant is that it is not like the old covenant. The old covenant required certain actions on the part of the people in order for them to receive the blessing of God. It required them to be obedient to certain external rules. If they successfully kept those rules, then God blessed them.

Deuteronomy 28:1ff.

> And if you faithfully obey the voice of the Lord your God, being careful to do all his commandments that I command you today, the Lord your God will set you high above all the nations of the earth. And all these blessings shall come upon you and overtake you, if you obey the voice of the Lord your God.

Verse 15ff.

> But if you will not obey the voice of the Lord your God or be careful to do all his commandments and his statutes that I command you today, then all these curses shall come upon you and overtake you.

You can see from these verses that the old covenant was a conditional one. If the people obeyed the law and followed certain principles, God promised them that he would be with them and would bless them. The blessing required obedience to all of the commands. No lapses were allowed. Deviating in any way brought a curse (Galatians 3:10). The results were totally dependent on the people. If they were obedient, blessing followed; if they were disobedient, curses followed.

Needless to say, no one ever successfully keeps God's commandments or lives up to God's standards. This was the case throughout the different periods of Bible history as we showed in the last chapter. Even though the people of Israel had seen the miracles of God and how he led them through the wilderness, through the Red Sea, and through the Jordan River, they still rebelled and eventually ended up captives in foreign lands. The curses which God had pronounced came to pass.

Now God is announcing a new agreement which will NOT be anything like the old agreement. The whole concept of being obedient in order to merit God's blessing is finished. God is not going to base his earthly blessings, nor the blessing of being in Heaven, on the degree to which we meet his expectations. That is because his standards cannot be achieved. That is the main lesson of the Old Testament. He is going to provide all the blessings of his New Covenant to his people without requiring certain behaviors from them as a condition for receiving the blessings. It will not depend in any way upon the behavior of the people or how well they keep God's laws.

This is the point at which many people stumble. It was at this very point that the nation of Israel stumbled. Romans 9:31 states:

> Israel who pursued a law that would lead to righteousness did
> not succeed in reaching that law. Why? Because they did not
> pursue it by faith, but as if it were based on works. They have
> stumbled over the stumbling stone.

Many people are still stumbling over this stumbling stone
because they are setting up a standard of righteousness which they
feel they ought to reach. If they reach it, they feel that God will
then look favorably on them. As we have said over and over again,
the problem is that the only standard righteous enough is the
perfection of God himself, and there is no one who is capable of
reaching that standard. God either has to condemn all for not
living up to his requirements, or he has to provide a way to make
the unrighteous righteous while maintaining his own righteous
character and justly dealing with the guilt of sin.

Perhaps you are stumbling over this very same point. You can
discern this by looking at your motives. Do you go to church or
do good deeds in hopes that God will look at you favorably and
reward you accordingly? Do you find yourself looking at others
and feeling that, compared to them, you are rather good, and so
you must have a good chance of making it? If so, you are stumbling
over the stumbling stone. God's salvation is promised totally
independently from our behavior. It is a free gift, received by faith.
Have you ever received the righteousness of Christ as God's gift
to you? Don't plan on being good enough. Just receive it from him
by faith.

Paul explains this more in Galatians 3. Verses 7 and 8 tell us
that God announced the gospel in advance to Abraham when God
told him that all nations would be blessed through him. Those who
have faith are blessed along with Abraham (v. 9). In comparison to
this, those who are under the law are under a curse. Paul quotes
Deuteronomy 27:26, which says, *"Cursed be anyone who does not
confirm the words of this law by doing them."* The promise to Abraham
came 430 years before the law was given to Moses. Paul tells us
that the law does not cancel the promise God made to Abraham.
Even in our own legal system, once a contract has been ratified,

additional conditions can't be added. God gave an unconditional promise to Abraham. He couldn't justly add the condition of the Ten Commandments to an oath he had previously given without condition. The promise stands.

He goes on in Galatians 3:26-29:

> For in Christ Jesus you are all sons of God, through faith. For as many of you as were baptized into Christ have put on Christ. There is neither Jew nor Greek, there is neither slave nor free, there is no male and female, for you are all one in Christ Jesus. And if you are Christ's, then you are Abraham's offspring, heirs according to promise.

From this passage, we see that those who belong to God are heirs of the unconditional promise made to Abraham because they are Abraham's spiritual offspring. People who believe in Christ and receive his gift are the seed to whom the promise was given, and no additional requirements that the law might contain can nullify the promise. Like the promise God gave to Abraham, the New Covenant is an unconditional promise. It does not depend on what we do, but only on our believing God and receiving the message for ourselves. Those who do so are heirs of the promise.

God's law will be written on the mind and heart. This is a new heart, a new spirit. The old will have been replaced.

God states that in the New Covenant he will give people a new heart, a heart of flesh rather than a heart of stone. On this new heart he has promised to write the Law of God. This is one of the major differences from the old covenant: the old covenant included externally imposed laws and religious observances which were impossible for the unrenewed heart to fulfill. You will remember that God wrote the law on the two tablets of stone that he gave to Moses. These were external rules and regulations imposed from the outside. But, under the New Covenant, God has promised to write the laws on a new heart which he would provide. How does this make a difference? The new heart is a heart which is inclined toward God. It does not contain the hardening deceitful influences of sin within it. It is a heart which enjoys the things of God. It enjoys communication with God and the fellowship which only comes through a relationship with him. The law, written on such a heart, is a delight rather than a burden.

Have you ever considered the impossibility of obeying the command that we should love the Lord with all of our heart, soul, and mind? There is no way that the natural man can come up with that kind of love. However, the heart that comes from the new creation is capable of loving God the way he expects. It is not the sinful natural heart we had at birth that can do this, but the new heart which God provides his people.

Listen to what David writes in Psalm 42:1,2:

> As a deer pants for flowing streams, so pants my soul for you, O God. My soul thirsts for God, for the living God. When shall I come and appear before God?

Or in Psalm 122:1:

> I was glad when they said to me, "Let us go to the house of the Lord!"

Or listen to what Paul writes in Romans 7:22, even as he struggles with sin:

> For in my inner being I delight in God's law.

In this latter passage, Paul is acknowledging a wrestling match that takes place within him. But it is not a wrestling match in his heart. It is a struggle between his renewed heart, which delights in the law of God, and sin, which is still present in his flesh. Some of you may say, "I don't know if I ever could work up that kind of love for God or develop that attitude in my own heart." Of course you can't! We are talking about a supernatural change, brought about by the Spirit of God, recreating and renewing the spirit of man, making it alive to God.

Another effect of the new heart is faith toward God. Romans 10:10 tells us that it is with the heart that a person believes and is justified. You remember our earlier discussion concerning the fact that God reckons faith as righteousness. But where does that faith come from? Is it possible for a hardened, stoney heart to believe? Can blinded eyes see without the miracle of the regenerating work of God? Hardly! Lydia was described as a worshiper of God, and yet the Lord had to open her heart in order for her to respond to the message of Paul (Acts 16:14). She had worshiped God even before her heart had been opened, but worshiping God is not a requirement for salvation. Many people worship God each week in church and yet have an unregenerated heart. Perhaps this is the situation with you. A regenerated heart is necessary. Only in that way can someone worship God in spirit and in truth.

This very point is at the crux of many problems church leaders have in working with people, and it's a problem many people have with themselves. We often try to get people to act like Christians when they are not. Many times we will try to reform our own behavior. We may recognize that some habit or attitude that we have is improper. We may try in our own energy to reform ourselves so that we can act more like Christ or be "more Christian." The fact that efforts like these result in repeated failure may be due to the lack of internal change. The old heart cannot be reformed. It has to be replaced!

A person who has been changed from within has the streams of life-giving water bubbling and flowing from within him (John 7:37). The faith that receives all of these blessings from God comes from a heart which has been changed by the mighty power of the Spirit of God.

God has promised that all who call upon him will be saved (Romans 10:13). There are no exceptions. Calling upon the Lord to save us is the cry of a believing heart. An unbelieving heart is a sinful heart (Hebrews 3:12), and therefore can't, and doesn't want to lay claim to the promises of God. The unregenerate heart is deceitful above all things and desperately wicked (Jeremiah 17:9). So what we need is that God in his mercy would regenerate our heart and make us new creatures. Only then will we be able to receive all he has promised to those who believe.

God will be their God and they will be his people.

This portion does not need much expansion because we have discussed it quite extensively already. It is important just to note that it is in the new birth, under the New Covenant, that a person becomes one of the people of God and he becomes their God. Those who remain in their unregenerate state remain enemies of God and in rebellion against him. God doesn't make them rebellious. We all are rebellious and at war with God when we enter this world. We are that way because we desire to be. If we begin to hate the old way and desire to be rightly related to God as one of his children, we give evidence of the fact that God is performing a mighty miracle within our soul. Our heart will cry out for the living God, and we will seek his face and fellowship with him, our heavenly Father.

God's spirit will be in them.

The New Covenant further states that God will put his spirit in his people. This is different from giving them a new heart. The new heart is man's regenerated spirit. It is a human spirit. But God goes further and also gives his children his own Spirit. That means that God himself dwells in them. Listen to what Paul writes in 1 Corinthians 2:11,12:

> For who knows a person's thoughts except the spirit of that person, which is in him? So also no one comprehends the thoughts of God except the Spirit of God. Now we have received not the spirit of the world, but the Spirit who is from God, that we might understand the things freely given us by God.

You don't know what I am really like or what I am really thinking. I (my spirit) am the only one who really knows me. In the same way, nobody really knows what God is like or what he thinks. Only his Spirit knows. In this passage we learn that God has given us his Spirit so that we might know the things which God has given to his children.

So under the New Covenant, God changes the heart, writes his law on it, and then gives his own Spirit to dwell in the heart of man. There is communication between his Spirit and our spirit! In Romans 8:16 we read: *"The Spirit himself testifies with our spirit that we are God's children."* There is an ongoing fellowship that the unregenerate can never understand. The dead spirit has been made alive, and there is communication once again as God speaks to our spirit through his word. For those who have been born again, this is one of the strongest sources of assurance there is. As the Spirit of God witnesses with our spirit that we are children of God, we can have the assurance that God is working.

It is the presence of the Spirit in the life of the Christian that produces the characteristics that God is interested in. They aren't produced by our ingenuity or our efforts to be obedient to the law of God. They are produced by the Spirit of God actively at work in our lives. The fruit of the presence of the Spirit of God is listed for us in Galatians 5:22-23:

> But the fruit of the Spirit is love, joy, peace, patience, kindness, goodness, faithfulness, gentleness, self-control; against such things there is no law.

The fruit which a plant produces depends on what kind of plant it is. You can't get apples from a grape vine, nor can you get oranges from a peach tree. A healthy tree brings forth fruit because of the life of the tree. In the verse we are looking at, God gives us a list of the fruit (singular) of the spirit. This is the fruit which the Spirit produces in the life of a believer. A child of God will exhibit this fruit as the life of God works and grows inside.

Look in John 15:1-8. Verse 5 says:

> I am the vine; you are the branches. Whoever abides in me and I in him, he it is that bears much fruit, for apart from me you can do nothing.

107

Notice that Jesus says that he is the vine. His children are the branches. There is unity of life in the vine and the branches. In looking at a grape vine it might be difficult to distinguish between the vine and the branches. We sometimes refer to the entire plant as the vine. The life and nutrients that flow through the vine are the same nutrients that flow into the branches where the fruit grows. If there is no connection between a branch and the vine, then the branch will not be capable of producing fruit. Jesus states very clearly that a branch that remains attached to the vine will bear fruit. There is no question about it. God will prune the vine so that it produces the fruit he is interested in. It will happen. There is no bearing of fruit unless the branch is attached to the vine. The same thing is true of our relationship with Christ. His life so thoroughly becomes the life of the Christian that the fruit of the spirit is the natural result. If there is no fruit of any kind, it must be because the branch is not connected to the vine. If the fruit of the Spirit is not working out in your life in some measure, there is great cause for you to be concerned about whether or not you are connected to the vine – to Christ. Bearing fruit is the glory of the Father (v. 8) and gives evidence that a person is a disciple of Christ.

The full glory of the plan which God has designed begins to become clear now. Man is not capable of living the kind of life which God desired. So God changes the heart and comes in to dwell within the life of the person. In doing so, he produces the characteristics that he desires to see. At the same time, the individual involved knows a greater joy and peace than he has ever known before. He experiences this joy because he is living a life which conforms to the way God created him. So much of the sorrow and despair we feel in this life is due to the fact that we are living a life totally contrary to the kind of life our body and soul were designed for. Under the New Covenant, there is the freedom of knowing that all that God demands of us he himself works in us by his spirit. Consider these statements from Scripture:

> Now may the God of peace … equip you with everything good
> that you may do his will, <u>working in us</u> that which is pleasing

in his sight, through Jesus Christ, to whom be glory forever and ever. Amen. (Hebrews 13:20,21, emphasis added.)

For it is God who works in you both to will and to work for his good pleasure. (Philippians 2:13, emphasis added.)

For this I toil, struggling with all his energy that he powerfully works within me. (Colossians 1:29, emphasis added.)

They will be moved to follow the laws of God.

The final thing mentioned in the New Covenant was that its recipients would be caused to follow God's law. That means that there is a change in motivation. We, in our natural state, are not capable of following God's laws the way God intended. We do not have the desire to abandon self and put God and others first. We do not have the inclination to do what is right out of the proper motivations. However, once our heart has been changed, God's Spirit given, and the law and principles of God written on our heart, we are inclined to follow God's way. He has provided the motivation and the cause for right behavior.

I was teaching this material in a Sunday School class one time and we were thinking about this portion of Scripture. We were discussing the fact that God promises to cause his children to walk in his ways. I asked what that meant. Different people commented on what they thought it was saying. Then there was a long pause as the truth of it began to sink in. One lady said suddenly, "God doesn't do that for all Christians, does he? I know a lot of Christians who God isn't working in that way. He isn't causing them to follow his ways."

We need to think carefully about this: If there actually are Christians who are attached to the vine, but the life of God is not producing fruit in them, or if there are Christians whom God is not causing to walk in his ways, then his Word is not true. But God's Word is true! Therefore, if there is no fruit in someone's life, that person is not connected to the source of all life, Jesus Christ.

Perhaps we have fooled ourselves into thinking that Christianity is what we do or what decision we make instead of whether God has made us spiritually alive. That new life will result in a living dynamic faith.

The new heart and spirit are gifts of God. They are not deserved or earned by those who receive them. Their hearts had been just as wicked as everyone else's. God does not grant a new heart as a result of obedience because there is none righteous, no not one. The new heart is not given as a result of faith; faith is the result of a new heart. Faith cannot come from the natural heart, because *"the natural person does not accept the things of the Spirit of God, for they are folly to him, and he is not able to understand them because they are spiritually discerned"* (1 Corinthians 2:14). We all need God's gift of a new heart before we can believe in him.

It is time to dethrone man and respect the rightful place God has reserved for himself. Without God, we are all lost and condemned sinners. We do not deserve the grace which God provides. If God had not stepped in to rescue us, we would all be consumed (Lamentations 3:22). Everything we have and are has resulted from the work of God in his mercy.

When God gives a new heart and writes his law on it inclining our nature toward him, does that mean that sinning is finished? No. Even though our basic nature has changed, sin is still a powerful force, and a born-again person sometimes acts like a natural man. Paul had struggles with right and wrong, but he wrote: *"For I have the desire to do what is good, but I cannot carry it out. For in my inner being I delight in God's law"* (Romans 7:18,22 NIV).

In 1 John we read:

> No one born of God makes a practice of sinning, for God's seed abides in him; and he cannot keep on sinning, because he has been born of God. By this it is evident who are the children of God, and who are the children of the devil: whoever does not practice righteousness is not of God, nor is the one who does not love his brother. (1 John 3:9–10)

110

> Therefore, if anyone is in Christ, he is a new creation. The old has passed away; behold, the new has come. (2 Corinthians 5:17)

We have studied the meaning and some of the applications of the New Covenant, but we need to bring it together so that you can understand how it relates specifically to you. We began the discussion of the new birth in the last chapter by referring to a conversation which Jesus had with Nicodemus. Let's turn back to John 3. With everything we have studied so far, we ought to be able to put this chapter into perspective.

In verse 5, Jesus told Nicodemus that if a man is not born of water and the Spirit, he would not be able to enter the kingdom of God. He then pointed out two kinds of birth. He told him that flesh gives birth to flesh, but the Spirit gives birth to spirit. He told Nicodemus that this should not surprise him. Why not? Because Nicodemus was a teacher of the Jewish people. He should have known all about the New Covenant and the implications which we have been discussing.

In verse 13, Jesus tells Nicodemus that the Son of Man (meaning himself) came from heaven. In saying this, he is indicating his deity. Then he goes on to tell Nicodemus that the Son of Man must be lifted up the same way the serpent in the wilderness had been lifted up. We discussed this incident earlier. The people sinned, and God punished them with venomous snakes. The remedy was a brass snake on a pole, and all the people had to do was to look at it to be saved from their snake bites.

Jesus tells Nicodemus that the Son of Man must be lifted up in the same way that Moses lifted up the snake in the wilderness. Just as those who looked at the snake lived, so those who believe in the Son will have life. Those in the wilderness were healed from their snake bites and received their natural life back. Those who look to the Son are healed from the sting of sin and receive their eternal life back – the life they lost in Adam centuries ago.

> For God so loved the world, that he gave his only Son, that whoever believes in him should not perish but have eternal life. (John 3:16)

Jesus told Nicodemus that the Son of God did not come to condemn the world, but that the world might be saved through him. The condemnation had already been pronounced. As he says in verse 18, "*Whoever believes in him is not condemned, but whoever does not believe is condemned already, because he has not believed in the name of the only Son of God.*"

And in verse 36, he says, "*Whoever believes in the Son has eternal life; whoever does not obey the Son shall not see life, but the wrath of God remains on him.*"

The wrath of God is already on the world of men. It is there because of sin. All of us have sinned, and the resulting consequence of that sin is death. But God tells us that he has lifted up his own son on a cross so that anyone may look to him and live. It may seem foolish. It may seem that it is too simple. But that is what God has done. Those who believe on the son HAVE eternal life.

In Jesus' concluding remarks to Nicodemus, he tells him that Light has come into the world, but men love darkness rather than light. However, life comes by admitting our need, by turning away from our own remedies, and looking at the cross where the Son of God took the penalty for our sin. Jesus refers to it as coming to the light. In verse 21, he tells Nicodemus that whoever lives by the truth comes into the light, so that it may be seen plainly that what he has done has been done through God. In other words, a believer knows his sinful past. He knows that salvation came as a gift from God and that he owes everything he is and everything he has to God. In coming to the light, it is obvious that what he is and what he does is because God has worked in his life. A change has been made. The old has been removed, and the new heart and new spirit have taken its place.

Salvation is a gift and is received by faith. What about you? Have you given up trying to be good enough for God? Have you accepted his offer of forgiveness and righteousness? Has God changed your heart from a hard, stony heart to one that is sensitive toward God? Has he given you his Spirit so that there is living communication between you and him? If not, I urge you today to come to him in faith and ask him to do for you what he has done for millions of others throughout history. He has promised that he would not turn any away that come to him. Whoever believes on the Son has everlasting life. Look to him today. In so doing, you will be received by God and discover that you are one of the ones he has called to be his very own.

Chapter 5
Dealing with Guilt

We have been discussing how God is in the process of calling out a people to be his very own. The human race has been lost in sin since Adam disobeyed God in the garden of Eden. Since that time, we have not been interested in knowing the true and living God. We don't want God to reign over us. We don't recognize that all we have comes from God, and so we aren't thankful and don't worship him. We want to make up our own rules and live according to our own agenda. Even though we have rebelled, God is in the process of regenerating and renewing people all over the world. He sent his only Son to pay the sin penalty so that anyone who comes to God by faith in Christ may be forgiven and be accepted as a son in God's family. And because we have a dead spirit and a corrupt nature, God's regenerating work includes creating a new heart within us and changing our motivation so that our desire is focused in the right direction. He is preparing a people for participation in Life with God.

The important message of this book is that God is at work. He is not frustrated by what is going on. He has a plan and a purpose, and he is working it out in the world. Being an infinite God, he is able to do this without making us into robots. Our real freedom ended when Adam sinned. It doomed everyone, and removed any chance of ever escaping, unless and until God stepped in and began to rescue people from death and judgment.

As God is carrying out his work, Satan too is busy. He is using our emotional needs, our conflicts, and the world's philosophy in an attempt to hinder the work of God. Even though he is not successful, there is a constant battle going on in which we all have a part. You see, we are not just third parties sitting on the sidelines of history, and looking at and analyzing God's plan for the world and for history. We are a part of and are involved in what is going on. Do you remember that in the second chapter, we noted that at the end of history there would be two groups of people – one enjoying God and praising him for all his wonderful works, and the other suffering severe punishment? There is no third group. You and I as we live today are a part of one or the other of these two groups. As we discussed in the philosophical chapter, there aren't multiple truths. What the Bible describes is the truth – not just for some people, but for all people everywhere in every generation.

In this and the next few chapters, we are going to discuss the implications of these truths in the area of our personal lives. If I'm one of those who is a member of his family, what effect does that have on my regular day-to-day life? How does it impact me personally (Chapters 5-7), my family relationships (Chapter 8), and my participation in the church (Chapter 9)? By discussing these three crucial areas, we are touching on the fiercest field of battle. If we can see how God's truth applies in these areas, we will find a greater degree of freedom to live a joyful godly life than we have ever had before.

First then, we begin a discussion of the implications of these truths for our personal lives. One of the biggest issues people face is that of guilt and guilt feelings. How can God relate to me if I'm guilty, and how does forgiveness fit in? And if God just forgives us of everything, doesn't that make for some wild living?

We have spent a lot of time demonstrating the fact that God has declared that the whole world is under the judgment of death. All have sinned and have fallen short of the glory of God (Romans 3:23). But in spite of this, God loves his creation, and desires fellowship with the creatures that he made in his own image. He desires that all the personal forces in the universe see how generous, gracious, and kind he is in taking us rebellious creatures, making us share in the divine nature (2 Peter 1:4), adopting us into his royal family (John 1:12; 1 Peter 2:9), and allowing us to share in the ruling of the universe (Revelation 20:6).

God tells us in Romans 3:20 that no one will be declared righteous in his sight by keeping the law. Before we even get a chance to feel discouraged about that truth, God announces in verse 21:

> But now the righteousness of God has been manifested apart from the law, although the Law and the Prophets bear witness to it— the righteousness of God through faith in Jesus Christ for all who believe. For there is no distinction. (Romans 3:21–22)

What he is basically saying is that God's righteousness is available, and can be counted as my righteousness. If you are one of God's children, God declares that the righteousness of God has been given to you. Even though all of us have sinned and fallen short of the expectations and demands of God's glory and righteousness, we are justified freely by his grace through the redemption that came by Christ Jesus (Romans 3:23, 24). So these promises include you if you are one who has trusted Christ and believed on his name.

You see, it would not be just for God simply to ignore your sins. If there were a local human judge who kept letting thieves and murderers off the hook out of supposed love and generosity, the public would not stand for it. He would not be a just judge. But in our case, since the penalty which was required has been paid by Jesus Christ himself, God can be just, because he has punished sin, and still he can justify you. To justify means to declare righteous, to pronounce clean and perfect in his sight. It's an exchange. God gives you his righteousness in exchange for your sin which has been blamed on Christ. Christ was then put to death for those sins.

Doesn't it depend upon how good I've been? No! Romans 3:27 asks: "Where is the boasting?" The answer is that there is none. You can't even boast about being smart enough to understand and

believe the gospel. If it were a matter of your being smart enough
or shrewd enough to have noticed the good deal which God was
offering, you would be able to boast. You would be able to stand
before your friends and say, "How come you guys aren't smart
enough to see that this gospel is a great deal?" Or, on the other
hand, you might say, "God has forgiven me because I have gone
to church more and read my Bible more than you have." Neither
of these boasts is possible. You didn't come to know the Lord
because of your insight or the strength of your faith. You may have
accepted it by faith, but you were only able to believe because God
has done a regenerating work in your heart, changing it from a
heart of stone to a heart of flesh, and granting you the gift of faith.
The Bible says, *"For by grace are you saved through faith, and that not of
yourselves, it is a gift of God not of works"* (Ephesians 2:8).

In Romans 4:3, we are told that Abraham believed God and it
was credited to him as righteousness. In verses 23 and 24 we read:

> But the words "it was counted to him" were not written for his
> sake alone, but for ours also. It will be counted to us who
> believe in him who raised from the dead Jesus our Lord.

God is saying that when you trust him, believe on him, and put
your faith in him, he credits that faith as righteousness for you.
That is, your record in the file of heaven declares that you are
righteous. Second Corinthians 5:21 states:

> For our sake he made him to be sin who knew no sin, so that
> in him we might become the righteousness of God.

> And be found in him, not having a righteousness of my own
> that comes from the law, but that which comes through faith
> in Christ, the righteousness from God that depends on faith.
> (Philippians 3:9)

We like to establish our own righteousness because we are
ignorant of God's righteousness. We typically create a list of rules
to live by and then seek to measure ourselves by those rules. We
often do that in association with our churches. Each church has its
own personality and standards and expectations. These are all

usually things that we can pretty much measure up to, especially outwardly. We can't conceive of a righteousness as perfect as God's. What we need to do is to submit to God's righteousness. By submitting, we acknowledge God's righteousness as the true standard, and we acknowledge that we need that righteousness or we are dead.

Aren't my sins going to detract from the righteousness God is giving me? The answer is "No." God replaces our sinful record with Christ's righteousness. No matter how good or wicked we have been, God says that all our righteousness is like filthy rags in his sight (Isaiah 64:6). It is necessary that they be totally replaced. That is what God has done for you if you are one of his children.

God says that so far as the east is from the west, that is how far he has removed our sins from us. Our sins and iniquities will be remembered against us no more (Jeremiah 31:34). John the Baptist, in announcing that Christ had come, called him *"The Lamb of God that takes away the sin of the world"* (John 1:29). Hebrews 9:26 tells us that, *"He has appeared to put away sin by the sacrifice of Himself."* The sin question has been completely and thoroughly dealt with.

If God allowed even one sin to remain on our record, it would separate us from him forever. If it took our conscious confession of each particular sin to have it erased from our record, most of us would constantly have at least a few sins remaining there because it is impossible to remember them all. In that case, we could not be saved. We like to think we can confess all of our sins because we are usually operating on the basis of our revised personal list of righteousness. That is pretty easy to keep up with, and if we struggle in an area, we adjust our list so that that behavior is not listed. But for example, if we really are to love the Lord our God with all of our heart, soul, mind, and strength, how are you going to keep track of the many times in a day where God only had 50% (or less!) of your mind or strength? You can't. Christ died because of your less than perfect love for him.

So how is confession related to forgiveness? Many of you have probably memorized 1 John 1:9 which says, *"If we confess our sins, he is faithful and just to forgive us our sins and to cleanse us from all unrighteousness.*" Some people carry guilt because they wonder about the sins which they have not confessed. Have those been forgiven? Let's take a few minutes to look at this passage. It would be helpful to have your Bible open as we work through this.

In 1 John 1:3, John is telling us about **the life**, Christ's life, which he had personally seen so that we might also have fellowship with God and with other believers. He tells us in verse 6 that if we claim to have fellowship with God and yet walk in darkness, we are lying. In other words, to walk in darkness is inconsistent with the Christian life. He is not talking about some Christians who are in fellowship with God and other Christians who do not have fellowship. He is talking about Christians who have fellowship with God, and others who claim to be Christians, but are not because their life is a life of wandering in the darkness.

If we walk in the light (verse 7), in other words, if we are true Christians, we have fellowship with God and with one another, and Jesus' blood cleanses us from ALL sin. That means past, present, and future sins. The promise of salvation is that God washes away all of our sins through the blood of Christ. There will be some people who claim to be without sin. It isn't necessary, they think, to be cleansed of sin because they don't have any. He tells us in verse 8 that if we claim to be without sin, we deceive ourselves, and the truth is not in us. In other words, someone who claims that he was born and continues to live without sin is not a Christian. A person who does not have the truth in him does not know God. You should be able to see that John is moving back and forth between saved people and lost people. Verses 6 and 8 are referring to people who walk in darkness, or those who don't have the truth. These are lost or unsaved people.

In contrast to this kind of person, the person who walks in the light (verse 7), and who confesses his sin (verse 9), and who admits that he is a sinner and agrees with God about the character of his natural life, receives forgiveness and cleansing from the faithful God. I don't believe the main emphasis of this verse is on the day-to-day confession of sin as though it takes such confession of each sin to cleanse each sin. A person who has come to God in faith, trusting the finished work of Christ on the cross, is one who has agreed with God's assessment of his former life and his continual need for God to work in his life, and therefore will be open and regular in his confession. He doesn't deny his sinfulness but acknowledges it. Someone who trusts Christ in this way has all of his sins forgiven – past, present and future. Forgetting to confess one won't leave that one unforgiven. If it was unforgiven, we could not be saved.

In saying that, I am not implying that it is unnecessary to confess our sins. Often when we sin, we have a guilty feeling, knowing that we have done something wrong and then tried to hide it from God. It seems to put a wall between God and us. The wall isn't there as far as God is concerned, but it is there as far as we are concerned. If we honestly admit to God that we have sinned, we can once again know the joy of the forgiveness that has already been ours all along. But the confession of each individual sin doesn't bring the forgiveness for that particular sin.

Turn to Hebrews chapter 9. There are a few verses here that will be of tremendous help regarding this whole question of sin and guilt. Look at verse 14:

> How much more will the blood of Christ, who through the eternal Spirit offered himself without blemish to God, purify our conscience from dead works to serve the living God.

> So Christ, having been offered once to bear the sins of many, will appear a second time, not to deal with sin but to save those who are eagerly waiting for him. (Hebrews 9:28)

God sent his son to die on the cross so that our sins would be forgiven and removed from us. He wants us to have a cleansed conscience. The cleansed conscience is not due to our faithful confession. The cleansed conscience is clear due to the fact that our sins have been removed from us and dealt with on the cross. That means our consciences should be free from the constant bombardment of guilt and despair that plagues so many people.

121

He wants us to be free to serve the living God. Being free to serve God is the goal. He doesn't want us to be burdened down in bondage to sin or its effects on the conscience. The sin question has been so thoroughly dealt with that when he comes again, he will not have to deal with the sin question again. He has already removed our sins from us.

Turn to Hebrews 10. In the first couple of verses, the writer mentions that if the Old Testament sacrifices had actually removed sins, they would not have had to be offered over and over. Those sacrifices were not able to make the people perfect (or complete). Watch that word "perfect." It comes up again. Continuing in verse 2:

> Otherwise, would they not have ceased to be offered, since the worshipers, having once been cleansed, would no longer have any consciousness of sins? (Hebrews 10:2)

Notice the two points: first, if the sacrifices had made the worshipers perfect, the sacrifices would have stopped being offered, and second, the people would no longer have felt guilty for their sins. Instead of helping the people not to feel guilty for their sins, verse 3 tells us that the sacrifices were a constant reminder of their sins. Over and over the people were reminded about how guilty they were because over and over they had to keep bringing sacrifices. Verse 4 tells us the reason it didn't work. It is impossible for the blood of bulls and goats to take away sins. They were offering the sacrifices in obedience to God, but the sacrifices themselves were accomplishing nothing. The blood of animals cannot take away sin.

Now look very carefully at verses 10-14. I am going to quote just verse 10 and 14 together so that you can see how it fits.

> And by that will we have been sanctified through the offering of the body of Jesus Christ once for all. For by a single offering he has perfected for all time those who are being sanctified.

The Old Testament sacrifices were not able to make the people perfect. If they had, the sacrifices would have stopped, and the people would no longer have carried the guilt of their sin on their consciences. But we are told in this passage that what the Old Testament sacrifices could not do, Jesus did once and for all by the sacrifice of himself. We've been made holy through his sacrifice, and we are told that we have been made perfect and complete forever through his sacrifice. Let these thoughts sink in deep, and meditate on them frequently. If the sacrifice of Christ accomplished what the old sacrifices could not do, then having been made perfect, the sacrifices should cease to be offered and we should not carry around a guilty conscience because of our sins. The verses state clearly that the sacrifice of Christ was once for all. That means no further sacrifice is necessary. Having been made holy and complete (perfect), there is no need to be reminded constantly of our sins, and there is no further need to be burdened down with the guilt of them. Our conscience can be clear, and we can serve God acceptably.

So often, we as Christians carry the guilt of our sin as though Jesus had never died. It is as though we don't believe what God has told us. Why do we insist on carrying our sins when God has told us explicitly that they have been dealt with once and for all and have been permanently removed from us? In effect we do what the Old Testament sacrifices did. We constantly remind ourselves of sin just like the continual bringing of sacrifices did for the people of the Old Testament.

To show that this all fits together with the Old Testament, the author of Hebrews goes on to explain the prediction of the New Covenant which we have already discussed in some detail. We now have the fulfillment of what had been promised so long ago.

Verse 17 of Hebrews 10 quotes Jeremiah 31:33 which says, *"I will remember their sins and their lawless deeds no more."* Verse 18 then says, *"And where there is forgiveness of these, there is no longer any offering for sin."* No longer any sacrifice for sin! Do you understand what that means? It is finished! The entire debt has been paid, once and for all. There is no more to pay. There is no more to do. The sacrifice has been paid.

Turn now to Romans 8:1. *"There is therefore now no condemnation for those who are in Christ Jesus."* This verse teaches us that there is no condemnation NOW for those who are in Christ Jesus. Who are those who are in Christ Jesus? They are believers, those who are called of God to be his children. There is no condemnation, no judgment for those who are in Christ Jesus. God isn't sitting in heaven counting our sins. We as God's children need to believe this just as much as we need to believe that Jesus died to give us eternal life. Many people struggle continuously with the guilt of sin, not realizing that Jesus Christ has paid for that sin. God has forgiven and forgotten it. We should have enough faith to forget it as well. Ask the Lord today to give you the faith you need to believe that your sins are no longer an issue with God. Ask him to give you that freedom of spirit that comes from knowing that your standing with God is one of perfect righteousness.

How does this work out in everyday life? Suppose it's been a long hot day. Things have not gone right at work, and now you are back home with the family. It isn't long before one of the kids does something irritating which sets you off. Suppose you get angry and send your children to their rooms so that you can have some time without interruptions and annoyances. Down deep you really love your children, and you know that you really should be treating them more kindly, perhaps even talking to them, playing games, or reading them a story. However, you feel like doing none of that tonight!

There are several responses which you might have in this situation. You may realize that this is not an appropriate way to act, but we are human and sometimes these things happen. The problem with that point of view is that it contradicts God's way of doing things. God tells us that we should be patient and kind. Scripture tells us that love is not easily provoked and is not abusive. So the problem is not in our humanness. The problem is sin. To respond this way to our children is sinful and self-serving and an offense toward God.

Another response then is to agree that it is wrong to act this way, but after all, God is loving and forgiving, and I can't help the way I act, so it will all turn out fine in the end. This too is the wrong response. Acknowledging the sinfulness of the behavior is a good first step, but God cannot just overlook sin.

The opposite response is one of overwhelming guilt. You realize that you've blown it again. So you go to your wife and apologize, and then you go to the children and apologize. However, you realize that you've done exactly the same thing two or three times every week for the last two months! So, after the apologies are over, depression begins to set in. You wonder if you feel sorry enough. You wonder how anyone could ever love someone as uncontrolled as you. You begin to wonder if you are a Christian after all. A Christian certainly wouldn't behave this way, would he?

So how does the truth of our forgiveness in Christ work in this kind of situation? First, it is certainly appropriate to confess the sinfulness of your behavior to your family, and to ask them for their forgiveness, and even ask what you can do to make it right. It's good to acknowledge that your behavior falls way short of God's standard for loving family relationships. But what about your relationship with God?

The gospel is good news because it not only promises eternal life, but it promises the removal of sin from us. So the moment I behave in the way I've just described, the sin is removed instantly. My actions are indeed worthy of punishment, the death penalty, but the sinful thoughts and acts I've just committed are blamed on Christ and charged against him. His death on the cross was the punishment for these outbursts against my wife and children. The sin is gone. Of course you should confess to your family. Of course you should confess to God. But those confessions are not prerequisites for the forgiveness God has provided in Christ.

Try to keep in mind the fact that your forgiveness doesn't depend on the thoroughness of your apology or the depth of your repentance, but on the mercy of God in Christ. Satan will use these feelings of inadequacy as an opportunity to accuse you of insincerity. He will try to point out that you don't look very sorry for the way you have behaved. You may not feel like you repented thoroughly enough. Remember, God isn't waiting for a certain level of remorse. Your faith in Christ, as weak as it may be, is what secures all the benefits of God's grace. There is no condemnation for the Christian.

In addition, you need to avoid bringing this sin to your mind every day for weeks. People tend to do that. They say, "Man, I can't believe what an idiot I was for the way I treated my family yesterday!" "There's no way I can be a Christian if I'm able to act that way!" God has removed our sin and buried it and so should we.

Now comes a crucial question: "If we are seen by God to be perfectly righteous; if he does not hold our sins against us, and our salvation doesn't depend upon what we do, can I go on sinning?" And what about other people? Don't we need to lay down the law?

Paul poses this very same question for us in Romans 6:1-2. He writes, *"What shall we say then? Are we to continue in sin that grace may abound? By no means! How can we who died to sin still live in it?"*

The answer is quite simple. A Christian has a new heart, changed attitudes, changed desires, changed motivations. Real Christianity is not a religion of unregenerated people who are trying to get by with using grace as license to sin. In fact, grace teaches us to deny ungodliness and worldly lusts, and to live righteous and godly lives (Titus 2:12).

Paul's answer to "Shall I continue in sin?" is this:

> By no means! How can we who died to sin still live in it? Do you not know that all of us who have been baptized into Christ Jesus were baptized into his death? We were buried therefore with him by baptism into death, in order that, just as Christ was raised from the dead by the glory of the Father, we too might walk in newness of life. (Romans 6:2–4)

Scripture teaches us that the reason that we do not continue to live a life of sin is because we have died to sin. God grounds our victory over sin in the reality of our death to it. Scripture tells us that those who were baptized into Christ Jesus were baptized into his death. Let us examine this portion in a little more detail. In 1 Corinthians 12:13, Paul says, "*For we were all baptized by one Spirit into one body.*" In saying this, he is telling us that baptism is the Spirit's operation to place us into the body of Christ.

The church is referred to as the body of Christ. When Christ was here on earth in bodily form, he ministered to those around him, but he was limited by the fact that his body was only in one place at a time. After he ascended into heaven, he sent the Holy Spirit to dwell in the hearts of those who were his. In 1 Corinthians 12:13, we are told that it is the Spirit's responsibility to baptize or place his children into the body of Christ. Each Christian has a particular function in the body of Christ. (See 1 Corinthians 12 and Romans 12.) With the Spirit of God indwelling individual believers, Christ is able to minister all over the world at one time. His eyes, ears, hands, and feet in the form of individual believers are in many different places all at the same time.

When the Holy Spirit puts us into the body of Christ, the Scriptures call this baptism. I believe this is the baptism that is being referred to in Romans 6. In being baptized into Christ, we were also baptized into his death. What does this mean? Someone who is in Christ is a member of Christ's body. Christ died on the cross almost two thousand years ago. If we are a member of Christ, then God says that we died when he died. This is a mystery, to be sure, but it is still true. Paul goes on to say in Romans 6:5, that if we have been united with him in his death, we will certainly also be united with him in his resurrection. Our identity is in Christ. When he died, we died. Sin's penalty has been meted out; sin's power has been broken.

Paul writes in verse 6:

> We know that our old self was crucified with him in order that the body of sin might be brought to nothing, so that we would no longer be enslaved to sin. (Romans 6:6)

When Jesus died, he was no longer exposed to Satan's temptations. We know that even when he was alive, Jesus was not conquered by sin or the temptations that came his way. Yet, the battle was fierce. Once he had died, the battle was over. Sin had lost. Paul is telling us that we also have died to sin. That is an accomplished fact. That is why a Christian cannot continue in a life of sin. The victory has been won, and sin no longer has its power. When God looks at us, he sees us as part of the resurrected body of Christ. We are to look at ourselves in the same way. In fact, in Ephesians 2:6 we learn that we were raised with Christ and are seated with him in heavenly places by virtue of our union with Christ.

To some, this may seem like a mental trick. But God is saying that it is a fact. We are to trust what God says even though it does not seem to be logical. We need to resist the temptation to go by our feelings, and we must begin to act on what God's word says. Since we are a part of Christ's body, and since God knows Christ already died, that means that we too have died. If one died for all then we are all dead (2 Corinthians 5:14). The death has occurred. We are to live in the truth of this fact. That's what Paul meant when he wrote in Romans 6:11, *"So you also must consider yourselves dead to sin and alive to God in Christ Jesus."* This means we are to live this way. Count it as true. When sin's temptation seems so strong, you need to say to yourself, "I've died to this." When you say this, you are not making something up; you are stating a fact. Paul goes on to tell us not to allow sin to reign in our bodies. It can't demand obedience. It is not our master. It has lost its power no matter how strong it seems. We don't need to submit to it. Sin has been defeated.

Other scriptures support the fact that you can't live in sin once God has changed your heart and placed you into Christ. Look at the following verses from 1 John:

> If we say we have fellowship with him while we walk in darkness, we lie and do not practice the truth. (1 John 1:6)

128

Whoever says "I know him" but does not keep his commandments is a liar, and the truth is not in him. (1 John 2:4)

Everyone who has this hope in him purifies himself, just as he is pure. (1 John 3:3)

You know that he appeared in order to take away sins, and in him there is no sin. No one who abides in him keeps on sinning; no one who keeps on sinning has either seen him or known him. (1 John 3:5–6)

No one born of God makes a practice of sinning, for God's seed abides in him; and he cannot keep on sinning, because he has been born of God. (1 John 3:9)

Sin's greatest strength comes through the law (1 Corinthians 15:56), but the law no longer has jurisdiction over the Christian because, having died with Christ, the Christian is no longer subject to the penalty which the law demands. Understanding this principle is a great help in our personal fight against sin. But more on that in the next chapter.

Every one of us begins life as a slave to sin. But when Christ died, that bondage was broken and the law that went with it ceases to apply. Paul tells Timothy in 1 Timothy 1:9, *"Understanding this, that the law is not laid down for the just but for the lawless and disobedient, for the ungodly and sinners...."* Once someone becomes a child of God, he is no longer a sinner. (I didn't say he never sins.) Paul tells us we are not under law but under grace (Romans 6:14).

There's another truth that needs to be included in this discussion about being baptized into Christ. Every person is either in Adam or in Christ. When we are born into the world, we are in Adam. That is, we can trace our ancestry back to Adam. Adam serves as our representative. Adam's decisions are counted as our own. When Adam sinned, you sinned because you were in Adam. However, when you come to Christ, you are reborn. God regenerates your life. You become a new creature in Christ. When this happens, you are taken out of Adam and put into Christ.

Being in Christ, you are credited with the righteousness of Christ. His righteousness is counted as yours just as Adam's sin had been credited as yours. Since God sees you as having died with Christ when he died, your history in Adam has ended. When God looks for your record as a member of Adam's family, he finds that you have already died. The new you is a member of Christ. You possess eternal life. You are a child of God, a co-heir of Jesus Christ. Your life is hidden with Christ in God. Christ is your life, for when he appears, you will appear with him in glory (Colossians 3:3, 4). Your identity is not your choices or your sins. It is Christ!

You may still be wondering how all of this fits together. You know about the facts we've been discussing, but it sure doesn't seem like you're dead to sin, does it? We still want to know what happens if we continue to live a sinful life even though we have trusted Christ.

Paul goes on in verses 16-23 of Romans 6. He begins talking about slavery. He is not talking about slavery to a human master, but slavery to either sin or righteousness. He tells us in verse 16 that we are a slave of whomever we obey. If we continually offer ourselves to sin, then we are a slave to sin. But if we offer ourselves to God, we are a slave of God and righteousness. In this regard, it doesn't matter that we are not under the jurisdiction of the law. Even though you've been set free, if you freely offer yourself as a slave, you are a slave. Jesus said in another place that we cannot serve two masters (Matthew 6:24). We are therefore either a slave of righteousness or a slave of sin, one or the other, but not both.

When I respond angrily to my wife, I am offering myself as a servant of sin at that moment. Moment by moment, I am offering myself as a slave of sin or of righteousness. God makes it very clear to us what the results are for slavery to either of these two masters. In Romans 6:16 he tells us that slavery to sin leads to death, but slavery to obedience leads to righteousness. He expands upon this in verse 19 where he tells us that slavery to sin is slavery to impurity and to ever-increasing wickedness, but slavery to righteousness leads to holiness.

Notice something in verse 17. He says that his readers used to be slaves to sin, but they wholeheartedly obeyed the teaching, and have been set free from sin, and have become slaves to righteousness. Notice that they wholeheartedly obeyed the teaching. That is because their heart has been made new. Can the same thing be said about you?

He summarizes the results again in verses 21 and 22. Slavery to sin leads to death, but slavery to God leads to holiness which results in eternal life. There is no middle ground between these two alternatives. What kind of death is he talking about here? Ultimately, eternal death. We embrace death every time we choose the sin side. The other alternative, slavery to God, leads to eternal life. We might diagram it as shown:

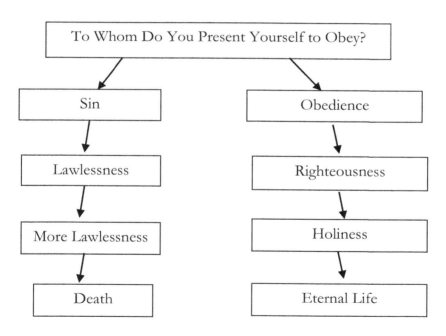

I think we should be very clear about this. Put verses 16, 19, and 22 together. Slavery to obedience leads to righteousness, which leads to holiness with the result of eternal life. There is no other way to eternal life than this. There are some who would have us believe that because they raised their hand in a church service, or made a profession of faith as a Christian, or were baptized as an infant or an adult, or became a member of the church, that therefore they inherit eternal life no matter how they live. There are those who make the profession of faith in God's gracious gift of salvation, but they still live their lives in slavery to sin. Does their profession alone guarantee them eternal life? NO! IT IS NOT POSSIBLE!

When God comes into someone's life and transforms it by his grace, that person is then motivated to do those things which are pleasing to God, and not to try to get away with as much sin as possible. When God rescues someone from slavery to sin, that person is set free to be a slave of God and righteousness. The result in such a person will be ever-increasing righteousness and holiness which is the only road to eternal life. There is no other.

The grace of God teaches us to deny ungodliness and worldly lusts, and to live soberly, righteously, and godly in this present world (Titus 2:11). The grace of God doesn't teach us to get away with as much sin as we can. Rejecting temptation, turning our back on ungodliness, and living godly lives are characteristics developed by the grace of God in our lives. Not having these basic characteristics of God's nature is a sign that God's saving grace is missing from that life.

So what I should think about when I'm tempted to sin, or even when I give in to that temptation, is that in taking that step, I am taking a step toward judgment and death. As a believer, that is not the road I want to be on. If I am truly a believer, God will not allow me to persist on that road. He will take me home to heaven before he would let me get to the end of that road because that way ends in death.

> That is why many of you are weak and ill, and some have died. But if we judged ourselves truly, we would not be judged. But when we are judged by the Lord, we are disciplined so that we

may not be condemned along with the world. (1 Corinthians 11:30–32, emphasis added.)

But what about backslidden Christians? Only God knows those who are truly his. The point we are trying to make is that salvation results in a changed life. Those who constantly yield to sin move on to greater wickedness and eventually eternal death. Those who yield themselves to God find ever-increasing righteousness in their life, and their life is increasingly characterized by holiness. This is the way to eternal life. Does that mean we are saved by our works? No! Do we have to achieve a certain level of perfection before God will save us? No! What it means is that when God changes a heart and comes to dwell in a life, the attitudes and motivation change accordingly. Love for God and obedience to him become the hallmarks of our lives. The change in behavior comes about from a change from within by the Spirit of God, not a change caused by efforts of self to live like a Christian. This change may be slow and take many years, but it will take place.

I can hear someone saying something like this:

> This all sounds way more complicated than the simple gospel we read about in the Bible. Didn't Paul tell the jailor, "Believe on the Lord Jesus, and you will be saved"? It doesn't sound like he needed to understand all of this about yielding to the flesh or spirit. Paul didn't tell him he needed to worry about whether he was sinning more than a real Christian would. He basically told him to trust Christ and he would be saved. Right?

Absolutely right. At the risk of being too repetitious, let me just say this: The gospel is simple. Believing on Christ saves us. Period. But what we are talking about in these chapters is what happens *when* you believe. It must be important because the Bible dedicates a lot of space to these teachings. When we believe something is true, it changes our behavior. If someone tells us a devastating hurricane will arrive tomorrow, if we believe it, we will make preparations.

When a person actually believes that he is condemned, but that trusting in Christ will save him, his behavior changes. At the same time, God has said that he will completely change believers from the inside out. But it will take time because sin is deeply entrenched in our flesh: our physical bodies, minds, will, and emotions. God is committed to that transformation. If no such transformation is taking place even at a slow pace, it is probable that our belief was false or superficial. That is what this whole discussion is about.

Here is where we touch base again with the purpose of this book. Is there any "Rhyme or Reason" to what God is doing? Is there any way to understand what is going on? God is active in the whole process of salvation, not just in its beginning in someone's life.

We'll begin with Philippians 1:6:

> And I am sure of this, that he who began a good work in you will bring it to completion at the day of Jesus Christ.

This verse gives us a couple of very important truths. First of all, it tells us that God is the one who began a good work in us. We didn't start the work. God did. The verse goes on to promise that he who began the good work will carry it on to completion. That means that he is not going to give up in the middle of the job. There is nothing that will hinder God from doing what he intends to do. He does not do a half-baked job no matter what the circumstances are. We have all visited the homes of people who began projects only to get involved in other things, and the half-finished project sits there for months waiting to be completed. There are some projects that never get completed. God is not like that. He accomplishes everything he sets out to do.

The verse goes on to tell us that he will continue the work which he began until the day of Jesus Christ. It will take that long. There is a lot to be done in each one of our lives. None of us is anywhere near what God would like us to be. Throughout our lifetime, God will continue the work he began in us. God is making us like Christ so we will glorify him.

I can hear someone say, "Yes, but he might not succeed with me since I might do something which would turn him off forever. Or, I might end up rejecting him or denying him." If you had put yourself into Christ, then certainly you might end up removing yourself from Christ and be lost in the end. If your being a Christian was due to your own intelligence or dedication, you might change your mind or rethink the decision which you had made. But the truth of the matter is that if you are in Christ, you are in him because of the work and will of God. "*And because of him you are in Christ Jesus, who became to us wisdom from God, righteousness and sanctification and redemption*" (1 Corinthians 1:30 emphasis added).

So first of all, you would never have turned to him on your own. It takes the re-creating power and work of God to change a hard heart like yours was. Secondly, God knew ahead of time what he was getting. All time – past, present, and future – is in God's eternal present. He knew how stubborn or weak you would turn out to be, and he began a work in you anyway. He will follow through on what he has begun. We have God's word on that!

Look at Romans 8:29, 30:

> For those whom he foreknew he also predestined to be conformed to the image of his Son, in order that he might be the firstborn among many brothers. And those whom he predestined he also called, and those whom he called he also justified, and those whom he justified he also glorified.

And then Ephesians 1:4-6:

> Even as he chose us in him before the foundation of the world, that we should be holy and blameless before him. In love he predestined us for adoption to himself as sons through Jesus Christ, according to the purpose of his will, to the praise of his glorious grace, with which he has blessed us in the Beloved.

Let your heart meditate on the truths contained in these passages. God predestined us to be conformed to the image of his Son. To predestine means to determine ahead of time. God determined that his children would be conformed to the image of his Son. That conformity to the image of Jesus Christ will bring glory to God. Anyone who can take sinful rebellious creatures such as we were and change them into the likeness of the Son of God deserves the glory and praise of the entire universe. This is God's goal, but it is more than a goal. He has predestined it. That means he has made it certain.

God has no intention of losing any of his children. How is that possible? It is possible because of the discipline God the Father is bringing to bear on our lives. God does not want us to be condemned with the world. He will not allow us to be condemned with the world. If we don't judge ourselves, then he will judge us.

This is why Hebrews 12:5, 6 tells us:

> And have you forgotten the exhortation that addresses you as sons? "My son, do not regard lightly the discipline of the Lord, nor be weary when reproved by him. For the Lord disciplines the one he loves, and chastises every son whom he receives."

We are not to make light of the discipline of the Lord. We are not to live disobedient lives with the flippant attitude that God might give us a slap on the hand. God's discipline is a serious thing. We are also not to get discouraged. We are to realize that we are under the care of a loving father who is working out all of our circumstances for our good and for his glory. Verse 10 of Hebrews 12 tells us why God disciplines us: *"that we may share in his holiness."* Why is that important? Look at verse 14. *"Strive for peace with everyone, and for the holiness without which no one will see the Lord"* (Hebrews 12:14).

Are you a professing Christian who is not walking with the Lord? Are you walking in a life of sin that is separate from the will of God? The first concern is whether you really know God or not. Has God regenerated and changed your heart, given you a new spirit that loves the things of God and has fellowship and communication with him? Has he given you a love for the truth? If not, it sounds like you are not really one of his sheep. If you can hear him calling you through the truth of his Word, why not turn to him today and accept him as your Lord and Savior. He will save you. He has promised to receive all those who call on his name.

Perhaps you are truly born again. You know that you have the Lord living in your life, but you are not walking with him. You need to know for a fact that God is disciplining and will continue to discipline you so that you will develop the character and likeness of God in your life. You also need to know that if you stubbornly refuse that discipline, God may take you home prematurely in order to prevent your being condemned with the world. He has promised to be gracious and to complete what he has started, and if he needs to do it that way, he will. Why don't you confess your stubbornness to him, and receive the joy of full fellowship and forgiveness that are yours in Christ?

You might be thinking, "But, isn't it possible that I might lose my salvation?" In John 6:37 we learn that everyone the Father gives to the Son will come to Christ. There are no exceptions. Verse 39 tells us that Christ will lose none of those the Father has given to him, but he will raise him up on the last day. There are no "ifs" in this verse. It does not say he will raise him up *if* he stays with Christ. He will definitely raise him up on the last day.

Turn now to Romans 8:37-39. In this passage, we learn that neither death nor life, neither angels nor demons, neither the present nor the future, nor any powers, neither height nor depth, nor anything else in all creation will be able to separate us from the love of God in Christ Jesus. The salvation which we have is from God himself. He gives it and he has promised never to take it back. Look at Ephesians 1:13-14:

> In him you also, when you heard the word of truth, the gospel of your salvation, and believed in him, were sealed with the promised Holy Spirit, who is the guarantee of our inheritance until we acquire possession of it, to the praise of his glory.

God has given every believer the Holy Spirit as a seal and down payment of the inheritance yet to come. When someone receives a down payment as a pledge, he gets to keep the payment whether or not the purchaser comes through with the rest of the deal. It is "earnest money" to prove the good intentions of the buyer. This is the idea of the word "deposit" or "earnest" used in this passage. God gives his Holy Spirit as a down payment for our inheritance. If for some reason God would decide not to follow through with his side of the deal, we would still have the Holy Spirit. Obviously, God is not going to allow us to go to Hell with the Holy Spirit living in us! That is how we can know without a doubt that our salvation is secure. God has sealed it with his Spirit.

There is no danger in our being lost once we are saved. The real danger is in the possibility that we might think we are saved when we are not. Jesus said there will be people coming to him on the day of judgment telling him that they have done miracles and preached in his name, and yet he will tell them that he <u>never</u> knew who they were (Matthew 7:23). How is it possible that someone could do many good works for Christ and still not belong to him? We're not saved by the works we do or the home we are raised in. It is very simple to do things out of obligation or in order to try to earn the favor of God. Many people know the motions that Christians go through. We are creatures of habit and imitation. The faith of our parents won't save us, and acting like a Christian won't save us. What we need is the transforming work of God in our soul that causes us to cast ourselves totally upon Christ, trusting him completely for our salvation. It all depends upon him.

Turn in your Bible to Matthew 13. In the first part of this chapter, Jesus tells his disciples a parable about a sower who went out into the field to sow seed. In scattering the seed by hand, the seed didn't always land in the best places for growth. Some of the seed fell on the path where people walked. Because the path was trampled down, the seed just lay on top and birds soon came and picked up the seed before it could germinate. Other seed fell on rocky soil where there wasn't much depth. Here the seed germinated but as soon as the sun came up, the plants died. Some other seed landed among thorns. It sprouted well enough, but it was soon choked out by the weeds. Finally, some of the seed fell on good ground where it was able to germinate and grow to maturity.

The interpretation of this parable begins in verse 18. Matthew tells us that the seed is the gospel of the kingdom. When some people hear this message and don't understand it, Satan is right there to snatch it away. It produces absolutely no effect in the heart. It doesn't stay long enough to sprout. There are others who hear the word, but it has no root. It does not go down deep into their soul. It is a surface understanding. It is a very dangerous thing to have just a mental understanding of the facts about Christ. We can believe that he exists, we can understand that he died on the cross, but until it takes root and becomes part of our being, it quickly dies. All it takes is a little trouble or persecution and the whole thing is quickly forgotten. Another kind of person hears the word and it does take root. However, the daily cares of life and its associated worries, or perhaps the deceitfulness of riches, quickly choke out the young life that had started.

Finally, there is the fourth kind of man who hears the word and understands it. It develops strong roots in his innermost being. In his case, the cares of life or riches are not allowed to have an impact on the young faith. Solid growth takes place that results in the production of fruit. In each case the word was the same. The seed that fell on the path was just as capable of producing life as the seed which fell on the good soil. What was different? Obviously, the difference is in the type of soil. In the case of the soils, how does the good soil become good? Have you ever planted a garden? Is the soil good by nature? I mean is it clean, aerated well, without weeds? Does the soil prepare itself for planting? The gardener gets out there and tills the soil. He removes rocks and weeds from the area where he is going to plant.

In the spiritual sense, the same thing happens. God, through his Word and by his Spirit, reaches down and tills the soil of the hearts where the seed will be most effective. Who makes one to differ from another? (1 Corinthians 4:7). It is God. If God is the gardener, do you think that he is not going to be successful at raising a good, fruitful garden? Is he going to have a plant come almost to the point of bearing fruit and then give up on it? In the good soil, the plants will all bring forth fruit. In Isaiah, God tells us that just as the water that comes down from heaven waters the earth before it returns, his word also does the same thing. He promises that his word does not return empty. It always accomplishes whatever task he sent it out to accomplish (Isaiah 55:11). We can rejoice to know that whoever is born again by the living word of God will be saved forever. There is no failure with God. He will make them stand (Romans 14:4).

What we've seen in this chapter then is that as Christians we have been completely forgiven of all of our sins, past, present, and future. These sins have been removed from us to such an extent that our consciences should not be constantly badgering us about how sinful we are. Jesus actually did take away our sins. We have also seen that such forgiveness is not an open door to sinful living, because God's work is not just a work of forgiveness; it is a work of transformation. God changes our hearts and our motivations. He continues the work he began in order to conform us more and more to the image of Christ. It is his work, not ours. Paul says it well in 1 Corinthians 1:30, 31: *"And because of him you are in Christ Jesus, who became to us wisdom from God, righteousness and sanctification and redemption, so that, as it is written, 'Let the one who boasts, boast in the Lord.'"*

It is God's doing that we are saved. It is God's doing that we are sanctified. And it is God's doing that we are redeemed. Therefore, the glory goes to God. And while he is doing that work, and as we are learning how to defeat sin, we have the assurance that there is no condemnation. This assurance is an umbrella for us as we grow. And how does this relate to the big picture? Christians all over the world testify of the forgiveness and freedom of guilt they have found in Christ. As a result, God's fame is increased, and his grace and glory are made known everywhere.

Chapter 6
The War Against Sin

The next question that confronts us as we think through what God is doing is this: What remedy has God given us in our fight against temptation and sin? Yes, we have been forgiven, but what about the ongoing pressure we feel to do wrong? God's intent, and indeed all of his work in us, is toward the goal of ever-increasing righteousness for the praise of his glory. Titus 2:14 tells us that God is purifying for himself a special people. But failure to overcome sin seems to be a daily reality for us. Even in the last chapter, we learned about the freedom from guilt that forgiveness brings, but in the next breath, we talked about making sure we pursue righteousness so as not to find ourselves on the path to eternal damnation. Even our stumbling efforts to pursue righteousness can be guilt-inducing. But the truth is, if God is at work calling out a people for himself, and if we as his people are to be for the praise and glory of God in this life, then God will certainly provide the means for our increasing victory over our fallen nature. And I, for one, need to know what that strategy is, and how to access it.

The place we'd like to start is with an understanding of the role of the law in all of this. The Bible tells us that the law gives sin its power. 1 Corinthians 15:56 reads: *"The sting of death is sin, and the power of sin is the law"* (emphasis added). When sin stings you, it is a fatal sting. Death is the inevitable consequence because guilt separates us from God, and separation from God is death! And sin gets its power from the law. In Romans 7:5, Paul writes, *"For while we were living in the flesh, our sinful passions, aroused by the law, were at work in our members to bear fruit for death".* He goes on to say in verses 7-11:

> Yet if it had not been for the law, I would not have known sin. For I would not have known what it is to covet if the law had not said, "You shall not covet." But sin, seizing an opportunity through the commandment, produced in me all kinds of covetousness. For apart from the law, sin lies dead. I was once alive apart from the law, but when the commandment came, sin came alive and I died. The very commandment that promised life proved to be death to me. For sin, seizing an opportunity through the commandment, deceived me and through it killed me.

That is a pretty clear statement of what we are up against. Romans 5:20 tells us that the law was added so that the <u>trespass might increase</u>. We all know what it feels like to have someone tell us we can't do something. Immediately, there is aroused in us the desire to do it anyway. We may not have even thought of it before, but now that someone is trying to tell us what to do, we rebel against anyone having that kind of authority over us. Sin, then, is empowered by the law. The law declares that the soul that sins must die. But what happens after that punishment has been carried out? Can the law demand a punishment more severe than death? Can it demand a punishment after death? No! Once the sentence has been carried out, law must be still. It can make no further threats. It can demand nothing more.

This is exactly what has taken place. In dying for us, Jesus Christ has silenced the law. The law's demands have been completely met. Sin entered the world, the law's sentence was announced, and that sentence was carried out. There is nothing further that it can say. There is no further punishment to be imposed. John Newton expressed this truth in his hymn *Let Us Love and Sing and Wonder*: "He has hushed the law's loud thunder; he has quenched Mt. Sinai's flame." If you've trusted Christ, that is the case with you. The law cannot demand an additional penalty. Romans 8:33 says,

> Who shall bring any charge against God's elect? It is God who justifies. Who is to condemn? Christ Jesus is the one who died—more than that, who was raised—who is at the right hand of God, who indeed is interceding for us.

The Bible compares the transition from law to spirit as being similar to that of going from childhood to adulthood. When a person is a child, he must be given all sorts of rules and guidelines to keep him safe. Parents say such things as, "Don't play in the street," or "You have to eat your vegetables." When a child grows up, by and large he has internalized most of those rules, and is able to regulate life for himself without someone telling him everything to do.

In Galatians 4, Paul makes the comparison to spiritual life. He says that even though we are an heir along with Abraham of the promises God has given, we are under the guardianship of the law during our youthful stage. When is that? Notice what he writes in Galatians 4:3-5:

> In the same way we also, when we were children, were enslaved to the elementary principles of the world. But when the fullness of time had come, God sent forth his Son, born of woman, born under the law, to redeem those who were under the law, so that we might receive adoption as sons.

So what he is saying is that the period of childhood and elementary things was before Christ came. It has nothing to do with our own personal chronology or spiritual growth. Now that Christ has come, and the law has been fulfilled, we are no longer under its guardianship. We, in this age, are adults. We have been given the Spirit of God, and the laws and principles of God are written on our hearts. This is analogous to being adult and knowing inside yourself what you should eat and what dangers to avoid.

So, the guardianship of the law is finished. You are not under it anymore. You are under grace. The law has no jurisdiction anymore because all of its demands have been completely met in the death of Christ. Carefully read the following passages:

> For sin will have no dominion over you, since you are not under law but under grace. (Romans 6:14)

> Or do you not know, brothers—for I am speaking to those who know the law—that the law is binding on a person only as long as he lives? For a married woman is bound by law to her husband while he lives, but if her husband dies she is released from the law of marriage. Accordingly, she will be called an adulteress if she lives with another man while her husband is alive. But if her husband dies, she is free from that law, and if she marries another man she is not an adulteress. Likewise, my brothers, you also have died to the law through the body of Christ, so that you may belong to another, to him who has been raised from the dead, in order that we may bear fruit for God. (Romans 7:1–4)

In the beginning of Romans 7, Paul discusses the woman who is free to marry another man since her first husband has died. She has been freed from the law of her first husband. The law forbade her from being married to another while her first husband was still alive. But now that her first husband has died, that law does not apply. In marrying this new husband, she may legally follow his direction in life, and bear his children. Paul then compares this to our relationship to Christ and the law. He states that we have died to the law in the same way that the woman had died to the law of her first husband. When that husband died, she had no more responsibility to him. That relationship had been severed.

The same thing is true of the law and sin. As we saw in the last chapter, we are in Christ and we died with him. Therefore, we have become dead to both the law and sin. God made him to be sin for us, and that sin was nailed to the cross: "*And you...God made alive together with him, having forgiven us all our trespasses, by canceling the record of debt that stood against us with its legal demands. This he set aside, nailing it to the cross*" (Colossians 2:13–14).

When Jesus Christ died on the cross, all responsibility to the old masters sin and the law ceased. They have no authority. Paul continues in Romans 7:

> For while we were living in the flesh, our sinful passions, aroused by the law, were at work in our members to bear fruit for death. But now we are released from the law, having died to that which held us captive, so that we serve in the new way of the Spirit and not in the old way of the written code. (Romans 7:5–6)

Notice that Paul is using the past tense to describe the situation. He says, "when we *were* living in the flesh." Before our regeneration, we were living in and controlled by the sinful nature — the flesh. But that is in the past. Notice too how the two oppressors, sin and the law, work together to bring fruit for death. The sinful passions are aroused by the law. James describes this entire sequence: "*But each person is tempted when he is lured and enticed by his own desire. Then desire when it has conceived gives birth to sin, and sin when it is fully grown brings forth death*" (James 1:14-15).

First, we notice that temptation results when we are lured and enticed by our own evil lusts. There is something in us attracted and enticed by deceiving temptations. No one can say that he is completely free of this influence in this life. We can learn how to resist through the Spirit, but those lusts seem to stay. Next, we see that when the drawing away of the lust conceives, it brings forth sin. Sin is the child which results. And finally, as sin matures and grows up, it results in death. You can see that the relationship we had with our former "husbands," sin and the law, resulted in an offspring that produces death. There is an inevitability and a natural progression about it all. We discussed the same thing in the last chapter where we recognized that continued yielding to sin results in greater unrighteousness and finally death.

Back in Romans 7, Paul begins verse 6 with the wonderful word, "But." He says, "But now." It had been the case that we bore fruit to death, but now – there is a difference now. The old abusive husband died when Christ died. By dying to what once bound us, we are free to serve our new husband, and to bring forth his fruit, his offspring. The resulting offspring of our former husband resulted in nothing but death, destruction, and despair.

But we are free from that husband. The law has nothing more to say to us. Our new husband is none other than Jesus Christ. He is the creator of the universe and has been given all power and all authority. We bear fruit to God! Our offspring (our deeds) are of a godly character. They are the result of our union with Christ and his work in our lives through his Spirit. Our good works don't come from our own determination and will power. They come from our union with our new husband. They bear the marks of his life because they are his offspring in us.

Look at verse 6. Paul says that we now serve in a new way. It is the way of the Spirit and not the old way of the law. Here we begin to see how it all is going to work. Paul will go on to describe how difficult the struggle with sin is, and when we get to chapter eight, he will describe in greater detail how we serve in the Spirit. The way that we bring forth fruit to God is through the Spirit. It is by the activity of the Spirit of God in our life that righteous deeds result.

Paul tells us in 2 Corinthians 3:6: "*[God] has made us sufficient to be ministers of a new covenant, not of the letter but of the Spirit. For the letter kills, but the Spirit gives life.*" God knows that the efforts to please him by trying to keep the letter of the law will not work. It only brings frustration and discouragement. It is the ministry of the Spirit in our lives that accomplishes it all. Continue in 2 Corinthians 3 beginning with verse 7:

> Now if the ministry of death, carved in letters on stone, came with such glory that the Israelites could not gaze at Moses' face because of its glory, which was being brought to an end, will not the ministry of the Spirit have even more glory? For if there was glory in the ministry of condemnation, the ministry of righteousness must far exceed it in glory.

The announcement of the law came with bright lights and lots of thunder. When Moses came down from the mountain, his face shone. He had been with God himself on the mountain. Because of that face to face contact with God, Moses' face glowed and radiated with a heavenly glory. That is the glory that is talked about in this passage. What was Moses doing up there on the mountain? He was receiving the law from the hand of God. The law is good, but it enabled sin to cause death (Romans 7:13). It gives sin the opportunity it is looking for to destroy us. That old arrangement had a lot of glory, but the whole thing is being brought to an end (v. 17). But how much greater glory will be provided under the New Covenant by the ministry of the Spirit in our lives! Look at how Paul continues the discussion in 2 Corinthians 3:17-18:

> Now the Lord is the Spirit, and where the Spirit of the Lord is, there is freedom. And we all, with unveiled face, beholding the glory of the Lord, are being transformed into the same image from one degree of glory to another. For this comes from the Lord who is the Spirit.

Where the Spirit of the Lord is working, there is a glory that is unveiled and will be evident to all. The glory that the Spirit brings is an ever-increasing glory. It is a glory which doesn't need a veil. Moses put a veil over his face because he did not want the people to see that the glory he had was fading away. It was temporary. The glory that the Spirit gives is permanent and constantly increasing as we are being transformed into his likeness. Victory is assured because it is the Lord's victory. He will accomplish his work in our lives as we yield to him. It is a result of the outworking of the New Covenant which we discussed in detail in an earlier chapter.

Turn to Galatians 5:19-26. In verses 19-21, Paul lists some of the deeds of the flesh. These are the death-producing acts produced by the combined power of sin and the law in the life of an unregenerate person. These are the offspring Paul talked about in Romans 7. When we were married to our first husband, this is the kind of natural offspring which resulted. They are called the deeds of the flesh. How do I know that someone who does these things is unregenerate? He tells us plainly in verse 21: "*I warn you, as I warned you before, that those who do such things will not inherit the kingdom of God.*" People who live like this are not born again.

Let's take a minute and look at these deeds of the flesh. They are listed for you beginning in verse 19 of Galatians 5. First of all, he calls them obvious. It should be easy to tell which activities have their source in the flesh and which have their source in the Spirit of God. All of these deeds of the flesh deal with activities that God has always condemned. He includes immoral sexual sins, idolatry, witchcraft and hatred. He also includes jealousy, rage, selfish ambition, party spirit, drunkenness, and things like that. All of these things find their source in the fallen human nature, the flesh. When things like this are characteristic of someone's life, Paul says that such a person will not inherit the kingdom of God. Someone who still has these characteristics as dominant in his life has never had the change we are talking about in this book. If you are reading this and sense that your way of living is characterized by these kinds of sins, you have every reason to question whether you are rightly related to God.

In verse 22, Paul describes the fruit of the Spirit. This is the natural result of the Holy Spirit's presence in someone's life. This is the kind of fruit which results when we have died to the old and are married to another: to God, to bring forth fruit for him. Look at the list – "Love, joy, peace, patience, kindness, goodness, faithfulness, gentleness and self-control." Wouldn't it be great to be clothed with these characteristics as we live our lives? You can be and you will be if you turn to Christ in faith and trust his saving power toward you. You can't produce them on your own. You can't say to yourself, "Now I see what a Christian should look like. I will now begin living this way!" No! These traits aren't produced by you. They are produced in you. They are the fruit of the loving relationship you have with your new husband, Jesus Christ.

I know some of you are thinking something like this: "That's all easy to say, but I know a lot of Christians who don't live like this. In fact, they seem to be a lot more like non-Christians than Christians. In fact, my own life is not so peaceful, loving, faithful, and self-controlled as it should be."

No Christian ever lives the Christian life perfectly. But please notice what verse 24 says: "*And those who belong to Christ Jesus have crucified the flesh with its passions and desires.*" Even this crucifying of the flesh is accomplished by the Spirit, as Romans 8:13 says: *"But if by the Spirit you put to death the misdeeds of the body, you will live."* Do you see what this is saying? Someone who comes to Christ realizes the bondage of his old way of life. He realizes the deadly results of continuing in a life of sin. He turns to Christ as his savior from sin, and reckons his old self to be crucified on the cross with Christ because he has become one with Christ. The cross is a place of death: it is the place where sin and death were taken away and crucified. It is the place where our "old man" was taken. Paul said, *"I am crucified with Christ"* (Galatians 2:20). When we were placed into Christ, we were placed into his death. Turning to Christ is a dying to the "old" and a rebirth into the "new." There is no other way it can be.

Let's turn back to Romans 7 and pick up the discussion. We have already stated that law and sin work together to bring about death. But before we come down too hard on the law, we need to recognize a couple of things. First of all, the law is not sin. Paul tells us very clearly in verse 7 that we would not know what sin is if it weren't for the law. Perhaps some of you think that it would have been better not to know what sin is. The thing to remember, though, is that sin will accomplish its work, and will ultimately result in death whether or not you recognize it.

We live in a day when many people do not feel bound to any law. Whatever they feel like doing, they do. They do not recognize the authority of the law of God in their lives. Even though they may not recognize sin, they nevertheless are affected by it, and it will result in death. It will produce heartache and despair throughout their life and will result in ultimate separation from God.

Therefore, it is very important to know what sin is. That is the purpose of the law. Paul tells us in Galatians that the law is a schoolmaster to bring us to Christ (Galatians 3:24). It has a lofty and noble purpose. The real culprit is sin. Paul tells us in verse 8 of Romans 7 that sin seized the opportunity offered by the commandment, "Thou shalt not covet." Sin produced in Paul every kind of covetous desire. Sin gains its power and life from the law. He says, *"For apart from law, sin is dead."* Paul told the Corinthians that the power of sin is the law (1 Corinthians 15:56). If the law had never come, sin would have still been there, but it would not have been obvious. The law reveals the depth of our fallen nature. But even so, the law is holy, righteous, and good. Paul told Timothy that the law is good if one uses it lawfully. The lawful use is not to try to quell sin with it, but to expose sin. If you try to use it to conquer sin, sin will just be empowered in its assault against you (Romans 7:12, 13).

In verse 15, we get to the very bottom of the issue. It is a point which every Christian needs to reach in order for his life to become truly effective for God. Through all the circumstances of life, God is at work in every Christian to bring us to this point. In verse 14, Paul comes to the end of himself. He senses that though the law is spiritual, he is unspiritual, sold as a slave to sin. I believe that this is the initial phase of regeneration. We come to see and acknowledge who we are and what kind of person we really are.

Paul has done what most of us do in our Christian life. We recognize that a change has occurred in our life. We now have the desire to do what is right. We want to please God. We want him to be glorified by our lives, and so we set out to please him. We look at the law to determine what is right and what is wrong, and then determine that we will live in conformity to it. The law we try to observe may be the commandments of the Old Testament. They may be rules of our church or of our parents. They may be the commands which Jesus Christ himself gave. Wherever they come from, they become our rule of life, and we determine to follow them.

Before long, we find out that there is a problem with us. Even though we've been born again, no matter how hard we try, we do not seem to be able to live up to an acceptable level in keeping our commitments to Christ. We begin to have the same feelings Paul had as he describes them in verse 15: *"For I do not understand my own actions. For I do not do what I want, but I do the very thing I hate."* And in

150

verse 19: "*For I do not do the good I want, but the evil I do not want is what I keep on doing.*"

Sometimes even the passages that we have been studying can produce guilt in us. We read about all the changes that God has promised to bring about in our lives, and then we take a hard look at ourselves and decide that God doesn't seem to be working. Sometimes we are even tempted to believe that we are not Christians because we don't seem to be coming along in our growth as fast as we think we should. We are constantly looking at the external to try to evaluate our lives.

Is someone who feels like this really a Christian? Look at verse 16: "*I agree with the law, that it is good*"; and verse 18: "*I have the desire to do what is right*"; and especially verse 22: "*For I delight in the law of God, in my inner being.*" I believe that these are descriptions of a Christian. An unregenerate person certainly does not delight in the law of God in the inner man! On the other hand, in verse 14, he describes himself as sold as a slave to sin. We have already discussed the fact that Christians have been released from sin, so how can he say that he is sold to sin? How do we handle this apparent contradiction? I believe that Paul is describing the situation early in his Christian life. His heart had been changed by the Spirit of God, and his alertness to sin had been intensified. However, he had not yet come to grips with the depth of his sin, and the total forgiveness of God, and the work of the Spirit to accomplish victory in his life. I believe these are the struggles of a babe being born. But the interesting thing is that many of us stay babes a long time. We may be into the Christian life 20 or 30 years and still have the Romans 7 struggle.

Why then is there a problem? Why is it that someone whose heart has been changed, who is a new creature, in whom the seed of God dwells, cannot carry out the desires that come from this new nature within him? The answer is SIN. In verse 23, Paul states the problem:

But I see in my members another law waging war against the law of my mind and making me captive to the law of sin that dwells in my members.

Paul sees that sin is present in the body of every Christian. It is sin that is causing the problem. We should notice something very clearly. Paul is not saying that this evil is part of our nature. No, a person who is in Christ is a new creation. Old things are passed away and behold, all things are become new (2 Corinthians 5:17). We are his workmanship. We possess a new spirit, a changed heart, and the Spirit of God dwells within us. Sin is not a part of that new nature.

Even though our inner man has been changed, we are still living in an unregenerate body with an unregenerate mind, will, and emotions. The Bible refers to this as our "flesh." Those last two sentences were important. Read them again. Our mind, will, and emotions are part of our flesh. Our Spirit is new, but it is going to take time to transform our mind, will, and emotions. There is a renewing of the mind that needs to take place (Romans 12:2). In Romans 7:18, Paul says that he knows that *"nothing good lives in me, that is in my flesh."* The flesh has not been regenerated. Sin still finds a place of refuge there. In describing what has happened to him, Paul almost rejects his responsibility for the things which he does wrong. In verse 17, he writes, *"So now it is no longer I who do it, but sin that dwells within me."* And then in verse 20, *"Now if I do what I do not want, it is no longer I who do it, but sin that dwells within me."*

We must be careful not to carry this line too far, but it is important to recognize that as Christians, the sin Paul refers to is not part of our nature. In verse 21, we see this principle: *"When I want to do good, evil lies close at hand."*

You will often hear people describing this conflict as a conflict of the two natures. They describe it as a new nature and an old nature. I don't want to be too picky about this, but I think there is a danger here. The danger with this terminology is this: By calling the flesh and sin the "old nature," we give it legitimacy as part of us. That is, we recognize it as an official extension of our nature.

Rather than believing God when he says that old things are passed away, we believe the lie of Satan when he continues to accuse us of being basically sinful and unsaveable.

Before we receive Christ and become a child of God, our nature is disobedient and sinful. But all of that changes when God regenerates us. Our hearts are made new. Paul speaks of this when he writes to the Ephesian Christians. In Ephesians 2:3-5, Paul writes:

> Among whom [the disobedient] we all once lived in the passions of our flesh, carrying out the desires of the body and the mind, and were by nature children of wrath, like the rest of mankind. But God, being rich in mercy, because of the great love with which he loved us, even when we were dead in our trespasses, made us alive together with Christ—by grace you have been saved.

Notice the past tense in these verses. We <u>used</u> to live among them, gratifying the cravings of our flesh. We <u>were</u> by nature objects of wrath. But now things are different. We are no longer that way. Because of his great love for us, our nature has been changed. We are new creations in Christ. Let's not give legitimacy to a nature that is not a part of us. Let's speak of it the same way Paul does. When we would do good, evil is right there with us. Sin is there, and it is at fault. But it is our responsibility to put it to death, to reckon ourselves dead to it, and not to offer ourselves as slaves to it. Those are our responsibilities. So we're not off the hook by just flippantly saying, "It wasn't me! It was sin."

The problem can now be stated this way: As a Christian, I have a new nature that desires to be obedient to God. The more I recognize what I should be doing, the more I find that sin is right there with me with great power pushing me to do things I really don't want to do. My motives and desires have changed, but how can I defeat this enemy within? Is there any way to squelch its influence? Can I get to the point where I don't have to say, "The things I want to do, I cannot do"?

The answer to this question is the same one we have seen several times throughout this book. The solution to the problem is in God. What on earth is God doing? He has been, and is, working by his power and might to enable his children to have the victory which they should have over this enemy called sin. When Paul asks in desperation, *"Who will rescue me from this body of death?"* in verse 24 of Romans 7, he answers the question in verse 25. He says, *"Thanks be to God – through Jesus Christ our Lord!"* He knows where the solution lies.

We'll now examine the crucial teaching regarding our source of victory. We begin in Romans 8:1. The verse uses the word "therefore." We are hit with the good news immediately. *"There is therefore now no condemnation for those who are in Christ Jesus."* Notice the word "now." At this moment, there is no condemnation for those who are in Christ Jesus. Are you one of those believers who feels like the Apostle Paul? Do you find yourself wanting to do what is right, but somehow do not know how to bring it about? Do you delight in the law of God in your inner man, but for some reason the acts of your body don't seem to follow through with your inner desires? There is good news for you. You are not under the condemnation of God. God does not go around condemning his children. He knows our makeup, and he recognizes that we are dust (Psalm 103:14). His son Jesus Christ paid the penalty of sin. God has taken it out of the way and removed it as far as the east is from the west. There is no condemnation for those who are in Christ Jesus.

Paul goes on to explain the reason for this in verse two. It is not because we have performed well enough. It is not because God ignores sin. It is not because we are no worse than the average believer. It is because, through Christ Jesus, the law (principle) of the Spirit of life has set us free from the law (principle) of sin and death.

What is the law of sin and death? It is the principle which says that the soul that sins shall die. It is the law which says that the wages of sin is death. For the Christian, these principles do not apply. Why? Because Jesus Christ bore the death penalty for all his children. He became sin for us so that we might be made the righteousness of God in him. But there is more to it than that. Verse 2 tells us that the law of the Spirit of life set me free from the law of sin and death.

If you were to step off the roof of a skyscraper, your body would follow the law (principle) of gravity. Your body was following that law when you were standing on the roof, and your body will follow it when you step off the roof. The law of gravity is merciless. It would apply to anyone who would step off a tall building. What if you were to step off the roof with a hang glider over your head? Would the law of gravity cease to exist? No, but a different law would be put into effect – the law of aerodynamics. The law of aerodynamics would set you free from the law of gravity in the sense that you would not go plummeting to your death. If you do not have the law of aerodynamics working on your behalf, you would face certain death in your fall to the ground. This is probably not a good example since the law of gravity works in conjunction with the law of aerodynamics to produce the motion of the hang-glider whereas the law of sin and death contribute nothing to the law of the spirit of life. But it gives you the idea.

It is like this in spiritual matters as well. The Spirit of God in a believer brings him under a different principle. The Holy Spirit in the life of a believer provides a stronger principle than that which sin has available. As the Spirit does his work, the believer will find sin having less and less of an influence in his life. In those instances where the Christian does fall into sin, he has the assurance that there is no condemnation. The point is that it is the Spirit of God who helps the Christian to keep from living a life consumed by sinful ways. Our new nature is not inclined toward sin, but the presence of sin in our lives is a powerful force. The Spirit is there to confront and counter that force.

The law, the good commands of God, was not capable of providing the power to live the kind of life which God wants from each one of us. Paul writes in verse 3: *"For God has done what the law, weakened by the flesh, could not do."* There was nothing wrong with the law, but it was not capable of bringing the flesh into conformity with what God expects. The flesh, remember, is the unregenerated body along with certain aspects of our soul such as our mind, will, and emotions that have not been regenerated. We find that what the law could not do, God did. Notice it does not say that what the law could not do, we did. It says, what the law could not do, GOD DID!

How does he do it? God did it by sending his own Son in the likeness of sinful flesh to be a sin offering. Jesus came in a body like ours, but apart from sin. He lived those thirty some years in a human body, and never once gave in to the temptations of sin. Sin did not have a part of him. He defeated sin in his perfect life. What is more, he gave it a fatal blow by dying on the cross as the ultimate sin offering. He died without ever sinning, and he rose again the third day triumphing over sin's partner, death. So God did what the law could not do. He condemned the sin. He robbed it of its power. And what's more, he succeeded in doing this in a human body. That is what he means by "He condemned sin in the flesh." He essentially proved that the human body, per se, is not the problem. Christ defeated every temptation, and he did it in a human body! That should give us great encouragement.

What else was it that the law could not do? It could not cause the flesh to perform according to the righteous requirements of the law. But what the law could not do, God did. Look at the end of verse 3 and into verse 4. Paul says, *"He condemned sin in the flesh, in order that the righteous requirement of the law might be fulfilled in us, who walk not according to the flesh but according to the Spirit."*

First notice what God condemned. He condemned sin in sinful man (sin in the flesh). Verse one told us that we are not under the condemnation of God, but we learn that sin is condemned. That sin in you that seems so powerful so much of the time, is under the condemnation of God, but you are not under that same condemnation if you are one of his children. The sin is condemned, but not you! Sometimes that sin will get the best of you. Even though you didn't want to do wrong, you did it anyway. God condemns the sin, but not you! Understanding this is extremely freeing. I mentioned it before, but I look at this truth as a spiritual umbrella. It's a protection from the wrath and judgment of God. As I learn and grow and put the truth of the Bible into practice in my life I will fail. But as I fail, there is no condemnation. In the old covenant, a person had to be perfect and not sin once, otherwise he was under the curse of God. The New Covenant is different.

Why did he condemn sin in the flesh? He did this so that the righteous requirements of the law might be fully met in you. You are not capable of living up to the righteousness of the law. There is no way for you to do well enough to become acceptable with God or to keep yourself acceptable to God. But God himself will meet the righteous requirements of the law in you by his Spirit. As we look to God and keep our focus on him instead of on our surroundings, we will find him giving us the victory he wants us to have. He does this as we walk in the Spirit rather than in the flesh.

But you say, "He doesn't do that for all Christians, does he? I mean, what about the Christian who doesn't walk in the Spirit? What about the Christian who lives for himself and not for the Lord?" We'll look at this in a moment, but remember the promise of the New Covenant: God promised to give a new heart and a new spirit. He gives us his Spirit. He promised to write his law on our hearts and to cause us to follow his ways. Did you hear that last line? He promised to cause us to follow his ways. If there really is a Christian who goes through life living for himself to gratify his own flesh rather than to live for the glory of God, then either God has promised something he did not intend to provide, or he intended to keep his promise, but found that the stubbornness of man was too great to overcome. Either way, we are imagining a god that doesn't exist. You will remember that God will discipline his children so that they may share in his holiness. They cannot see the Lord without holiness, and God has ways of developing it in our lives.

Let us continue in Romans chapter 8 to see if we can find some further answers to the question at hand. God promises that the righteous requirements of the law will be fulfilled in those who do not live according to the flesh, but according to the Spirit. Who are these people that live according to the flesh, and who are the ones who live according to the spirit? Is he talking about two different kinds of Christians – Christians who live according to the flesh and Christians who live according to the Spirit?

Verse five tells us that those who live according to the flesh have their minds set on what the flesh desires. Verse six tells us that the mind of the flesh is death. Verse seven tells us that the mind of the flesh is hostile to God. It does not submit to God's law and is not able to do so. Verse eight states that those in the flesh cannot please God. Are these verses describing someone who is a Christian, but who is just living a fleshly sort of life? I don't think so. Verse nine confirms it for me. It says that you are not in the flesh but in the spirit if the Spirit of God lives in you. If someone does not have the Spirit of Christ, he does not belong to him. What we can see from these verses is that a person who lives according to the flesh is someone who does not have the Spirit of God living in him.

Let's look at the same passage from the positive side. Verse five says that those who live according to the Spirit have their minds set on what the Spirit desires. Verse six says that the mind controlled by the Spirit is life and peace. Verse 9 says that if the Spirit of God lives in you, you are controlled by that Spirit.

The interpretation is clear. The Spirit of God, dwelling in a believer, produces in him the characteristics which God's law requires. It is not because a person decides that he should obey the law in order to prove that he is a good Christian, but rather, the very presence of the Spirit of God in his life will produce the kinds of behavior which God himself expects. *"God ...works in you, both to will* and *to work* of his good pleasure (Philippians 2:13, emphasis added).

As in every other aspect of our Christian life, the important principle which is crucial here is faith. No one is justified by keeping the law, and he does not maintain his Christian character by keeping the law. He maintains his Christian character by trusting the God who promised to work out his life in us.

This is exactly the point in Galatians 3. Paul writes in verse 2, *"Let me ask you only this: Did you receive the Spirit by works of the law or by hearing with faith?"* The correct answer is that the Spirit was received by faith. He then says, *"Are you so foolish? After beginning with the Spirit, are you now trying to attain your goal by human effort?"* Obviously, the answer he wants is that we cannot attain the goal of righteousness by human effort any more by than we could be saved by human effort. It is all a matter of faith and the work of the Spirit.

But what about the sin that has taken up residence in our bodies? Paul explains in Romans 8:10, that if Christ is in you, your body is dead because of sin, yet your spirit is alive because of righteousness. Our bodies will continue to contain the vestiges of sin and its effects for a long time. Sin is a mortally wounded enemy, but it takes up residence in our flesh. Even in its weakened condition, it can deceive us into believing that it is stronger than it is.

We are given the promise that the same one who raised Christ from the dead will also give life to our mortal bodies through the same Spirit that now lives within us (Romans 8:11). The day will come when our bodies themselves have been raised and renewed; they will no longer provide the haven for sin. Victory over sin will then be a reality in practice.

Paul is always on guard to make sure we don't understand him to be saying that we can continue to sin so that grace may be more abundant. In Romans 8:12-13, he emphasizes this fact: *"So then, brothers, we are debtors, not to the flesh, to live according to the flesh. For if you live according to the flesh you will die…."* We know that a regenerated child of God does not face eternal death. But yet he says that if we live according to the flesh we will die. What is he saying? He is saying that if you are the kind of person who thinks he has believed in Christ, you have accepted forgiveness of sins, and you interpret that forgiveness as an excuse to sin as you please, you will die. In other words, you have not been born again. You will not see the kingdom of God. Those in whom God works have a change in attitude that gives them a love for God and a desire to please him as much as possible.

Continuing in verse 13, *"For if you live according to the flesh you will die, but if by the Spirit you put to death the deeds of the body, you will live. For all who are led by the Spirit of God are sons of God."* A Christian is a person who puts to death the misdeeds of the body through the Spirit. He is someone who has the Spirit of God living within him, and who is led by the Spirit of God. If you claim to be a Christian, but you are not led by the Spirit of God, then you have been deceived.

These verses also answer the question of responsibility that we left hanging earlier. Paul had said that when he did wrong, it was not he himself, but sin that lived in him. It sounded as though Paul was unwilling to take the responsibility for the things he had done wrong. However, in verses 12 and 13, we see that it is our responsibility through the Spirit to put to death the misdeeds of the body. Sin itself is the source of the evil in our lives. It has significant strength left, even though it has been mortally wounded, and is under the condemnation of God. But we have the responsibility of yielding to the Spirit, and putting to death the deeds of the body in the power of the Spirit to gain the victory over sin.

In Ephesians 5:18, Paul tells us not to be drunk with wine, but to be filled with the Spirit. Someone who is drunk with wine is controlled by the wine. Someone who is filled with the Spirit is controlled by the Spirit. We are to give the Spirit free reign in our lives to produce the godly life he wants to produce. We are not to grieve the Spirit (Ephesians 4:30) or quench the Spirit (1

Thessalonians 5:19). We grieve and quench the Spirit when we try to run our lives in our own strength, and with our own ingenuity, and when we give in to the cravings of the flesh.

How do we work this out in practice? Let's suppose a temptation enters your mind. You have several choices available. You could tell God that you don't care what he says, you are going to give in to the temptation this time. That is blatant disobedience, and you can expect the disciplinary hand of God on your life. But let's suppose that as soon as the temptation enters your mind, you recognize it and determine that you will not give in. If you focus on the temptation and attempt to drive it away, you will almost certainly end up defeated. By focusing on the temptation, you end up trying to fight it in your own strength, the strength of the flesh. Your flesh has no capability of being obedient to God and resisting the temptations. The longer you focus on the sin, the stronger it becomes. Moreover, if you try to use the law as a tool, you will be doomed to failure as well, because the law is not capable of putting down sin. The law actually gives sin more power to defeat you.

What then are you to do? Our passage in Romans 8 tells us that we are to put to death the misdeeds of the body <u>through the Spirit</u>. You already recognize that the thing you are being tempted with is against the law of God, so it is definitely sin. Focus your attention on God and what he has done about sin. Realize that whether or not you succumb to the temptation, your standing with God does not change. You continue to be free from his condemnation. God is telling you that he has paid for that sin, should you fall into it. Immediately the power of the temptation decreases. As you continue to focus your thoughts and prayer on God, thank him that although you are not under condemnation, the sin in you which is giving power to this temptation has been condemned. Acknowledge that the temptation is attracting strong desires that are coming from within you and are part of the residue of sin remaining in you. It's not from outside. We are tempted when we are drawn away by our <u>own lusts</u> (James 1:14). Confess those lusts. The temptation is coming from an enemy of God, a defeated enemy. Do you want to take sides with something that is against God – a losing side at that? Thank God that your connection with Adam has been severed in your death and resurrection with Christ, and therefore this sin has no power to trap you except the power you give it. Refuse to offer the members of your body as weapons of unrighteousness, but rather offer them to God as instruments of righteousness (Romans 6:13). Do you really want to participate in what is bringing condemnation on the world? (Ephesians 5:6; Colossians 3:6). Allow the Spirit of God to have the victory over the temptation. Say in effect, "God, I cannot fight this one. I'm giving it to the Spirit to handle." It is by the Spirit that we are to put to death the deeds of the body. Ask him to bring defeat to this temptation and to slay the sin.

Paul tells us in Romans 5:10 that we were reconciled to God while we were still enemies. How much more, now that we have been declared righteous, we will be saved by his life. In other words, the life of God is at work in our lives, and it is his life that will save us. Salvation is not just going to heaven when we die. Salvation is our being released from the power of sin in our present life now by the life of Christ in us.

Suppose you know all of this, but you purposely ignore it in order to pay more attention to the temptation. Suppose you ultimately fall because you refused to put these Scriptural principles into practice. First, you need to confess the sin and claim God's forgiveness as we have already discussed. Then what you will find is that the battle will increasingly take place prior to the actual full force of the temptation. Sometimes we are suddenly tempted with no time to prepare ourselves. As you begin to act in faith on God's word, you will find that you recognize the approaching temptation before it hits. As this happens, the intensity of the battle actually increases each time, and you begin to get a new sense of how sinful and devious your flesh really is. You will find yourself scheming of ways to circumvent the work of God, thus revealing to yourself that the sin problem is deeper than you ever imagined. As these tendencies come more and more to the forefront, you will see that the battle is not really with a specific sin but with a more subtle, much stronger force coming from deep down. This is Sin that is embedded in your unregenerate flesh. It is this Sin that needs to be defeated more than just the superficial temptation you are experiencing.

Many Christians feel trapped by sins of various kinds. Some of the more dangerous or addicting temptations can be handled by removing the temptation from the house. This makes it somewhat easier, except we must realize that the sin in our flesh is capable of tricking us into bringing the material back into the home or leading us to the place where the temptation can bring forth sin. You will learn to recognize the devious nature of the sin in you when you sense something inside is plotting to bring the sin back. But God can, in fact, give you victory over drinking or smoking or pornography or anger or lust, as long as you rely on the Holy Spirit's power to put sin to death.

If you are a Christian and you desire the things of God, you know that your heart has been changed, and that God lives in you by his spirit; you know your sins have been forgiven in Christ, and you are discouraged because of your lack of victory. Trust God for that victory and faithfully follow him each day. Thank him for what he is doing in your life. Meditate on his word and let him know all of your thoughts. Walk in the light, confessing your sins to him every time you fall. You will find that the Spirit of God will have great freedom in your life to work against the sin that is there. You don't have the power to fight against it. God has that power.

There are a couple of verses in Galatians that I have interpreted incorrectly for most of my life. Look with me at Galatians 5:16,17:

> But I say, walk by the Spirit, and you will not gratify the desires of the flesh. For the desires of the flesh are against the Spirit, and the desires of the Spirit are against the flesh, for these are opposed to each other, to keep you from doing the things you want to do.

In the past I read this to say that because the flesh and the Spirit were working against each other, you would not be able to do the good things that you wanted to do. One day I was using my interlinear Greek New Testament. Underneath the Greek words (which I don't understand very well), the writers have included English translations. It doesn't read very well because the words are in a different order than they would be in standard English. Here is what verse 17 says in this Greek interlinear:

> for flesh lusts against the spirit, and the spirit against the flesh, these for each other opposes, lest whatever things ye wish these ye do.

What it is saying is exactly the opposite from the way I had always read it. It says something like this: "The flesh lusts against the Spirit and the Spirit against the flesh so that you <u>don't do</u> the evil things that you otherwise <u>would do</u>." Paul makes this statement immediately after saying, "But I say, walk by the Spirit, and you will not gratify the desires of the flesh."

Now there is certainly truth to the way I used to read it. Romans 7 is ample evidence of that. Paul complained that he couldn't do the things that he really wanted to do. But the introduction to the truth about the Spirit's role is seen in chapter 8 as the solution to the problem Paul was expressing in Romans 7. It is not the intention of God for us to stay in the situation where we are defeated by sin. He doesn't consider it normal for the Christian to live in constant defeat by the power of sin. He does want us to reach a Romans 7 experience so that we will realize that we cannot do what is right through sheer human will power and the effort of the flesh. I believe, however, that the Romans 7 experience should occur in the infancy of our Christian life, and we should basically grow out of it as we learn to trust God more and more in our daily lives. Some of us, unfortunately, spend a long time there, struggling, studying, and asking questions.

But what the law and the flesh are not able to do, God is able to do and will do in his children. He intends to accomplish all of his own demands in our lives. Through his Spirit he brings forth in us the fruit which he longs for. Just as a husband rejoices when his wife presents him with a child, likewise God rejoices when his bride, the church, presents him with the fruit which is pleasing to him. This fruit, like the child, is the result of the life of the husband at work within the life of the wife.

What then is our responsibility? Do we just sit around passively like puppets waiting for the Spirit of God to move in our lives? Are we like robots? Don't we have the responsibility to get up and get going for God? Sometimes I think we try to compartmentalize ourselves too much. We try to analyze which part of us is doing one thing, or which part of us is doing something else. Let's look at a couple of passages of Scripture.

Ephesians 4:22 says, "*You were taught to put off your old self, which belongs to your former manner of life and is corrupt through deceitful desires.*" Colossians 3:5 tells us to put to death whatever belongs to our earthly nature. These verses put the responsibility squarely on us to put off and put to death the parts of our old fleshly nature. Romans 8:13 tells us how this is accomplished – by the Spirit. We are to do it by the Spirit. It doesn't happen to us as we sit passively in our chairs. God's salvation and the work he is accomplishing in us involves us. It is a change in us, a recreating of us.

Let's look at another example. Philippians 2:12 tells us to work out our salvation with fear and trembling. Left alone, that verse sounds awesome and threatening. It sounds as though we've been given an impossible challenge. But look at the next verse: "*For it is God who works in you to will and to work for his good purpose.*" The verse starts with the word "for." The reason I am to work out my salvation is because God is working in me. As I take steps to obey God's commands, as imperfect as my obedience may be, God's work in my life is being accomplished.

One more passage: John 3:19 says, "*And this is the judgment: the light has come into the world, and people loved the darkness rather than the light because their works were evil.*" There is the general indictment of mankind again. Verse 20 tells us that everyone who does evil hates the light and does not come to the light for fear of having his evil deeds exposed. We might expect then that the passage would go on to tell us that those who live righteously come to the light so

165

that God and everyone else might see all of the wonderful things they are doing. What it actually says is that those who live by the truth come to the light – but not so that they will be praised for their good deeds. They come to the light so that it may be plainly seen that what they have done has been done through God (John 3:20). What that means is that as we live our lives and serve God, we are not afraid to come to God's light, and live in the brightness of his glory, because we know that our sins have been forgiven, and anything we do that is right is being done through God's power in us. It is God who works in us. We live daily by faith, trusting God, doing what we know we should do, confessing things that are wrong, and joyfully thanking God for all the forgiveness and victory he brings.

We've been looking at some very heavy truth in these passages. They are meant to help us understand where the victory lies. When we are first discovering the truth, however, it can be a difficult thing for us because we don't always know how to put it into practice. I believe the secret can be summarized best in the words of the familiar hymn, "Trust and Obey." We face all types of circumstances every day that we must respond to. We respond to members of our families; we make decisions at work; we are constantly interacting with people in our churches. If we simply believe God when he says that he is working in our lives to accomplish his will, and then obey him sincerely from the heart as we go through the day, we will know victory. And then be thankful. Be thankful not only for God and all he has done to forgive you, but be thankful for situations where God's grace is at work. As you walk faithfully with God, you will be amazed at the times when his grace is evident in the midst of the temptations and struggles of life.

Chapter 7
God's Plan for Your Life

Now that we have laid the foundation describing God's purposes for doing what he does, and have described how God has provided forgiveness and victory over sin for his people, we are going to focus in this chapter on how God's overall purpose relates to us personally, and to our meaning in life. There will be some repetition here because we have discussed some of these things in theory, but I want you to think about yourself. How does God's purpose of glorifying himself through his people affect some of the normal issues and struggles in your life?

We've already talked about several topics that should be of immense help in living life as a Christian. The fact that we've been forgiven of all our sins is of tremendous help in overcoming feelings of guilt. The fact that God loves us and is involved in our lives gives us support and encouragement through all the twists and turns of life. If we've been truly born again, we will want to live obedient, moral lives, and we have discussed God's provision for gaining victory over habits and sin.

In this chapter, we want to think about unchangeable or difficult things that sometimes trip us up and cause us to complain or be discouraged. We'll think about such things as how we look, our innate abilities, where we're born. We'll also think through our response to the authorities in our lives. In addition, God uses sickness, disasters, and other so-called negative circumstances to help us grow. And finally, we'll consider things that affect our emotions – things such as self-esteem, discouragement, and depression.

Let's start by looking at a couple of passages:

> And we know that for those who love God all things work together for good, for those who are called according to his purpose. For those whom he foreknew he also predestined to be conformed to the image of his Son, in order that he might be the firstborn among many brothers. (Romans 8:28, 29)

> In him we have obtained an inheritance, having been predestined according to the purpose of him who works all things according to the counsel of his will, so that we who were the first to hope in Christ might be to the praise of his glory. (Ephesians 1:11–12)

God's ultimate and overriding purpose in your life, assuming that you are one of his children, is to conform you to the image of his Son, Jesus Christ, so that you can be to the praise of his glory, both as an individual, and as part of the church. This is the reason God made you! This declaration of the glory of God through us is not just for the audience of other people, but, according to Ephesians 3:10, it is *"so that through the church the manifold wisdom of God might now be made known to the rulers and authorities in the heavenly places."* The principalities and powers are able to see the majesty of God as you model the character of Christ in ever-increasing ways as part of the body of Christ.

What that means is that God's goal is to recreate you to be like Jesus Christ; and he will accomplish that goal! He wants you to worship like him, think like him, care like him, act like him – be like Jesus. And the reason he wants this is so that he will be glorified as your creator and savior.

We need to understand that there is purpose in our lives. There is a God who actually exists, who has a purpose in mind for you. You are not like someone all alone on a raft at sea. The verses we just read tell us that God works his purpose in our lives using all the circumstances of our lives to accomplish it. Notice that he does this for those who love him, those who have been called according to his purpose. If you are one of God's children, you have been called; he is working through the circumstances of your life to accomplish his goals in you. God designs all of our circumstances to accomplish these goals.

So, the first thing we need to understand is that God made us individually, particularly, and specifically the way we are.

> For you formed my inward parts; you knitted me together in my mother's womb. I praise you, for I am fearfully and wonderfully made. Wonderful are your works; my soul knows it very well. My frame was not hidden from you, when I was being made in secret, intricately woven in the depths of the earth. Your eyes saw my unformed substance; in your book were written every one of them, the days that were formed for me, when as yet there was none of them. (Psalm 139:13 – 16)

The next thing we need to understand is that God is in control of your place in history. In Acts 17:26 we read:

> And he made from one man every nation of mankind to live on all the face of the earth, having determined allotted periods and the boundaries of their dwelling place.

You had no control over the time and place of your birth. You had no control over your heredity. God designed your entire DNA pattern himself. He didn't consult with you about how tall you would be or what color your skin or hair would be. You also had no control of who your brothers or sisters would be, or what they would be like, or how they would treat you. Romans 8:28 tells us that God works all things together for good to them that love God. That means that all the circumstances of life, both good and bad, are used by God to increase godliness in you personally.

There are times in life when we groan and complain about the circumstances in which we were born. Some of us don't like how we look. You yourself may feel that you are just ordinary rather than spectacular like some movie star or athlete may be. You may not like the fact that you were born in a rural area rather than in the city. But God has determined your time and the exact places where you would live. There is a purpose in it. That purpose is to become like Christ for the glory of God. You need to embrace this truth. The next time you look at yourself and say, "I wish I had ...." or "I wish I was more ...", remember that you are the way you are because God made you exactly as he wanted you to be.

One of the facets of God's positioning you exactly where he wants you in time and place is that of authority. One of the hardest areas of life for some people is that of authority. Young people often have difficulty dealing with the authority of parents or schoolteachers. Wives sometimes have difficulty with the authority of their husbands in the home. People are often resistant to the authority of their boss at work or the authority of the government. In each of these areas, we often feel like we know more or have better ideas than our authorities have. This leads us to complain about the way things are being handled, especially things involving us!

One of the difficulties with authorities is that they impose their will on our lives in many ways. They tell us what to do or what not to do. When we don't see eye to eye on a matter, we get frustrated. When things don't go right at work, and we are mistreated, we tend to carry the bitterness home with us.

The thing that you need to remember is that in placing you in time and space where he wanted you, God has placed you under specific authority. You had zero choice as to who your parents would be. You didn't choose to be born to an unwed mother. If you were born in the United States, you aren't under Roman authority in 25 A.D. You are under U.S. authority in 2000 something. Your authorities, with all their faults and flaws, were designed by God to perfect you. God would have us realize that our response to authority has nothing whatever to do with whether the authority is Christian or not, or whether the treatment is fair or not. Look at these passages for example:

> Children, obey your parents in the Lord, for this is right. (Ephesians 6:1)

> Let every person be subject to the governing authorities. For there is no authority except from God, and those that exist

have been instituted by God. Therefore whoever resists the authorities resists what God has appointed, and those who resist will incur judgment. For rulers are not a terror to good conduct, but to bad. Would you have no fear of the one who is in authority? Then do what is good, and you will receive his approval, for he is God's servant for your good. But if you do wrong, be afraid, for he does not bear the sword in vain. For he is the servant of God, an avenger who carries out God's wrath on the wrongdoer. Therefore one must be in subjection, not only to avoid God's wrath but also for the sake of conscience. (Romans 13:1–5)

Servants, be subject to your masters with all respect, not only to the good and gentle but also to the unjust. For this is a gracious thing, when, mindful of God, one endures sorrows while suffering unjustly. For what credit is it if, when you sin and are beaten for it, you endure? But if when you do good and suffer for it you endure, this is a gracious thing in the sight of God. For to this you have been called, because Christ also suffered for you, leaving you an example, so that you might follow in his steps. (1 Peter 2:18–21)

Let all who are under a yoke as bondservants regard their own masters as worthy of all honor, so that the name of God and the teaching may not be reviled. (1 Timothy 6:1)

We can see from these examples in Scripture that God has placed authorities over us, even those that may be harsh and unkind. Our responsibility is to accept those authorities and to be obedient, except of course in those cases where we are being told to do things which are against the law of God. The example of the disciples tells us that we ought to obey God rather than man (Acts 5:29).

As a believer, you are a part of a chosen people, a royal priesthood, and a holy nation. Your purpose is to declare the praises of God. The reason God put you under authority is because we as human beings have proven repeatedly that we are not inclined to do what is best and right. Therefore, God instituted authorities of all kinds. All powers that exist are ordained of God

(Romans 13:1-5). God gave us government, for example, to maintain order and punish evil doers.

When we disobey and reject the authority that is over us, we are being disobedient to God. What about the husband who is just ornery? God is seeking to develop holiness and other godly characteristics in your life through your husband. He determined that the best way to develop those characteristics would be for you to have the kind of husband you have. This is true even if you are in your situation because of sin or disobedience. Perhaps you married a man who was not a Christian. You broke God's commandment about being unequally yoked together with an unbeliever. God will still use that individual in your life to accomplish his purposes.

Men, the same thing is true for you. In order to help you on the road to holiness, he gave you the particular wife you have and the particular employer you have.

When you reject the authorities in your life and complain about what they ask you to do, you are complaining and rejecting God's direction (Romans 13:2). After he saved us, he didn't just go away and allow circumstances to unfold. He is actively at work on your behalf even through the most godless employer or the most stubborn police officer who stopped you for speeding. These are God's agents. Don't reject them.

God's people got into a great deal of trouble in the Old Testament when they complained against Moses. They murmured because there was not enough water and not enough bread (Exodus 15:24; 16:2; 17:3; Numbers 14:2) Later on in their history, the people of Israel complained to Samuel that they wanted a king. When Samuel took this to the Lord, God told him, *"They have not rejected you, but they have rejected me from being king"* (I Samuel 8:7).

"But I can't stand it on the job. I am constantly belittled. My ideas are never followed. It seems as though my boss is always checking up on me to see if I am doing a good job. How am I supposed to remain joyful and enthusiastic?"

You can't change where you were born or who your parents were, but you have the freedom to change jobs. But let's assume that God has not opened the door for such a change. How might you respond to being belittled by your employer? You could become angry because you don't like being ignored. You don't like being treated like a second-class citizen. You don't like your good ideas being overlooked, right? Why do we have these feelings? We want to feel loved and wanted. We want to know that we are appreciated, that we are worth something. We do not want to believe that we are nothing, that there is no value in what we can contribute to the world.

Those feelings are unavoidable. The problem is that we are searching in the wrong place for affirmation. The truth of the matter is that there may well be other people who could do a better job. Even if your boss were paying more attention to you and listening to your ideas, it's such a small part of the overall operation of the company, and the company is such a small part of the overall operation of the country, and the country, as big as it is, is a small part of the overall world situation. But even if your boss does listen to you, does that make you important? Is your worth and significance in the world dependent on whether people pay attention to you or not? No! Just because people pay attention to you doesn't mean you are doing a good job. And just because people are ignoring your ideas, does not mean you are doing a poor job. Your value does not come from the responses of people to you or to your work. Don't lie to yourself.

When I became a high school principal, an interim principal in another building gave me advice that turned out to be amazingly accurate. He said, "Don't be too full of yourself and what you are able to accomplish. A couple of years after you leave this job, your policies, procedures, and protocols will be largely forgotten and replaced by those of the new administration." He was exactly right. It's always right to do a good job and to make improvements, as in my case, in my school. But to imagine that doing so is going to have an eternal impact in my community is naïve. But the ways I might impact people for Christ — that's a result that has eternal consequences.

Here's what's important to remember: Your value comes from being created in the image of God. It comes from your having been set apart by God for his glory to be one of his adopted children. It comes from knowing that the all-powerful God has chosen to live in your life, to guide you and lead you. It comes from knowing that the all-wise God has specifically designed and allowed circumstances in your life so that you would become more like his Son, Jesus Christ. Your value comes from your relationship to God. Your growth in Christ-likeness is assured by the God who designed your life circumstances in just the way he did in order to produce optimum growth in you.

You may be a fine, upstanding employee at your company, but do you realize that if you are doing a good job to impress your boss, or to get a promotion, or so that your neighbors will see you as a success, or any other similar reason, you are doing it for the wrong reason? God will work to wean you away from those motives in order to cause you to be more like Christ. Christ would work at your company in order to cause God to be praised. It is God we are working for.

> Bondservants, obey in everything those who are your earthly masters, not by way of eye-service, as people-pleasers, but with sincerity of heart, fearing the Lord. Whatever you do, work heartily, as for the Lord and not for men, knowing that from the Lord you will receive the inheritance as your reward. You are serving the Lord Christ. (Colossians 3:22–24)

> Bondservants, obey your earthly masters with fear and trembling, with a sincere heart, as you would Christ, not by the way of eye-service, as people-pleasers, but as bondservants of Christ, doing the will of God from the heart, rendering service with a good will as to the Lord and not to man, knowing that whatever good anyone does, this he will receive back from the Lord, whether he is a bondservant or is free. (Ephesians 6:5–8)

From all this we learn that God has designed authority in our lives to create growth in godliness in us. Let's work with God on this and not chafe against his design for our good.

Besides difficult authority situations, there are always many other questions and struggles. Sickness and death seem to come close to us way too often. Natural disasters or crime in our neighborhood often produce fear and worry. Poverty is a real struggle for many people. How does knowing the truth of God's Word and his purpose in the world help in these situations?

Remember the key truth that God is working all things together for good for them that love him and are called according to his purpose. As hard as it is to believe, God uses sickness, the death of loved ones, and our status in life to accomplish these ends.

There is an incident recorded in Scripture where Jesus helped a man by healing him of his blindness (John 9). This man had been born blind, and Jesus healed him. People were asking who had sinned to cause this man to be born blind. Jesus said that neither the man nor his parents caused him to be born blind. He tells the people that the reason that the man was born blind was so that God would get the glory through this circumstance.

Jesus wanted to be able to perform this particular miracle at this specific time. He knew it would be appropriate for his ministry, and he knew that it would be appropriate in the life of this man and his family. It was for this reason that the man was born blind. We don't know how old the man was, but just think of what he had been through. When he was a child, he could not go out and play with the other children and join in their games because he could not see. He probably was often discouraged and frustrated because his blindness kept him from becoming as active as he would like to be. And what was the reason that he had to suffer this way? So that Jesus could perform a miracle and glorify God many years later.

Think about the man's teen years. The other young people were enjoying their teen years. They were perhaps going places together. They were seeing what their prospective husbands or wives might look like. They enjoyed the music and other recreations of their day. And yet, here was this young man, unable to fully participate in those activities because of his blindness. And the reason for the blindness was so that Jesus could perform a physical and spiritual miracle in his life many years later. Jesus said specifically that the man was <u>born</u> blind *"that the works of God might be displayed in him"* (v.3).

My immediate response is that this doesn't seem fair. Didn't he deserve a better childhood than this? No. None of us deserves everything we have. All the benefits that we have – our life, our health, our mental abilities – all we have are gifts from God. He gives them or doesn't give them as he chooses, but we don't have any natural right to any of them. We are naturally enemies of God and deserve judgment and condemnation. We are not worthy of any benefits, except as God permits by his grace. "Wow!", says someone, "That's really depressing."

It is depressing, but it is the truth. Our worldview revolves around ourselves and, according to our evaluation, we deserve a lot of attention and acclaim. But we are naturally enemies of God and under his sentence of condemnation. Anything good which he allows us inmates to have is a blessing.

In Luke 13:4, Jesus tells of eighteen people who died when the tower in Siloam fell on them. He asks if these people were more guilty than all the others living in Jerusalem. In other words, "Had these people been terrible sinners, and that is why they were punished by having this tower fall on them?" Jesus' answer is "No." He goes on to say that unless you repent, you will also perish. Did he say that these people were innocent, and therefore it was an unfair accident? No. He implies that none of us deserves anything better than this. Unless we repent, we will also perish. Does that mean if I don't repent, a tower might fall on me? Probably not, but Scripture does teach us that it is appointed unto men once to die, and after that comes the judgment (Hebrews 9:27). These eighteen people died through an "accident." We don't know why God allowed these particular people to die at that time.

But we do know that the punishment of sin is death. There is a time of death appointed unto all of us and the judgment will follow. Repentance, turning from our old way and turning to Christ, is the only way we can know that no matter what happens to us, we are the Lord's (Romans 14:8).

What is the point? The point is that we have a heavenly father who oversees everything that happens to us. He is not the source of everything that happens to us, but all of it has to go through his hands. He only allows what will cause us to mature.

> No temptation has overtaken you that is not common to man. God is faithful, and he will not let you be tempted beyond your ability, but with the temptation he will also provide the way of escape, that you may be able to endure it. (1 Corinthians 10:13)

This verse is telling us that no matter what comes into our lives, it is not more than we can bear. Not because we are so strong, or because if we put mind over matter, we will be able to handle it. We will be able to bear it because God, who knows all about us – all our weaknesses, experiences, and strong points – God will not permit into our lives any trial or temptation that is greater than what we can handle through his power in us. Therefore, it becomes a matter of whether we will believe God or trust our own thinking.

Paul writes in Romans 5:3, "*Not only that, but we rejoice in our sufferings, knowing that suffering produces endurance.*" Joy is not something you put on. It is something that comes from down deep. Paul is saying that he is so certain of the truth that suffering produces perseverance and all the other resulting characteristics, that when he is suffering, he rejoices. He knows what the ultimate outcome will be. He understands how it is God's way of working out the character of Jesus in our lives. The Scripture says that even Jesus learned obedience through the things that he suffered. Suffering and trials are good for us.

James says it this way in James 1:2: "*Count it all joy, my brothers, when you meet trials of various kinds for you know that the testing of your faith produces steadfastness.*" God is not afraid to allow just the right amount of suffering into your life to mold you more and more into the image of Jesus Christ.

When God talks about suffering, he isn't just talking about taking it well when we receive suffering for something sinful or foolish that we have done. He is talking about suffering, even when we were perfectly innocent. In talking about slaves, Peter writes:

> Servants, be subject to your masters with all respect, not only to the good and gentle but also to the unjust. For this is a gracious thing, when, mindful of God, one endures sorrows while suffering unjustly. For what credit is it if, when you sin and are beaten for it, you endure? But if when you do good and suffer for it you endure, this is a gracious thing in the sight of God. (1 Peter 2:18–20)

This passage is talking about slaves, but in our day, it applies to employers, parents, or any authority God places over us. Christ suffered for us leaving us an example that we should follow in the same path that he walked.

Peter goes on to tell us in chapter 3:

> Verse 14: But even if you should suffer for the sake of righteousness, you are blessed.

> Verse 17: For it is better to suffer for doing good, if that should be God's will, than for doing evil.

> Chapter 4:12: Beloved, do not be surprised at the fiery trial when it comes upon you to test you, as though something strange were happening to you. But rejoice insofar as you share Christ's sufferings, that you may also rejoice and be glad when his glory is revealed. If you are insulted for the name of Christ, you are blessed, because the Spirit of glory and of God rests upon you. But let none of you suffer as a murderer or a thief or an evildoer or as a meddler. Yet if anyone suffers as a Christian, let him not be ashamed, but let him glorify God in that name. For it is time for judgment to begin at the household of God; and if it begins with us, what will be the outcome for those who do not obey the gospel of God?

The circumstances of life are not arbitrary. Things don't just happen. God is working actively on your behalf. The difficult things and sufferings you may be experiencing are part of his plan. Will you respond with joy, believing that God is actually accomplishing good in your life through it, or will you become bitter and adopt a complaining attitude? If you choose the latter course of action, it doesn't mean God's plan has failed. He has allowed the suffering and will use even your negative reaction to show you the depths of rebellion and discontent that are lodged in your heart. Don't forget, God knows what he is doing. We sometimes don't know ourselves very well. It sometimes takes "bad" things happening to us for us to recognize the ungodly attitudes still lurking down deep in our hearts. It is like using a foaming cleaner on the upholstery. All the churning down deep in the fabric is bringing up the imbedded dirt which has been trapped there for years. Our complaining and bitterness show both us and God exactly what kind of hold sin still has on us. It is time to begin the confession process and the other steps toward victory that we have already discussed. As you suffer, thank and praise God that he is still interested in you enough to allow this to happen to build character and the nature of Christ into you.

Someone with a non-murmuring attitude is an amazing witness to the world. Paul tells us in Philippians 2:14 to do all things without murmuring and complaining so that we can shine as lights in a dark world. Lost and sinful people murmur and complain, but Christians should not. As God uses these various principles from his Word to build your faith and strengthen your obedience, you will shine brighter and brighter. And, as we have been learning in this book, that is the reason we are here.

Another thing that God is doing in your life is providing guidance and direction. In order for God's purposes to be realized in your life, God has to lead you in the right path, and he has promised to do just that. In Proverbs 3:5-6 God says, "*Trust in the Lord with all your heart, and do not lean on your own understanding. In all your ways acknowledge him, and he will make straight your paths*" (Proverbs

3:5-6). He also tells us that a man devises his plan, but it is God that directs his steps (Proverbs 16:9). God has a ministry of service designed just for you. It is his intention that you be an instrument of his grace in the lives of others.

Way back in the early part of this book, we talked about 1 Peter 2:9, which says:

> But you are a chosen race, a royal priesthood, a holy nation, a people for his own possession, that you may proclaim the excellencies of him who called you out of darkness into his marvelous light.

At that time, we talked about the fact that God's people are priests. That is, they have a ministry to perform in helping to reconcile others to God. God is at work in your life in such a way that you will be a faithful minister of God in the lives of others. In 2 Corinthians 5:18, we read *"All this is from God, who through Christ reconciled us to himself and gave us the ministry of reconciliation."* In the verse from 1 Peter quoted above, we are told that we are to declare the praises of him who called us. It is our responsibility and privilege to be ambassadors for Christ, to declare his praises so that others might hear the truth of the gospel of grace and turn to the Savior and have faith in him.

Paul's attitude in Philippians 1 is such a good example to me and to all of us. Paul says that to depart and be with Christ is better than continuing to live on in this body. But realizing that God is not ready to take him yet, Paul says, *"Convinced of this, I know that I will remain and continue with you all, for your progress and joy in the faith"* (Philippians 1:25). Wouldn't it be great if we all could take that attitude, to see as our mission the encouragement of others in their joy and in their progress in the faith?

Some people have an impractical view of God's leading. It is almost as though they expect signs in the sky to tell them what to do. God has promised to lead his children. He has told us that he would guide us with his eye (Psalm 32:8). In Isaiah 30:21, God says, *"And your ears shall hear a word behind you, saying, 'This is the way, walk in it,' when you turn to the right or when you turn to the left."* If we have been born again, we should live our life of faith, being aware of the fact that God is at work in our circumstances, guiding and directing in such a way that we might be able to minister his grace to others. Abraham's servant who went to seek a wife for Isaac said, *"As for me, being on the way, the Lord led me"* (Genesis 24:27 NKJV). This man wasn't sitting around the house waiting for a sign. He went forward with as much as he knew about God's will. As he continued his mission, God was leading both providentially and directly so that he might find the wife which God had in mind for Isaac. The Scripture says, *"The heart of man plans his way, but the Lord establishes his steps"* (Proverbs 16:9).

In the book of Esther, we find that Esther, a Jew, was the queen of the land. The situation had developed where her people were on the verge of extinction because of the decrees of the king. Mordecai persuaded Esther to intercede on behalf of her people, telling her, *"And who knows but that you have come to royal position for such a time as this?"* (Esther 4:14). God had worked in Esther's life in such a way as to put her in this position just for that very time. She was not aware of it until the crucial moment came, and by Esther's intercession, God's people were saved from destruction.

In the story of Ruth, we find Naomi telling Ruth to go out and glean in the fields to provide for the food they needed. The Bible says that she *"happened upon the field of Boaz"* (Ruth 2:3). Ruth was to become David's great-grandmother. This did not just happen. God was obviously at work in this entire incident, but to her it appeared to have happened, we might say, "by chance." So even though God does not speak directly to us, he is definitely leading us through the normal, everyday decisions of life.

If you are one of God's children, God is working in your life in the very same way. Don't look for big signs in the heavens. Just follow the Savior day by day in faith and obedience. As you do so, demonstrate in your life and by what you say, that God's grace is real to you. In so doing, you will be a faithful servant and a faithful priest of God. *"Let your light shine before others, so that they may see your good works and give glory to your Father who is in heaven"* (Matthew 5:16).

As we live our lives in the normal everyday routines, we are a testimony for Christ. Consider this interesting passage in 2 Corinthians 2:14-17:

> But thanks be to God, who in Christ always leads us in triumphal procession, and through us spreads the fragrance of the knowledge of him everywhere. For we are the aroma of Christ to God among those who are being saved and among those who are perishing, to one a fragrance from death to death, to the other a fragrance from life to life. Who is sufficient for these things? For we are not, like so many, peddlers of God's word, but as men of sincerity, as commissioned by God, in the sight of God we speak in Christ.

This passage tells us that as we live, we have an influence. Some people won't like it. But to those who are saved, the testimony of our lives will be like a sweet fragrance of life. They recognize the Spirit's work because they have that same Spirit within them.

Who is equal to such a task? None of us. Only because of the presence of the living Savior in our lives are we up to the task. It is not an easy thing to be the fragrance of death, and to knowingly turn people off by standing up for the truth. But on the positive side, it's exciting to know that, as the fragrance of life, we are an encouragement to believers.

What is God doing? He is molding you and making you like Christ through the circumstances and people he allows into your life. What else is he doing? He is leading you through life, allowing your life to be a witness and testimony to those around you. Some of them will be drawn by it, and others will be repelled. Either way, God receives the glory, and that is what it is all about. There is a purpose.

Knowing there is a purpose ought to help us with issues of self-esteem. We hear a lot these days about self-image or self-acceptance. The first and foremost problem in dealing with our self-respect involves having a thorough understanding of the gospel message. Most people in our culture have been educated in schools dominated by humanistic thinking. They have been subjected to a constant barrage of humanistic messages in the media. Why is it crucial to understand this? Because the humanist philosophy is false.

If the secular humanists are correct, each one of us is a product of random events, chance happenings, over billions of years. Any meaning we have in life is the meaning we give it. Each individual is responsible for establishing his or her own meaning, and that meaning can be different from person to person. It's a self-defined thing. Therefore, meaning is an illusion. A meaning that is just arbitrarily established is not real meaning. There are many people who know this. They know that money or prestige do not really supply meaning in life. It is impossible to bring true meaning to life while trying to maintain a totally secular point of view. There is no meaning because there is no purpose. Without God, there is no purpose. There is just randomness and chance. No purpose equates with no meaning. This results in a nihilistic, depressing, sometimes self-destructive or violent existence.

Some people try to maintain a secular naturalistic point of view most of the time, and then look for some emotional or mystical meaning in life through religion or other mystical experiences. They have given up hope of finding any rational basis for meaning, and so they abandon their rational side and look for meaning in the emotional experience that religion may give them. If they attend church at all, these people typically attend churches where the ministers themselves are barely more than secular humanists using religious terminology. They may talk about doing good without really understanding what "good" is, or without even believing that there is any real objective "good." The words "God" and "Jesus" are part of the religious vocabulary, but they don't mean there is a real God who can actually hear and answer our prayers. They don't believe in a real Jesus who is God and who died to pay all the penalty for sin.

Real meaning comes from knowing that the God who made the universe actually cares about the world he created, and more specifically, he cares about you personally. Even though his creation has rebelled against him and disobeyed every command he has given, he still cared enough to enter the world himself and take upon himself the frailty of human flesh. He cared enough to die in order to take the punishment that you and I deserved.

When you see yourself as one whom God sought out in order to regenerate and transform, the problem of poor self-esteem begins to diminish. To know that God is designing all circumstances for our good so that we will be conformed into the likeness of his son – to know that – is to be encouraged and built up in our self-esteem. What an amazing thing to think that the God who made the universe did not leave us to fend for ourselves, but rather is working actively on our behalf! That gives meaning to life.

Let's think about prayer for a minute. Saying prayers to fulfill some religious exercise is one thing, but to know that God's children have direct access to God is something else. As a son of God, I can go to him and share my concerns and frustrations with him. I can pray for others, asking God to regenerate them and to change their lives in the same way that he has changed mine. He has made each one of his children a priest to be an intermediary between God and his fellow men. What does that do to someone's self-esteem?

Do you remember how Moses felt when God called him to lead the children of Israel to the promised land? Moses said to God, *"Who am I, that I should go to Pharaoh and bring the children of Israel out of Egypt?"* (Exodus 3:11). After God had showed him some signs he could use and told him what he could say to prove his authority, Moses said, *"Oh, my Lord, I am not eloquent, either in the past or since you have spoken to your servant, but I am slow of speech and of tongue"* (Exodus 4:10).

Moses had a poor self-image. He was not sure he could do what God had asked him to do. The solution to his problem was not in building up more confidence in himself, but it was based on the confidence he could have in God. In Exodus 4:11, God asked Moses, *"Who gave man his mouth? Who makes him deaf or dumb? Who gives him sight or makes him blind? Is it not I, the Lord? Now go; I will help you speak and will teach you what to say."* Moses' strength was to be found in God, not in himself. Unfortunately, Moses did not learn the lesson right away and still asked for someone else to go in his place. God was angry with Moses, not because he was weak in his speech, but because he lacked faith in the God who would give him the help he needed.

Later in the journey toward the promised land, the people had forgotten what God had done and complained about the way they were being treated. God was about ready to destroy them. Psalm 106:23 tells us that Moses stood in the breach before him to keep God's wrath from destroying them. Moses was fulfilling his responsibility as a priest: he prayed for his people. God is a prayer-answering God. He has given his children the privilege of coming to him in prayer and asking things of him. He wants us to learn how to fulfill that priestly ministry. God can do for us what he did for Moses. Moses started out insecure and unsure of himself, and yet, because of the work which God did in his life, he changed him into a mighty intercessor.

Think too about the story of Joseph who was sold into slavery by his brothers. They had planned to kill him, but then they came up with the idea of selling him to slavery in Egypt. They sinned when they did this. It was obviously not God's will that they should sin against their brother this way. Over and over through Joseph's ordeal, the Bible says that God was with Joseph. But it sure didn't feel that way to him. But later, when Joseph became a ruler in Egypt and his brothers stood before him apologizing for what they had done, Joseph said this: *"You meant it for evil, but God meant it for good."* God is not the author of sin, but he used the sin of Joseph's brothers to accomplish his purposes. He needed Joseph in Egypt to bring about the salvation of the Israelites during a great famine. God used the sin of these brothers to accomplish that end. Satan was defeated by the very sin that he had engineered. God always does this for his children.

He did the same thing for Job. Job was a righteous man. He had a good home, a nice family, and great wealth. Satan asked permission to put Job through the test. God gave him permission to take his family and his health away from him. Through the process, Job suffered immensely. But he kept his faith in God, and in the end, he was placed in a better position than he had been before all the trouble started. God turned Satan's cruel scourges into victory. I'm not saying it was easy for Job. I'm saying that God was working, and that Job was better for it in the end, even though he couldn't see it during the process.

God did the same thing with Christ. In a sense, Satan put Christ on the cross, but ultimately it was that same cross that brought about Satan's defeat.

Think about the characteristics of Christ and then look at your own life. What areas need improvement? It could be that the circumstances you are facing are designed or allowed by God to develop these very characteristics in your life.

For many people discouragement, even bordering on depression, is a problem. I've been very discouraged, maybe even depressed at times. I am not a psychiatrist, but I suspect that the causes for depression are not all the same, and that there are some causes which are organic. However, in some cases, it is a matter of thinking about the wrong things, having a self-focus.

Depression often comes about by a focus on self. It is a self-pity situation. We somehow don't feel that "life" is treating us fairly. It may be set off by plans that we had which were hindered by another person, or by the weather, or some other circumstance. It may result from a fear that we are not measuring up to an expectation we have for ourselves. We may not be as good an athlete as we would like to be. We may sense that others have it better than we do. They may seem to have more fun than we think we're having. The list could go on and on, but basically it centers on the fact that we have some goal or desire which has not been met to our satisfaction. We may not even be aware of what that goal or desire is.

Social media isn't helping with all of this either. Almost everyone in our social media circle seems to be having more fun than we are. They seem to have more friends. Even the spinach souffle in the picture on Facebook makes life look more fun for them than it is for you.

First, we need to understand that deep discouragement is not part of the Christian life, the life lived in the power of the Spirit. God allows it certainly, but it is not part of victorious Christian living. This means that it is of the flesh and is a sin which needs to be confessed and forsaken just as any other sin should be.

Why sin? Because we aren't thinking about the right things. In Philippians 4:8, Paul writes:

> Finally, brothers, whatever is true, whatever is honorable, whatever is just, whatever is pure, whatever is lovely, whatever is commendable, if there is any excellence, if there is anything worthy of praise, think about these things.

God has been so good to us, and we need to focus our minds on those things. As I have already said probably too many times in this book, God is at work in our lives, and we need to believe him and focus on all he has done for us, in us, and through us.

Psalm 42 gives us some insight into the despair of the Psalmist. In verse 3, he says, *"My tears have been my food day and night, while they say to me all the day long, 'Where is your God?'"*

To add to the despair caused by the faithless questions of those around him, he remembers the past. He says in verse 4, *"These things I remember, as I pour out my soul: how I would go with the throng and lead them in procession to the house of God with glad shouts and songs of praise, a multitude keeping festival."*

Relief comes when he begins to talk to himself. He says,

> Why are you cast down, O my soul, and why are you in turmoil within me? Hope in God; for I shall again praise him, my salvation. (Psalm 42:5)

He knew where to look when he felt this way. The thing to do is to turn our gaze to God rather than focusing it on ourselves. God is the one who is in charge of our lives. He is the one who is working all things together for our good. Satan would have us look to the circumstances and become bitter and depressed. But we need to look to God and praise him even when we don't see how it is going to work out.

Paul explains in Philippians 3:7 that the Christian way of looking at things is totally different from the way the rest of the world looks at them. He tells us that those things that would normally have been considered gain to him he now considers a loss. Notice that. He is not saying that they have a lesser place, but that he considers them loss. The things the world considers a gain, the Christian considers to be a loss, a negative – something which holds him back from becoming all God would have him to be. He goes on to tell us that his supreme aim is to gain Christ and to be found in him, not having a righteousness of his own, but a righteousness that is from God through faith. That is the real goal. In order to accomplish this, verse 13 tells us that we must forget what is behind and strain toward the goal of the heavenly call of God.

We become depressed when some temporary or earthly goal is blocked. The gathering clouds of depression should tell us that we have our eyes on the wrong thing. We need to put our sights back on God and praise him for what he is accomplishing in us.

As we have looked at these areas in this chapter, has the thought entered your mind that the solutions almost seem too easy? You might be facing a problem unlike any that we have discussed here, and yet the principles are the same. However, you might be tempted not to give them serious thought because they seem to over-simplify everything. This comes about because we want so desperately to hang on to control. We insist on worrying about things we can't do anything about, because when we worry, we are at least doing something! God would have us trust him! It sounds too simple, but that is the truth of it. He has it all under control. He has designed the program necessary to train you to become like Christ. You need to learn to trust him and obediently walk with him each day. And the end result will be the glory of God now and in the ages to come.

Chapter 8
God's Plan for the Family

One of the most important relationships God has given us for our good and for his glory is the family. We've been discussing what it is that God is doing in this world and what his purposes are. The concept of family is an important part of that discussion. Why? Because family is the central training ground for raising another generation of people who will have the praise and glory of God as their central focus.

There are several questions we need to answer as we examine the Bible's teaching on this subject. What is the Bible's definition of family? How does God say a family should function? How does a family functioning on a biblical basis advance God's agenda in the world? This is not going to be a discussion of all aspects of marriage, child rearing, and family life. That would take an entire book. My intention in this chapter is to demonstrate the key role the family plays in God's plan for the ages.

It's important for us to ask these questions because this world is God's creation. He is the one who has designed it, and he is the one who is governing it. We live in a culture where everything seems to be decided on the personal level: Whatever seems right or feels right to me is what I should do. We are told that we as individuals can determine the structure of our life and family. We are told that we need to rethink what a family is, because not everyone has the same sort of family, and we need to give legitimacy to all family structures. The claim is that the individual is the final arbiter of form and structure when it comes to family.

Individual autonomy is the creed of the day. But since God exists and designed the family, we must submit our will to his in this as in all other areas of life.

All through the Bible, God compares his relationship with his people to that of a husband with his wife. Everything about marriage and family is a picture of Christ and the church. In addition, the family is to be a God-centered place where children can be raised *"in the nurture and admonition of the Lord"* (Ephesians 6:4). God hates divorce and expects strong faithful relationships between husband and wife. Why? Because *"he seeks godly offspring"* (Malachi 2:15). Why does he seek godly offspring? Because he is gathering together a people for his own name, and the more there are, the better.

The Bible tells us that God created us as male and female and he did that for a purpose. We find that purpose in Genesis 2:18. God said, *"It is not good for the man to be alone. I will make a helper suitable for him."* In Mark 10:6, Jesus says, *"But from the beginning of the creation, God 'made them male and female.'"* So right at the outset, we can see that God established the human marriage relationship as one involving two genders or sexes, male and female. They are different but complementary.

God had created mankind to be similar in many ways to animals. But, in distinction from the animals, he created them in his own image. God has attributes of personality, creativity, communication skills, and so forth. He loves and he hates; he sees and knows; he appreciates beauty. He created mankind to have those same characteristics. The fact that we have these traits makes us distinct from all the other creatures he has made. Because of this difference, Adam, at first, did not find another creature that was compatible with him. The only other beings he had for companionship and relationship were the animals. There were no others to love or to communicate and fellowship with. God, knowing that this was not good (Gen. 2:18), created a woman for Adam.

God described her as a suitable helper for him. That is, she was compatible with him. She was of his kind. Her help would be especially suited to the areas where he lacked. Neither one of them alone was the totality of what human beings could be. It took both male and female with their unique qualities to fully complement each other.

This doesn't mean that God doesn't call some people to a life of singleness. After all, Jesus was single, and no one can claim that Jesus didn't live a fulfilled life in his humanness. It also doesn't mean that a man or woman can't function on their own and live productively the life of faith. But God did say that it is not good that man should be alone. He did create a woman for him that had complementary and helpful traits. The two together, he said, were made in the image of God. "*So, God created man in his own image; in the image of God he created him; male and female he created them*" (Genesis 1:27). Men have a way of thinking, acting, and relating that is different from the way women think, act, and relate. There is a complementarity in the relationship.

I think our culture creates many problems by trying to force men to think like women or women to be like men. In fact, part of the challenge in marriage is for each partner to learn what the other means when they interact. Many women today, reacting to the apparent patriarchy and dominant role that many men have, believe that the way to achieve equality is to say that they can be like men. In doing so, they are denying their own nature. In saying this, I am not suggesting that women are unable to do many of the same things men do, but that women, in doing these things, cannot be what men are. A woman *can* be the president of a company, let's say, but a woman *can't be* a man when she does this job. She may do a better job than her male counterparts, but even then she is not a man in doing so. And a man can take care of children. Many men have to do it by themselves because of divorce or the death of their spouse. But even if they are doing a good job, they are not doing it like a mother would. Men and women each bring a kind of innate goodness and quality to the things they do. God designed them that way. Based on his design, God has given men and women differing roles in life. It's not a matter of value or ability, it is a matter of purposeful design by a skillful and loving creator.

God tells us in Genesis 2:24 that a man is to leave his father and mother and be united to his wife. The two are to become one flesh. True union of a husband with his wife is not possible unless there is a leaving. When someone enters marriage without cutting the emotional umbilical cord to parents, he or she is not fulfilling God's plan for marriage. And it should be noticed that the Bible specifically says that "a man should leave." Satan will do all he can to mar any of the creations of God, and marriage is one of his prime targets. The beauty of many a marriage has been spoiled by a husband or wife being overly emotionally attached to parents. There must be a definite letting go on both sides, but specifically, there is a crucial importance for the man to stand on his own. God explicitly says the <u>man</u> should leave his father and mother and be joined to his wife. As we shall see, God has given man the leadership responsibility in the home, and if he is emotionally attached to mommy and daddy, he won't be able to function in this important responsibility and calling.

God gave Adam and Eve a specific command and blessing in Genesis 1:28. He said that they should be fruitful and increase in number. They should fill the earth and subdue it. God wanted them to have children. He wanted the earth to be full of people. Why? So that there would be millions of his creation joyfully praising God for his goodness to them and giving him the glory that he deserves.

> He established a testimony in Jacob and appointed a law in Israel, which he commanded our fathers to teach to their children, that the next generation might know them, the children yet unborn, and arise and tell them to their children, so that they should set their hope in God and not forget the works of God, but keep his commandments. (Psalm 78:5–7)

> But did He not make them one, having a remnant of the spirit? And why one? He seeks godly offspring. Therefore take heed

to your spirit, and let none deal treacherously with the wife of his youth. (Malachi 2:15 NKJV)

God's intention was that as the angels looked down from heaven, they would see people using their creativity for creating masterpieces of art and architecture, and musical masterpieces with which to worship and praise their creator. The angels would also see people using their intellectual abilities to investigate the world around them. As they discovered more and more of the intricacies of the world God had made, they would rejoice and give him the glory. God wanted the earth to be filled with such people. That's why he designed it the way he did at creation.

But as we noted earlier, sin came and things began to fall apart. With the sin came the curse. Notice what God said to Eve after the fall:

> To the woman he said, "I will surely multiply your pain in childbearing; in pain you shall bring forth children. Your desire shall be contrary to your husband, but he shall rule over you." (Genesis 3:16)

First, God lets her know that there would be sorrow, pain, and difficulty in giving birth to her children. The thing that God had commanded, i.e., being fruitful, would now be more difficult.

Second, he said, "*Your desire shall be contrary to your husband, but he shall rule over you.*" What does this mean? There is an interesting passage in Genesis 4 that perhaps can shed some light on this. When Cain was angry with his brother and wanted to do him harm, God came to him and said,

> If you do well, will you not be accepted? And if you do not do well, sin is crouching at the door. Its desire is contrary to you, but you must rule over it. (Genesis 4:7)

The last part of what God told Cain has the same construction as what God told Eve. God told Cain that sin's desire would be contrary to him. That's not a good thing, because sin's desire was one of lordship and mastery. Cain's responsibility was to rule over sin.

God is telling Eve that her desire would be for her husband in a way that was not good. She would desire to be in charge, to have the responsibility for what took place in her marriage and family. God says that Adam was to rule. He's not directing Adam to be a tyrant. He is simply saying that in a fallen world where counter opinions can't always be resolved in the right way, someone has to be responsible for those decisions. God has directed that it be Adam, the man. Every organization of people ultimately has to have a means whereby someone is finally responsible for the implementation of the plan or program, otherwise nothing would ever get done. The responsible person can delegate the decision to others. He can accept the recommendations of others, but ultimately, he is responsible to make the decision.

The same thing is true in a family. Someone has to have the final authority and be the one who is accountable to God for the affairs of the family. God has appointed the man to be the one responsible.

Does the fact that God put man as head over the woman mean that he is superior or more intelligent? First Corinthians 11:3 teaches us that the head of the woman is the man. But it also teaches us that the head of Christ is God. Does that mean that Christ is inferior to God the Father? Does it mean that God the Father is more intelligent or wiser than Christ? Of course not. God wants us to distinguish between lines of authority and value or intelligence. They are not the same. The wife may be very intelligent and wise and there may be many intelligent and wise women in the church, but God has appointed the man to be the leader.

While this is all very controversial in our culture, it should not be controversial in the church. All through the New Testament we find these truths repeated:

> Likewise, wives, be subject to your own husbands, so that even if some do not obey the word, they may be won without a word by the conduct of their wives. (1 Peter 3:1)

> Wives, submit to your husbands, as is fitting in the Lord. (Colossians 3:18)

> Now as the church submits to Christ, so also wives should submit in everything to their husbands. (Ephesians 5:24)

> I do not permit a woman to teach or to exercise authority over a man; rather, she is to remain quiet. For Adam was formed first, then Eve; and Adam was not deceived, but the woman was deceived and became a transgressor. (1 Timothy 2:12–14)

> The women should keep silent in the churches. For they are not permitted to speak, but should be in submission, as the Law also says. If there is anything they desire to learn, let them ask their husbands at home. For it is shameful for a woman to speak in church. (1 Corinthians 14:34–35)

This would be a good place to make a very important point. Because of the culture we live in, these statements sound almost foreign. They sound like the vestiges of a dying, male-dominated culture that would keep women home as slaves and child-producers. As Christians, we need to decide. Are we going to believe the Bible is the Word of God or not? It is just at junctures such as this that people give up on the faith. You can't go through the Bible and pick passages and say, "This we like and believe to be true," and "This one is false and needs to be denied." Well, you actually can do this, but the whole structure collapses on top of itself.

I'd like to make some comments directly to the men. You have the responsibility to lead. We'll go into more detail later in this chapter, but you need to realize that you need to lead. Many men are afraid to lead. They are afraid to make decisions and to set the course of the family on a godly path. Many times, it is the wife who is the one who is serious about training the children, or about having a prayer time with her husband, or seeing to it that the children are in church. As Christian men, we need to focus on the spiritual responsibility of leading our families in the ways of God. Even when we delegate certain responsibilities to our wife, we need to check back to see how things are progressing to make sure growth in grace is occurring.

It's important for Christian husbands to see themselves as priests in their marriage and family. Paul tells us in Ephesians that a godly husband has the Christ-like responsibility to sanctify and cleanse his wife with the washing of water by the Word (Ephesians 5:26). Christ did this so that he might present his bride to himself in splendor without spot or wrinkle. Likewise, a godly husband would do well to spiritually lead his wife and use the Word of God to minister to her in ways that cleanse and beautify her in spirit. Such service to his wife will greatly improve the beauty of their marriage as well as the well-being of his family. The husband is to be the spiritual leader and overseer of his home. In one of the passages we quoted earlier, the Bible tells wives that they shouldn't ask questions in church. Rather, they should ask their husbands at home. Many wives would say, "I can't do that. He doesn't know anything about the Scriptures!" That would be a sad commentary. Men, get into the Word. Learn. Grow. Ask your pastor for help. Become the spiritual leader God wants you to be.

The role of home and family is particularly important in this age. Through the sexual relationship, God has given us the power to "create" new eternal souls. When a child is born, he is born into the world dead in sin and lost as far as God is concerned. The most important need for these children is not education; it is not social skills or physical abilities. The most important need is for them to hear the good news of salvation in Christ in such a way that they repent of their sin and turn to God in faith, trusting him to save them. In the meantime, they need to have their sinful tendencies held back as much as possible by wise, godly parents. God has told us that faith comes from hearing and hearing from the Word of God (Romans 10:17). They need to hear the gospel in words from their parents, and they also must see it in their parents' lives.

Children are not naturally drawn toward the good. John gives us the characteristics of the world in 1 John 2. The lust of the eyes, the lust of the flesh, and the pride of life are a dominant part of every child's character until God miraculously calls them to himself through the gospel. Wise but unsaved parents do a lot to stem the tide of ever-increasing selfishness in the flesh of a child when they apply, perhaps unknowingly, God's instructions of discipline. Teaching children good social behavior, teaching them to be honest and truthful, and to be respectful of others, provides them with the general knowledge of right and wrong that helps to prevent sin from over-running the child. God's intention is that a child grow up in a home where there is a father and mother who are godly in character, who will teach and discipline, guide and restrain, and nurture and admonish their children. He wants a father and mother to teach their children about their need for a savior and how Christ can satisfy that need. God desires godly offspring. Christian parents should not shirk their responsibility in this task.

The definition of a family is changing in our world, but Christian families must work diligently to reclaim God's design. God made the woman to be a complement for the man. The two together make one flesh. Children should see that complementary nature of marriage from infancy up.

Remember the Biblical truth that although God loves the world, he abhors its rebellion against his rule. Those who have not been reborn by the Spirit of God are under the judgment and condemnation of God (John 3:18, 36). God is judging the world by releasing people to their own sin to enter into ever-increasing bondage to the sin they have chosen.

We find the downward slide given to us in Romans 1. Here are verse 18-29. My summary comments are in bold type before each verse.

God's wrath is currently being revealed from heaven. It is in progress now.

> For the wrath of God is revealed from heaven against all ungodliness and unrighteousness of men, who by their unrighteousness suppress the truth. (Romans 1:18)

God's wrath is justified because God has revealed his character to everyone. There are no excuses.

> For what can be known about God is plain to them, because God has shown it to them. For his invisible attributes, namely, his eternal power and divine nature, have been clearly perceived, ever since the creation of the world, in the things that have been made. So they are without excuse. (Romans 1:19–20)

Although we know this about God, we do not glorify him, and are not thankful. This results in a futile mind and darkened heart.

> For although they knew God, they did not honor him as God or give thanks to him, but they became futile in their thinking, and their foolish hearts were darkened. (Romans 1:21)

We foolishly claim to be wise, yet lower the glory of God to that of the character of man or other created beings.

> Claiming to be wise, they became fools, and exchanged the glory of the immortal God for images resembling mortal man and birds and animals and creeping things. (Romans 1:22–23)

God's wrath for these crimes is in progress, and consists of God giving people up to uncleanness to dishonor their bodies among themselves.

> Therefore God gave them up in the lusts of their hearts to impurity, to the dishonoring of their bodies among themselves. (Romans 1:24)

But man goes further and exchanges the truth for the lie, and worships and serves the creation by putting self and material things first.

> Because they exchanged the truth about God for a lie and worshiped and served the creature rather than the Creator, who is blessed forever! Amen. (Romans 1:25)

God continues his wrath by giving them up to dishonorable passions. Women exchange normal relations to that which is against nature.

> For this reason God gave them up to dishonorable passions. For their women exchanged natural relations for those that are contrary to nature. (Romans 1:26)

Men, leaving natural relations with women, burn in lust for one another, and receive in themselves the penalty for this error.

> And the men likewise gave up natural relations with women and were consumed with passion for one another, men committing shameless acts with men and receiving in themselves the due penalty for their error. (Romans 1:27)

Because they do not like to retain God in their knowledge, God continues his judgment by giving them over to a debased mind so they end up doing things which are not fitting...

> And since they did not see fit to acknowledge God, God gave them up to a debased mind to do what ought not to be done. (Romans 1:28)

Such as:

> They were filled with all manner of unrighteousness, evil, covetousness, malice. They are full of envy, murder, strife, deceit, maliciousness. They are gossips, slanderers, haters of God, insolent, haughty, boastful, inventors of evil, disobedient to parents, foolish, faithless, heartless, ruthless. (Romans 1:29–31)

Although they know that God does not approve of these things, and know that the penalty is death, people still do them and give approval to others who also do them, thus compounding the condemnation.

> Though they know God's righteous decree that those who
> practice such things deserve to die, they not only do them but
> give approval to those who practice them. (Romans 1:32)

According to this last passage, not only do people sin in this way, they give hearty approval to others who are doing the same thing. Paul tells us that because of this additional step of approval, the condemnation is compounded!

The downward spiral, having begun with the refusal to recognize God and be thankful, continues until God gives them up to uncleanness and dishonorable passions. Letting people go their own way is the judgment of God, and releases people to demonstrate the utter depravity and rebellion of their hearts by pursuing passions that destroy the normal man-woman relationship. This, in turn, destroys the picture of the relationship between God and his people that marriage is supposed to portray. What started out in such an idyllic way in the Garden of Eden has been defaced and obscured beyond recognition.

God has given parents the responsibility to raise their children God's way. They are the representatives of God to their children. To be irresponsible in this task is to allow greater rebellion in their children and possibly the ultimate condemnation of that soul in hell.

Turn in your Bible to Deuteronomy 6. In this chapter, Moses explains that he will be giving the people God's law. In verse 2, he tells them the reason why these commands were being given:

> That you may fear the Lord your God, you and your son and
> your son's son, by keeping all his statutes and his
> commandments, which I command you, all the days of your
> life, and that your days may be long.

Notice that he applies this teaching to three generations. He wants the current generation to fear the Lord, but he also wants their children to fear the Lord, and the next generation as well. Here is where things usually break down for us. Many of us teach our children well enough so that they are well-behaved and fear the Lord, but we don't teach them well enough so that they are able to pass this same thing on to the next generation. God wants us as parents to look two generations down the road when we teach our children. They need to be told how to live and how to pass this on to their own children in the future.

In verses 6-9, we find out how we are to handle the commandments and teaching which God provides. First, he tells the people that these commandments are to be upon their hearts. That means that the commandments must be internalized. It means that people must have a heart that is soft toward God, a regenerated heart that loves God and puts him first. Then it also means that the commands and teachings themselves must be on that heart. That can only come about as a person spends time with God in prayer and in meditation on God's words. You can't have the commands in your heart if you don't know what they are. This is not an optional part of the plan. Unless you have this part of the system working, the rest will fail.

There are many parents who take time to teach their children many skills. Some teach them how to play ball or play the piano. There are many fathers who teach their children how to do wood working or how to fix cars. Most parents are concerned about their children's education. They want them to get a decent education so that they can get a good job when they get out of school. But salvation does not come through any of these things. Salvation doesn't come through sending the children to Sunday School or church.

The parents need to have God's truths deeply implanted in their hearts so that they can then "impress them (God's truths) on their children." From the time they are infants, we should talk about God, his plan for the world, and what he expects of us. Children need to understand that they are responsible to God as well as to their parents for their behavior. They need to understand that God is really there, and that he has an interest in them. They need to understand that if they remain in the condition that they were born in, they will be lost for all eternity. They must be kept aware of the fact that a regenerated life is not a sinful life. A life of lying, cheating, hatred, greed, and adultery is a life without God. Those who live like this are not heirs of God (1 Corinthians 6:9,10).

Deuteronomy 6:7 tells us the extent to which we should take this teaching of our children. The commands and teachings of God are to be talked about while we are sitting at home, while traveling, upon going to bed, and first thing upon rising. Parents cannot talk with their children about the things of God at the appropriate times if they are never together. Some families never eat together or work together. When they are together, the TV is often on so that little conversation takes place. In our current culture, it is not the one screen but rather multiple screens. Many families provide screens for each child so that everyone can view or listen to what they want without having to interact or cooperate with others. How are we supposed to follow God's instructions in this passage if we don't make time to be with our children?

Verses 8 and 9 tell us that there should be symbols of our faith in God all over the house. If these symbols are without heart reality, they are meaningless. But godly reminders of the fact that we belong to God are an appropriate part of the home. Verse 20 says, "*When your son asks you in time to come, 'What is the meaning of the testimonies and the statutes and the rules that the Lord our God has commanded you?' then you shall say to your son, 'We were Pharaoh's slaves in Egypt. And the Lord brought us out of Egypt with a mighty hand.'*"

This passage highlights the kind of discussions that parents and children should have. It is not a matter of preaching at the kids once or twice a year. Rather, it is a daily dialogue about the things of God. It should be as natural a part of the conversation as any other topic normally discussed at home. When children see plaques, verses, and other Christian symbols around the house, they may bring up questions about what the verses mean and why they are important. These times will give us the opportunity to have many important life-changing discussions with our children.

In 1 Samuel 2, there is an account of a priest named Eli. In this passage, we are told about two of Eli's sons who were also priests. Eli's sons were wicked men: They had no regard for the Lord. They treated the worshipers with greed, and often forcefully took meat for themselves that should have been offered to God. In verse 22, we find that they slept with the women who served at the gate of the meeting place. In verse 23, we find Eli rebuking his sons for the things that they were doing, but they did not listen to their father. Eli belonged to a privileged family – privileged because God had chosen the family specifically to minister at the tabernacle where people came to bring their sacrifices (verse 27). In verse 29, God accuses Eli of scorning the altar and of honoring his sons more than God. He explains to Eli that the ministry of his family will be cut short because of the activity of his sons.

In chapter 3 verse 13, God revealed to Samuel what he had told Eli. In this passage we find some interesting things. God told Samuel that the judgment was coming because Eli knew of the sin of his sons, and he had failed to restrain them. Yes, he had told them that he was disappointed in their behavior, and he made a little speech about their bad behavior, but Eli did not take a stand against the sinful activities of his children. He did not restrain them! God gives parents the responsibility of restraining their children. It appears that in this particular case, the children were grown, and God still held Eli responsible to make sure they were behaving themselves. This was because not only was Eli their parent, but he was the high priest, the supervisor of the other priests. He had spoken to his sons, but there should have been more. He probably would not have been able to physically restrain them, but he certainly could have removed them from the priesthood.

God's view of the situation was that Eli respected his sons more than he did the worship of God. We know that Eli did not agree with what his sons were doing. He certainly disapproved of their behavior, but because Eli did not go far enough in rebuking them and restraining them, God accused him of being an accessory to their sin and respecting them more than God.

How many times do we do the same thing? We know that what our children are doing is not right, but we do not put a stop to it.

We are afraid of how they might react. We don't want them to look bad in the eyes of their friends. We don't want our friends to think that we are too strict with them or too narrow-minded, and so we don't do anything about the way they behave. I have seen fathers in a doctor's office tell their child to pick up the toys three or four times. Finally, they got down on the floor themselves and picked up the toys the three-year-old refused to pick up. In doing so, the parents are accomplices to the children's sin against God.

God says that disobedience to parents is a capital offense in his eyes (Romans 1:30-32). The natural state of children born into the world is one of separation from God. Sin and the flesh work together to bring out all kinds of characteristics that are fundamentally opposed to the principles of God. It is the responsibility of parents to be a restraining force in the lives of their children. In modern humanistic philosophy, the children should be allowed to explore and indulge themselves in just about anything they would like. According to God however, a child left to his own ways will only bring about heartache and despair for the parents and disaster for the child. Scripture teaches that *"Folly is bound up in the heart of a child, but the rod of discipline drives it far from him"* (Proverbs 22:15). God equates not disciplining a child with hating the child, and enforcing discipline as loving the child (Proverbs 13:24).

Because we are born sinners, our natural state is inclined in a direction opposite to that which God commands. It is the responsibility of the parents to discipline children in such a way that they come to the place of recognizing their need for a savior. God wants them to put their faith in him, having their hearts regenerated by the spirit of God. Parents who do not participate in godly discipline of their children are a party to the eternal death of their own children. Proverbs 19:18 says: *"Discipline your son, for there is hope; do not set your heart on putting him to death."*

Proverbs 29:15 tells us that a child left to himself will be a disgrace to his mother. God tells us in I Samuel 15:23 that rebellion is like the sin of witchcraft in God's sight, and arrogance is like idolatry. I think you realize God's hatred for those two sins. He equates rebellion to this kind of sin. We as Christian parents are priests of God, responsible to mediate between God and our children with the goal that they too will receive Jesus Christ as their savior and find new life in him. In the meantime, the tendencies of the flesh must be kept under control so that God's Word can do its work in their lives.

All the philosophy and psychology of our day has resulted in only tragic consequences for families, for our society, and for culture as a whole. Biblical truth alone offers real hope and real answers to the problems we face. Only the Biblical solution gives the rhyme and reason for what is happening. A wise parent will pass along not only the religious training concerning the gospel, but will also help the child to understand the basic principles of God's Word. How is a child going to learn to stand up against peer pressure unless he is taught to resist from a very young age? When you buy your child every trinket that is advertised on TV or that all the other children in the first grade have, you are not helping your child to resist peer pressure. Having what everyone else has in first grade may not appear to have a dangerous side to it. However, as your child grows along with those other children, he will always want to have what they have and do what they do. How are you going to suddenly put a stop to it when he is thirteen or fourteen years old?

We've talked a lot about the family in general and the raising of children. What does God specifically say to husbands and wives? In Ephesians 5:25, he tells the husbands, *"Love your wives, just as Christ loved the Church and gave himself for her."*

In 1 Peter 3:7, he says, *"Husbands, in the same way be considerate as you live with your wives, and treat them with respect as the weaker partner and as heirs with you of the gracious gift of life, so that nothing will hinder your prayers."*

Husbands are to love their wives like Christ loved the Church. He loved the Church so much that he died for her. He gave his all for his love of the Church. He tells husbands that they should love their wives in that same way. A husband should give himself willingly for his wife. He should be considerate of her. That means he should treat her politely and with respect. There is no room here for the abusive or demanding husband. A husband who expects his wife to do all the work while he sits around and watches TV is not loving her like Christ loved the Church. He is not showing her respect and consideration. Christlike husbands don't abuse their wives physically or verbally.

In addition to loving their wives, Paul told husbands not to be harsh or bitter against them (Colossians 3:19). Because of sin, there is a tendency for men to become bitter toward their wives. The flesh wants its own way, and when a man begins to feel that his wife is tying him down and becoming too demanding, he will often go along with it but will allow bitterness to grow up. Jesus Christ came as a servant. He laid aside his heavenly splendor in order to take upon himself the form of man. In addition, he did not become a man of high society, but he came as a servant. He wants us to have the same kind of mind that he has. He wants to develop a servant spirit within us. If we are to be like Christ, we will become servants. A husband is put in the unique position of being head in the home and, at the same time, being called upon to be a servant. God has put him in charge and given him the ultimate responsibility for all that goes on in that home. Then along with that he says he should be humble; be like Christ; be a servant. Don't look on your own interests, but look on the interests of your wife and children. It's a very difficult job, but God is able to accomplish it in the life of men who will submit to him.

To the wife God says, *"Wives, submit to your husbands as to the Lord."* God expects women to have a beauty that comes from the inner self – a gentle and quiet spirit, which God says he highly values (1 Peter 3:4). How are we training young ladies today? We seem to be training them to be loud and boisterous, to be like the boys. In today's culture, outward beauty is more to be praised than the inner beauty that God requires.

Look at what Paul writes to Titus about instructions for women. He told him to teach:

> Older women likewise, that they be reverent in behavior, not slanderers, not given to much wine, teachers of good things – that they admonish the young women to love their husbands, to love their children, to be discreet, chaste, homemakers, good, obedient to their own husbands, that the word of God may not be blasphemed. (Titus 2:3–5 NKJV)

Now that is certainly a controversial passage for our day and time! I would like to focus on the word "homemakers." The Greek word comes from a combination of the words for *home* and the word *work*. So what the Bible is saying is that older women, among other things, should teach younger women to be home-workers or workers at home. I know there can be extenuating circumstances and one short chapter on biblical family life cannot touch every possible circumstance, but it seems obvious to me that in general, God places the woman's central focus as the home. The man's central focus is out, working, governing, etc.

I'm just asking Christians to think about this. When Christian women are out in the workplace, they are, in many cases, under the authority of a man who is not their husband. There are opportunities for working together in close proximity, having lunch together, interacting in ways that can create a closeness of communication that might be missing in the marriage back home. In the Titus 2 passage quoted above, and many other passages, a wife is encouraged to be submissive to her <u>own</u> husband. It's hard to be submissive to your own husband if you are under the authority of another man in the workplace. No matter what anyone says, this is a dangerous situation.

When Christian women are out in the workplace, their children are often in day care or with babysitters who help the child eat, help him learn to walk, or hear his first words. Is this really what we want to take place? And what happens to all of the discussions throughout the day that God commanded us to have in Deuteronomy 6?

None of this has anything to do with claiming that women are not as capable as men or aren't able to solve problems or manage a team. In fact, many women are more successful at these things than their husbands. Many women I know earn more, or earn the fringe benefits for the family, and this is used as the justification for doing it this way. Sometimes this enables the man to pursue hobbies and toys, or to pick away at part-time work which then enables him to neglect his responsibility for supporting the family. I think we need to give these things very serious thought.

Can you imagine the beauty of a marriage where the man loves his wife like Christ loves the church and the woman is quiet and gentle; where both fulfill their God-given roles complementing each other's characteristics and thus showing their children what true humanity was meant to be? Out of a godly marriage relationship, then, God expects to see godly children being raised according to his rules. He gives promises of success, such as Proverbs 22:6 *"Train a child in the way he should go, and when he is old he will not turn from it."* God wants people to follow him, to be committed to his ways. He wants parents to train their children to follow those principles. When they do, he promises that when the children are old, they will not depart.

Our problem is that we don't do it God's way. Then, when things go wrong, we say, "See, you can do your best and it doesn't always work." God doesn't tell us to do our best. He tells us to train the children in the way they should go. A parent needs to discern where the child is spiritually and work accordingly. If they are believing children, God has given certain gifts that he will eventually use in ministry to the rest of the body of Christ. A wise parent will train a child with those gifts in mind. The Bible says to train up a child in the nurture and admonition of the Lord (Ephesians 6:4). "Train up" means to give them patterns to follow similar to training a plant to follow a string. Nurture means to provide the right spiritual and emotional nutrition that each particular child needs. This is demanding and time-consuming work. It doesn't leave much time for parents to pursue their own selfish interests.

A wise parent will help a child to understand how sin is present whenever he would do good. How can the child learn to reject sin in his life, and learn where the victory lies, if his parents don't help him with this? How will the child learn how to pray if the parents never teach him? How will he learn to love and meditate on God's word if his parents don't do it and show him how?

If the children are still unbelieving, there needs to be prayer for God to regenerate them and change their life. We need to pray that God would work faith in their heart that they might trust him with all their heart and soul and mind. We need to pray that God would grant them repentance (2 Timothy 2:25). This passage in 2 Timothy, although written to church elders, is a wonderful reminder of the importance of godly training in the home as well. We need to recognize that a child without God in his life is lost. The flesh will be dominant and will need to be controlled. That is the purpose of discipline.

Ephesians 6:4 tells fathers not to exasperate their children, but to bring them up in the training and instruction of the Lord. Nowhere does God condone abuse of children. Even though God encourages spanking, it is certainly not a beating or something done in anger. God's discipline of his children is done in great love and with tenderness. Our discipline of our own children should be done in the same way. Belittling children or telling them they are not wanted, or that they are worthless, is not a Christian way of disciplining. Being cruel and excessive in our punishment is not what God is asking for. God wants us to recognize sin in the lives of our children and to train this out of them through our disciplinary program. In this way, the children will learn how to discipline themselves so that their flesh wins fewer and fewer battles.

Is there any rhyme or reason to the breakdown in the American family and the increase in child abuse and juvenile delinquency? Certainly. The land is filled with those who are in constant rebellion against God. They don't praise and worship God for all he has done and are not thankful. Therefore, he allows them to go their own way, and to reap the consequences of their behavior. What we see is that reaping. Does that mean we just chalk it off and say there is nothing that can be done? Let's hide our heads in the sand and look forward to a better time in heaven? No. God has put his people here as salt and light for the world. He has given us a priestly ministry of reconciliation. At every possible opportunity, we should explain what God wants from us as people. When people wonder what is going on, let's tell them the real causes and the real solutions.

Turn in your Bible to Malachi 2:13-16. In verse 13, the people are crying because the Lord is apparently not paying attention to their offerings and worship. They wonder why this is. The answer is given in verse 14. The Lord is acting as a witness between the husbands and wives. The men have broken the covenant they had made with their wives. A covenant is a solemn promise. Breaking a promise is abhorrent to God. These people have broken the covenant they had made on their wedding day. Millions of people today are doing the same thing and yet they expect that God will hear them.

God tells us in Ecclesiastes 5:5 that it is better not to vow than to vow and not pay. God has no pleasure in fools. Millions of people repeat marriage vows and then break them without the slightest thought of the repercussions this will have in their lives. Verse 15 of Malachi 2 tells us that it is the Lord who has made them one. Jesus said, "*So they are no longer two, but one. Therefore what God has joined together, let man not separate*" (Matthew 19:6). Malachi explains that ripping apart what God has joined together covers one's garments with violence. Divorce is a violent act that breaks what God has made. Divorce is a violent act and should not be taken lightly by the church.

Verse 15 of Malachi 2 tells us why God is so interested in this situation. He tells us that he was seeking godly offspring. All the way through the Bible you can see God's plan working. He is interested in a godly group of people who will worship and praise him and demonstrate his character throughout the world. Because of this, he hates divorce (verse 16) because it hinders the prospect for godly offspring.

When we do not provide our children with a godly example of fatherhood or marriage, we obscure God's word pictures. It is becoming increasingly difficult for people to understand what God is like because good quality pictures are becoming more and more rare. God tells us that husbands are to love their wives like Christ loves the Church. When we describe God's love for the Church to many people in our generation, they don't know how to understand it because they have never seen a loving husband's sacrificial love for his wife. God hates divorce and all other behaviors and attitudes that hinder the demonstration of his character to the world. God's plan to call out a people for himself is closely tied to the family unit. He depends on godly parents to pave the way for his work in their children. God's way is the only way that works because it is the only way. There is a Rhyme and Reason to it all.

Chapter 9
God's Plan for the Church

In this book, we have been examining the question "What in the World is God Doing?" We have answered that question by demonstrating that God is in the process of calling out a people for his own possession, a people upon whom he has set his love and affection, and from whom he receives praise, honor, and glory.

According to Scripture, the church is at the core of what God is doing. It is not an after-thought for God. It is the main event. Most people, when they hear the word "church," think of a building. You hear expressions such as "Where do you go to church?" or "My neighbors don't go anywhere to church." The Greek word for church is *ecclesia*, which means "called out group." Imagine that! This is precisely what we have been considering in this book. God is calling out a people for his name's sake, and this group is called "The Church."

The book of Ephesians will help us in our thinking about this. Turn to Ephesians 1:22. In this passage we learn that Christ has been raised from the dead, and that God has put all things under his feet, and has made him to be the head of the church, Christ's own body.

How literally does he mean that the church is the body of Christ? In Ephesians 5:30, Paul writes, "*For we are members of His body, of His flesh and of His bones*" (NKJV). That means that in some way we are literally part of the physical body of Christ. This people that God is gathering is united with Christ the head and with each other as part of his body. When our Lord was on this earth, he was present in a physical body confined to one physical location at a time. Now, through his church as his body, he is able to be physically present with hands and feet all over the world.

Another important factor to consider in relation to this is that the physical body is not a bad thing. God created us as physical embodied beings, and he placed us in a physical world. God created Adam of the dust of the ground and breathed into him the breath of life, and he became a living soul. We are spiritual beings in a physical body made of the elements of the earth. God is not against the physical. We know this because when God became embodied in Christ, he took on human flesh, and lived here among us. He was not afraid to touch the physical. This is very important, because many religious philosophies teach that the body is evil and the physical is bad. God would not have entered the world the way he did if that were so.

There is a tendency even for us as Christians to consider the body and the physical a negative thing. Granted, the earth is cursed, and we suffer the consequences of the fall in our body with pain and suffering. But the body itself is not a bad thing that needs to be escaped in order to set the soul free. Christ's coming in a human body teaches us that the body is good, and that the enjoyment of food and other physical blessings is a good thing. In the final resurrection, our soul will be given a new body which the Bible describes as a spiritual body, but it will be a body that is like Christ's body after his resurrection, both physical and spiritual. We know that his resurrection body was a physical body because he said to Thomas, *"See my hands and my feet, that it is I myself. Touch me, and see. For a spirit does not have flesh and bones as you see that I have"* (Luke 24:39). Then he went on to eat in front of them. Our body will be a physical body for a spiritual being, like his glorious body (Philippians 3:21).

In 1 Corinthians 15:44, Paul writes that *"There is a natural body, and there is a spiritual body."* The word he uses for natural is "soulish." The natural body is one God designed for us as soulish creatures. The spiritual body is a physical body like Christ had after his resurrection, but it is called a spiritual body because its primary environment will be spiritual.

How do people become part of the body of Christ? 1 Corinthians 12:13 tells us, *"For by one Spirit we were all baptized into one body."* It is the baptism of the Spirit which places someone into the body. Jesus said that John came baptizing in water, but he (Jesus) would baptize in the Spirit. That means that Jesus baptizes us in the Spirit into his body. Just as John placed people in water, Jesus, through the Spirit, places us into his body. In so doing we become part of Christ. This happens at the moment of salvation. It is not a separate thing that only some special super Christians receive. The verse said, *"We were **all** baptized into one body."* In addition to being part of Christ's physical body, Paul writes in 1 Corinthians 6:17, *"But he who is joined to the Lord becomes one spirit with him."* A Christian also shares the same Spirit Christ has. We need to see ourselves as we truly are – one with Christ.

> For who knows a person's thoughts except the spirit of that person, which is in him? So also no one comprehends the thoughts of God except the Spirit of God. Now we have received not the spirit of the world, but the Spirit who is from God, that we might <u>understand</u> the things freely given us by God. (1 Corinthians 2:11–12, emphasis added.)

This passage is telling us that I can't really know you to the extent that you know yourself. Only your own spirit really knows you. And only my spirit really knows me. You can't really get in and know me the way I know myself. The same thing is true of God. But God has given us his Spirit so that we might know the things freely given to us by God (1 Corinthians 2:12). Verse 16 of 1 Corinthians 2 goes on to tell us that *"we have the mind of Christ."*

So here is how I want you to think about this. God created the earth. He then took dust of the earth, and made it into a human being, and then breathed into this being the breath of life, and man became a living soul. Everyone sinned in Adam, and God condemned the entire lot of us. But then God took upon himself a body of dust like ours, and redeemed us to himself at the cross so that these bodies and spirits of ours could be connected to Jesus Christ, the son of God. Amazing!

Now go back to Ephesians 1:23. When Paul says that the church is Christ's body, he adds the fact that this body is the *"fullness of him who fills all in all."* Who is the "him"? God, of course, since only God fills all in all. That means that in some manner, the church is the fullness of God. God is complete in and of himself, and so the church doesn't complete God. Because the Spirit of God inhabits his people and they are part of Christ, then, in some way, the church is the fullness of God in this world. That is another amazing thought!

Why is God doing all of this? Paul addresses this in Ephesians 2:7: *"So that in the coming ages he might show the immeasurable riches of his grace in kindness toward us in Christ Jesus."* The purpose is so that through all the ages of the future, God will be able to demonstrate to any spectators who might be there, how rich and kind he is in his grace by rescuing a bunch of rebellious enemies whom he originally had created in his image. They rebelled, and now he has exalted them and given them his Spirit and made them part of Christ and co-heirs with himself. God not only will be able to demonstrate this, but the whole purpose of what he has done has been with that goal in mind. His purpose in saving us, and making us part of Christ, is so that there could be this eternal demonstration of his grace and kindness. This is so important that I am going to say it a third time. The reason why God makes believers part of his body, and indeed why he created us in the first place, is so that in the ages to come, he would be able to continuously demonstrate the glory of his grace.

Paul gives us another angle of this purpose in Ephesians 3:10:

> So that through the church the manifold wisdom of God might now be made known to the rulers and authorities in the heavenly places. This was according to the eternal purpose that he has realized in Christ Jesus our Lord.

God's intention has always been that the church would show forth God's many-faceted wisdom to an audience. Who is that audience? The principalities and powers. Who are they? I believe he is speaking of angels and demons and all powers that God has created that live in the heavenly places. In a different passage, Paul describes our struggle as not being against flesh and blood, but against principalities and powers in heavenly places (Ephesians 6:12). God wants these adversaries to see how generous, merciful, and kind he is, and he wants them to see this when they look at the church, the body of Christ. **And this has been his purpose since before he created the universe and people.**

And finally, in Ephesians 3:21, Paul writes, *"To him be glory in the church and in Christ Jesus throughout all generations, forever and ever."* The church brings glory to God. The root of all sin is that we don't acknowledge God, give him glory, nor give him thanks. The salvation that God gives to his people in buying them back, giving them new life, and placing them into the body of Christ, demonstrates his glory in all its many facets, and it gives people the opportunity to praise God as individuals and also as they corporately meet together.

The church is a body, not a club. Clubs have membership requirements, elections of officers, pot-luck dinners, and the like. The church may have some of these things as well, but the church is made up of individuals who have been called out by God, joined to one another and to Christ by the same Spirit, and each individual is part of the flesh and bones of Christ. A human club is nothing like this. The church is a living organism with a head, Christ, a body, the Church, and one Spirit indwelling the entire organism. There are people in the pews every Sunday who are not actually part of the body of Christ. They are there, and they may participate, but they are like club members. They've joined an organization, but they are not part of the body, organically and spiritually connected to it.

So how does this body grow and function? I ask this because all living bodies grow. Ephesians 4:16 provides part of the answer for us. It reads, *"From whom the whole body, joined and held together by every joint with which it is equipped, when each part is working properly, makes the body grow so that it builds itself up in love."*

There is a knitting and joining together of the members of the body. In knitting, the yarn is intertwined in such a way that it is difficult to pull it apart. It is joined to other parts of the yarn in multiple directions so that there is a three-dimensional unity. The body of Christ is the same way. The members are knit together into one whole.

Secondly, we learn that every joint supplies something to the growth of the body through its effective working. When part of our physical body doesn't supply what's needed or stops performing its function, the body is sick, becomes weak, and potentially dies. In the body of Christ, growth and health are produced by the effective working of each individual part. When some parts fail to function properly, the body becomes weaker and less effective. That should be a challenge to all of us to know what our function is, and then to carry it out faithfully. Not doing so creates weakness and sickness in the body. We should not neglect the importance of teaching people that as members of the body of Christ, they should be functioning, using their gifts for the growth of the body and the glory of God.

In the human body, as the stomach does its work, the body is helped, and in return, the stomach is helped. As the feet, hands, and mouth each do their jobs, the whole body grows and the feet, hands, and mouth are helped in the process. It is the same in the body of Christ. God's goal is that each one should be like his Son Jesus Christ. How is that accomplished? It is accomplished as each member of the body carries out its particular responsibilities, ministering and caring for the other members of the body. And so each member is personally strengthened as the body itself grows stronger.

Just as in your own body, your physical life permeates your entire body, so also the life of God within us accomplishes the growth of his Church. Your fingers share in the life of your body; your brain shares in the life, as do the other parts of your body. It is the same with the body of Christ. Each part of the body shares in the life of Christ. The Spirit of God permeates the body. Through the operation of that life in us, and the effective working of each individual part, the body grows and matures until "*we all attain to the unity of the faith and of the knowledge of the Son of God, to mature manhood*" (Ephesians 4:13). In our human body all the activity is directed by the brain. In the body of Christ, Christ himself is the head of the body. He directs all its activity.

Using a different metaphor, Paul describes the church as a building. He writes,

> Now, therefore, you are no longer strangers and foreigners, but fellow citizens with the saints and members of the household of God, having been built on the foundation of the apostles and prophets, Jesus Christ Himself being the chief cornerstone, in whom the whole building, being fitted together, grows into a holy temple in the Lord, in whom you also are being built together for a dwelling place of God in the Spirit. (Ephesians 2:19-22 NKJV)

Notice how he uses the phrase "fitted together." This is similar to "knitted together." The bricks are mortared together in such a way that the building is solid and strong. In the case of the building metaphor, Paul says that we become a dwelling place of God in the Spirit. This too is an amazing statement that the God of the universe would dwell in and among his people. But as we read in Revelation, that is really what God wants to do: "*And I heard a loud voice from the throne saying, 'Behold, the dwelling place of God is with man. He will dwell with them, and they will be his people, and God himself will be with them as their God*'" (Revelation 21:3). God wants to dwell with us. Isn't that what "Emmanuel" means – God with us?

Let's stick with the image of the church being a building for a minute. Look at 1 Corinthians 3:9-17. Here, too, Paul speaks of the church as God's building. In this case he warns us to be careful how we build. Paul isn't so much talking about how we build our lives, but is actually talking about how we build the church. In verse 9, Paul says that you (plural) are God's building, so be careful how you build. Every believer is to be contributing to the work of God in the church, but we are to be careful how we build. We can build with valueless substances, or we can build with more valuable and substantial materials. We need to be careful how we build. Are our efforts self-motivated, superficial, and careless? Or do we build with solid, spiritual activity that edifies others and nourishes them with the truth of the Word of God? It's up to every one of us to contribute to the construction or growth of the church.

Now back to the body metaphor. In 1 Corinthians 12, Paul explains that the body is not one member but many (verses 12-14). The Spirit of God working in the body gives each believer one or more gifts to be used for the health and growth of the body. These gifts and functions are assigned by God himself, not chosen by the individual. God knows what functions are needed in the body, and so provides the ability and energizing power to enable that gift to be used within the church to accomplish the growth that is needed.

Beginning in verse 15 of 1 Corinthians 12, Paul personifies parts of the body, and illustrates the case of the person who feels sorry for himself or feels like he has nothing to contribute. We can't imagine our actual foot saying, "Since I'm not a hand, I must not be part of the body." Even if it did say that, would it then be disconnected? The answer is obviously, "No!" Likewise, if someone has a gift that he or she feels is not as significant as the pastor, does that make him or her any less important to the functioning of the body? Of course not, but sometimes it is hard to help people understand how really important they are in the functioning of Christ's body.

Don't ever think that because your gift seems to be small, it is therefore insignificant. Understand this, that even if you think you are nothing to God, and that your part is insignificant, you continue to be significant anyway. Thinking you are not a part of the body does not make you any less a part of the body. Many of us spend too much time wondering if we are any use to God. What we think of ourselves or our position does not make us any less a part of the work which God is doing. He uses us. He molds us and

220

makes us and works through us to accomplish his will in the lives of others. Remember Moses? He said that he could not speak. God rebuked him by asking him who had made man's mouth. The God who calls us to work for him also has provided everything we need to accomplish that work.

On the other hand, in verse 21, Paul explains that the eye cannot tell the hand that it has no need of it. This is illustrating the case of someone who feels proud that he has a particular role in the church and looks down on others to whom God has given a different gift. Every part is needed, and when one part suffers, the entire body suffers. Or if one part is honored, then the whole body is honored (verse 26). In fact, God says that just as we take greater care of the vulnerable and private parts of our body, it is the same way in the body of Christ: "*Our unpresentable parts are treated with greater modesty, which our more presentable parts do not require. But God has so composed the body, giving greater honor to the part that lacked it*" (1 Corinthians 12:23–24).

We have a hard time really believing this, don't we? Just as in our physical bodies, we take great care for parts of our body that are easily injured, and we cover those parts of our body that are personal and private, God has given greater honor and care and protection for those parts of his body which seem to lack. If you feel like you are one of those weaker, less important parts, take heart in the fact that God is bestowing greater honor and protection on you.

Paul talks about this in great detail in 1 Corinthians 12. In verses 4-6, he tells us that the same Spirit has given various kinds of gifts within the body. The same Lord has given different kinds of service. And the same God gives different kinds of empowering to accomplish the service. The Spirit gives the gifts; the Lord assigns the place; God empowers the person appropriately. Some kinds of service are out in the spotlight. Some are more quiet and in the background. God is the one who decides who gets which kind. In verse 7, we have an important truth to remember. Paul teaches us that every believer has been given a particular gift or gifts to be used for the common good. As soon as the Holy Spirit puts a new person into the body, he gives him the abilities required to accomplish the task which that part of the body is supposed to perform. Through the Spirit, God uses the person in that position to help accomplish the common good. What is that common good? The edification of the body so that we all might attain unto the unity of the faith and the maturity that belongs to Christ himself. To edify means to build up. God wants his body to reach unity in the faith, and he wants it to gain the maturity that Christ himself has.

The fact that every believer has been given a gift of ministry means that you have such a gift. There is a place in the body of Christ for you. In fact, if you are a believer, there is not only a place for you, but you are already in that place in the body. God the Holy Spirit has put you there. There is some function or purpose which needs to be accomplished where you are in order to help the body of Christ to be edified. Verse 11 tells us that we don't decide what those ministries are, but rather that God himself decides on the ministries. He is the head of the body, and through the Spirit he has placed each one of us in the body where he thought best. Through his Spirit, he carries out the functioning of that particular part of the body so that the whole body might be matured. That's what God is doing. He is choosing a people for himself and making each individual a partaker of the life of God. He then uses them to produce maturity in the whole body.

In 1 Corinthians 12:7-10, there is a list where we find gifts for communicating the gospel and teaching the word of God. There are also the gifts of wisdom and faith. In verses 28-31, we see gifts which provide for teaching, working miracles, and administering. In Romans 12:6-8, we see that God has provided for serving one another, encouraging, leading, and contributing to the needs of others. The Spirit gives the gifts; the Lord directs the particular place of service; and God the Father provides the power to accomplish them.

Every part of the body is to work with all the other parts, functioning properly within its sphere of service. Therefore, it is important for you to find out how the Holy Spirit has gifted you, and to put your God-given ability to work for the building up of the body. Remember, the church is the core purpose of God in this world right now, and it has been his plan since before time began.

God has given a particular structure to the church with certain individuals being in leadership for a particular reason. Look at Ephesians 4:

> And he gave the apostles, the prophets, the evangelists, the shepherds and teachers, to equip the saints for the work of ministry, for building up the body of Christ, until we all attain to the unity of the faith and of the knowledge of the Son of God, to mature manhood, to the measure of the stature of the fullness of Christ. (Ephesians 4:11–13)

Notice the various positions given: apostles, prophets, evangelists, shepherds, and teachers. We understand "shepherds" to mean "pastors." Their responsibility is to equip the saints. What are they equipping the saints for? The saints are to be equipped so that they can do the work of ministry in the church. Sometimes someone will ask, "Who is your minister?" The proper answer is, "All of us members."

What are we as members trying to accomplish in our ministering? The goal is to build up the body of Christ so that we would all come to "the unity of the faith and of the knowledge of the Son of God," with the ultimate goal of reaching the mature "stature of the fullness of Christ." Now that is quite the goal!

What does this ministry consist of? Since you are part of the body of Christ, your sins have been forgiven, you have a new heart, new attitudes, and a spirit which is in communication with God. Through your ministry (or service) as an individual Christian, you will be able to help, encourage, admonish, serve, or help a brother or sister in Christ in some way. As you do so, the entire body is built up and develops toward maturity. God doesn't do this through angels. He does it through other people, who, like us, need to be built up and matured in the faith. As they minister to us and we to them, we all grow.

Another way the Bible describes the Church is with reference to marriage. The church is called the bride of Christ. Let's go back to Ephesians 5. In verse 22, Paul begins to compare marriage to the relationship between Christ and the church. He talks about wives submitting to their husbands, and about the concept of the husband as head of the wife as Christ is the head of the church. In verse 25, husbands are exhorted to love their wives like Christ loved the church. How did Christ do that? He gave himself for her, and sanctified her and used the Word to cleanse her, so that he might present to himself the church as a glorious bride, without spot or wrinkle.

When we get to verse 30, Paul writes, *"We are members of His body, of His flesh and of His bones."* But then he says something very interesting. He writes, "For…" The fact that he starts with "For" means it is connected to the previous verse about being members of Christ's flesh and bones. He says, *"For this reason a man shall leave his father and mother and be joined to his wife, and the two shall become one flesh."* This is a quote from Genesis 2:24 when God created Eve, but Paul uses it in Ephesians to say that the way we leave parents and join with our spouse is a picture of our being members of Christ and being joined to him. In both cases he says that "the two shall become one flesh."

When a man and woman marry, God says they are one flesh. God says the same thing about Christ and the church. In fact, in Romans 7, Paul explains that in Jesus' death, our relationship with the law is broken so that we might be married to another, Christ, in order that we might bring forth fruit to God. Marriage is a picture of Christ and the church. We are one flesh with him.

In Hebrews 10:22-25, the author ties a lot of what we have been talking about together:

> Let us draw near with a true heart in full assurance of faith, with our hearts sprinkled clean from an evil conscience and our

bodies washed with pure water. Let us hold fast the confession of our hope without wavering, for he who promised is faithful. And let us consider how to stir up one another to love and good works, not neglecting to meet together, as is the habit of some, but encouraging one another, and all the more as you see the Day drawing near.

Notice that this passage contains so many of the things we have discussed. We are to draw near with a sincere heart, that is a heart that is true toward God and not deceitful. It must be a changed heart. We are to draw near with the full assurance of faith, believing the promises God has made about our salvation in Christ. Our hearts have been sprinkled from a guilty conscience. The problem of guilt and guilt feelings has been dealt with. And finally, there is the admonition to encourage one another and continue meeting together. We don't attend church meetings because of law, but because we desire to worship our Savior, and to meet with other Christians to encourage and build them up and to receive the encouragement which they provide.

What God has provided in simplicity for Christ's body worldwide, we have generally abandoned when it comes to the operation of our local assemblies. We find ourselves succumbing to the world's plan for operating organizations. When attendance slackens, we attempt to come up with better advertising or a flashier program. To build up enthusiasm for Sunday School, we invent contests. We compete against other churches to increase our attendance. We offer prizes for the most visitors. We have begun to trust in our methods more than in the methods which God has ordained.

We spend a lot of our teaching time trying to talk people into doing things that they don't innately want to do. We are trying to talk non-Christians into acting like Christians, and we use basic human methods to try to coerce Christians into worshipping and serving God faithfully. We have forgotten the word of Zechariah the prophet: " *'Not by might nor by power, but by My Spirit' says the Lord of hosts"* (Zechariah 4:6). God would have us teach the truth about our natural separation from God. He would have us teach that his regenerating work produces real results in the lives of people, and does not result in stillborns. He would have us witness because of our joy in the gospel and not to earn a prize for a Sunday School contest. He would have us spend time in prayer, laboring with Christ and one another for the souls of men, rather than playing at worship.

God is active and at work in our world through his church, his body. We have not yet reached the unity of the faith, and we have not yet reached the maturity of the fullness of Christ, but that is the goal. In the end God will present the church as a bride to his Son. She will be spotless and without blemish. What an exciting day that will be!

Chapter 10
Where Will it All End?

Where will it all end? That is the question that concerns us in this final chapter. We've been studying and discussing what God is doing in the world and in our own lives. History is going somewhere. God had very specific purposes in mind when he created the world, and as we have seen, God is at work moving and working in such a way that ultimately history will be brought to a conclusion. And in that conclusion, God will have succeeded in his purpose of demonstrating his glory for all to see.

Let's begin at the end, and then we will back up a little bit to see how we get from here to there. This is not a book on prophecy, so don't expect me to answer your questions about the timing for the rapture or tribulation or millennium. We're just going to take what the Bible says without trying to delve into all the intricacies of order and timing.

Christ is the central focus of history, and everything will ultimately be gathered together in him.

> For by him all things were created, …and in him all things hold together. (Colossians 1:16–17, emphasis added.)

> In [Christ] are hidden all the treasures of wisdom and knowledge. (Colossians 2:3, emphasis added.)

> Making known to us the mystery of his will, according to his purpose, which he set forth in Christ as a plan for the fullness

> of time, <u>to unite all things in him</u>, things in heaven and things on earth. (Ephesians 1:9–10, emphasis added.)

> For in him the <u>whole fullness of deity dwells</u> bodily. (Colossians 2:9, emphasis added.)

Jesus Christ is creator and sustainer of all things. He is the repository of all wisdom and all knowledge. The entirety of deity dwells in him, in his body. And at the end of time, everything will be united in him. There is no greater person or thing in the universe than Jesus Christ. We can't come up with enough words to say he is the core, the focus, the culmination, and the center of all things and all history. Whatever you can think of — any object, or scientific knowledge, or mathematical equation — it has its being and focus and meaning in Jesus Christ!

Because the church is Christ's body and bride, it too is at the center of God's plan. God will demonstrate and display his glory forever in his kindness toward his people, the church.

> The church ... is his body, the fullness of him who fills all in all. (Ephesians 1:23)

> To me, though I am the very least of all the saints, this grace was given, to preach to the Gentiles the unsearchable riches of Christ, and to bring to light for everyone what is the plan of the mystery hidden for ages in God, who created all things, so that through the church the manifold wisdom of God might now be made known to the rulers and authorities in the heavenly places. This was according to the eternal purpose that he has realized in Christ Jesus our Lord. (Ephesians 3:8–11)

So for all eternity, this demonstration of God's grace to an undeserving people will be displayed continually as Christ reigns. Jesus Christ loved his bride so much that he sanctifies and cleanses her through the word so that he can present her to himself a glorious church, without spot or wrinkle. He <u>will</u> make her holy and without blemish (Ephesians 5:26-27). I know I repeat myself, but this is the reason the world exists. This is why *we* exist! But what happens before that? How do we get from this life to that life?

There is death, then a resurrection, then a judgment.

> And just as it is appointed for man to die once, and after that comes judgment. (Hebrews 9:27)

Before the judgment, there will be a resurrection of both the just and the unjust (Acts 24:15). Daniel also has written, "*And many of those who sleep in the dust of the earth shall awake, some to everlasting life, and some to shame and everlasting contempt*" (Daniel 12:2). The resurrection of the just is called the first resurrection (See Revelation 20:6). We know there is going to be an order to this resurrection: first is Christ, of course, and then those who belong to him.

> For as in Adam all die, so also in Christ shall all be made alive. But each in his own order: Christ the firstfruits, then at his coming those who belong to Christ. (1 Corinthians 15:22–23)

We also know that there will be an order for those who belong to Christ. Those who have died will rise first, and then, followers of Christ who are still alive will be caught up with them to meet the Lord in the air.

> For the Lord himself will descend from heaven with a cry of command, with the voice of an archangel, and with the sound of the trumpet of God. And the dead in Christ will rise first. Then we who are alive, who are left, will be caught up together with them in the clouds to meet the Lord in the air, and so we will always be with the Lord. (1 Thessalonians 4:16–17)

Colossians 3:4 tells us that when Christ who is our life appears, then we will also appear with him in glory. First Thessalonians 3:13 says that Christ is coming with his saints. There will be a grand reunion of Jesus Christ with all his people when he returns.

We know that there is a connection between the earthly body that we have had during our life here, and the spiritual body that we will receive, because we are told that those in the grave will hear his voice and come out (John 5:28).

Paul writes to the Corinthians:

> And what you sow is not the body that is to be, but a bare kernel, perhaps of wheat or of some other grain. So is it with the resurrection of the dead. What is sown is perishable; what is raised is imperishable. It is sown in dishonor; it is raised in glory. It is sown in weakness; it is raised in power. It is sown a natural body; it is raised a spiritual body. If there is a natural body, there is also a spiritual body. (1 Corinthians 15:37, 42–44)

The body is sown a natural body, one that is corrupted. Then it is raised a spiritual body. That doesn't mean it is ghost-like. It means it is raised a body fit for the dwelling of the Spirit. Christ himself will transform our lowly body to be like his glorious body (Philippians 3:21). And we know that Christ's body was made of flesh and bones and could eat (Luke 24:39), and so that is the kind of body we will have. There will be things to eat in the resurrected life, after all, for we read, *"On either side of the river [of life], the tree of life with its twelve kinds of fruit, yielding its fruit each month"* (Revelation 22:2).

We are told that from that point on his people will always be with him. From that moment when the bridegroom comes for his precious bride, through the wedding supper, the judgment of the lost, and the reigning in the kingdom, we will be with the Lord!

Jesus told the disciples in John 14:1-3:

> Let not your hearts be troubled. Believe in God; believe also in me. In my Father's house are many rooms. If it were not so, would I have told you that I go to prepare a place for you? And if I go and prepare a place for you, I will come again and will take you to myself, that where I am you may be also.

Jesus was looking forward to the day when his followers would be with him. Even in his prayer in John 17, Jesus said:

> Father, I desire that they also, whom you have given me, may be with me where I am, to see my glory that you have given me because you loved me before the foundation of the world. (John 17:24)

But there will be a judgment for everyone as well. We have already read Hebrews 9:27: *"And just as it is appointed for man to die once, and after that comes judgment."*

> For we must **all** appear before the judgment seat of Christ, so that each one may receive what is due for what he has done in the body, whether good or evil. (2 Corinthians 5:10, emphasis added.)

> When the Son of Man comes in his glory, and all the angels with him, then he will sit on his glorious throne. Before him will be gathered all the nations, and he will separate people one from another as a shepherd separates the sheep from the goats. And he will place the sheep on his right, but the goats on the left. Then the King will say to those on his right, "Come, you who are blessed by my Father, inherit the kingdom prepared for you from the foundation of the world." Then he will say to those on his left, "Depart from me, you cursed, into the eternal fire prepared for the devil and his angels." And these will go away into eternal punishment, but the righteous into eternal life. (Matthew 25:31–34, 41, 46)

Consider the plight of those who are lost:

> Since indeed God considers it just to repay with affliction those who afflict you, and to grant relief to you who are afflicted as well as to us, when the Lord Jesus is revealed from heaven with his mighty angels in flaming fire, inflicting vengeance on those who do not know God and on those who do not obey the gospel of our Lord Jesus. They will suffer the punishment of eternal destruction, away from the presence of the Lord and from the glory of his might, when he comes on that day to be glorified in his saints, and to be marveled at among all who have believed, because our testimony to you was believed. (2 Thessalonians 1:6–10)

We learn from this passage that the Lord is coming back in the future with judgment as his main intent. God has "suffered the neglect, derision, and disbelief of millions of people who have refused to believe the Gospel. They were born in sin, as everyone is, and continued to live lives of sin and disobedience to God. Throughout all their lives they have shown themselves to be in agreement with Adam and his defiance of God's moral law and character. God was under no obligation to save them earlier, and he is certainly not under any obligation to do so as he comes to bring judgment to the earth.

We are told in this passage that they did not know God. Even with all the natural wonders to see around them, and God's written Word available, they still did not know or acknowledge him. Isn't this what Paul teaches us in Romans 1:18-21? He tells us that what can be known of God is made plain to people through God's creation, but they have suppressed it. In addition, he tells us that they did not obey his gospel. God never intended anyone to be perfect or righteous to be saved. He simply holds out the message that if someone puts his trust in Christ, believing that his death on the cross was the payment for our sins, he would be saved. Very few are willing to bow their knee and admit that they are in need of a savior. For those in this position, God has promised everlasting destruction and complete separation from the glory of God. On that day, when God comes to be glorified in his saints, those who have not received him as savior will be shut out. All those who have believed will stand in awe as they watch the events unfold. They will see the vindication of all the persecution and ridicule that has been hurled at the people of God through the centuries. As these things take place there will come the horrible realization among the lost that they are lost forever. Notice, too, that this will happen on the day Christ comes to be glorified in his saints. This day is the focus of our discussion in this book. We were created to bring glory to God on that day.

We have no idea what that day of judgment will be like. We do know who the judge will be. Jesus says in John 5:22, "*For the Father judges no one, but has given all judgment to the Son.*" This is explained further in verse 27 where Jesus explains, "*And he has given him authority to execute judgment, because he is the Son of Man.*" Paul tells the pagan philosophers in Athens that God has "*fixed a day on which he will judge the world in righteousness by a <u>man</u> whom he has appointed; and of this he has given assurance to all by raising him from the dead*" (Acts 17:31, emphasis added). We are human beings, and we are going to all be judged by a human being, Jesus Christ.

Peter points out the utter inevitability of the day of judgment. He reminds us in 2 Peter 2:4 that God did not spare angels when they sinned; he did not spare the ancient world, but sent a flood. During that flood he saved only eight people. Eight people! He condemned the cities of Sodom and Gomorrah and yet spared Lot. If God did all this, he is able and willing to do it again. In verse 9, he tells us that he will rescue the godly from the judgment, but will hold the unrighteous in custody for the day of judgment, and will continue punishing them while holding them.

Everything was created by the word of God, and Peter tells us, "*But by the same word the heavens and earth that now exist are stored up for fire, being kept until the day of judgment and destruction of the ungodly*" (2 Peter 3:7).

God is a God of love, but he is also a just God. To be consistent with his character, he must punish the system which is against his rule, and he must also punish those who refused to be a part of his reign. The heavens and earth that we see around us are reserved. If you have a reserved seat at a ball game, that means that seat is set aside specifically for your use. It is waiting for you to come and sit in it. In the same way, the heavens and earth are reserved for the day in which God will destroy them by fire. We wonder what God is doing these days. From this passage, we know that all you see around you has been placed in reserve for <u>that</u> day.

Verse 10 of 2 Peter 3 tells us that the earth and everything in it will be destroyed. God is not going to preserve any of it. He is not going to preserve any of our architecture or art. He will not preserve any of our literature or inventions. Gone will be the Mona

Lisa, the Eiffel Tower, the Sears Tower, the St. Louis arch, computers, *Gone With the Wind*, iPhones, etc. Compared to God's work, none of it will be worth saving. All the time that we put into these things will be forgotten (Isaiah 65:17). On that day it will all be gone.

Peter asks the question, "*Since everything will be destroyed in this way, what kind of people ought you to be?*" It all comes down to a very personal question, doesn't it? There is a purpose to life, but it is not found in all the things we have and see. The purpose is in our relationship to the God who made all this and will take it all away when his purposes have been fulfilled.

Peter answers his own question: "*You ought to live holy and godly lives as you look forward to the day of God and speed its coming*" (verses 11-12). God wants a holy and godly people. Remember, he told us that his children are a chosen race, a royal priesthood, and a holy nation. He is purifying a people for himself (Titus 2:14). A godly life is a life as God would live it. He wants his character portrayed in hundreds and thousands, even millions of lives that declare the praises of him who called us out of darkness into his marvelous light (1 Peter 2:9).

There is a wedding day coming!

There is death and there is resurrection. Then, as we have seen, comes the judgment. Jesus says there is a "resurrection of life," and a "resurrection of damnation" (John 5:29). But for those who have been saved and justified by Christ, there is also a wedding day coming.

> Then I heard what seemed to be the voice of a great multitude, like the roar of many waters and like the sound of mighty peals of thunder, crying out, "Hallelujah! For the Lord our God the Almighty reigns. Let us rejoice and exult and give him the glory, for the marriage of the Lamb has come, and his Bride has made herself ready; it was granted her to clothe herself with fine linen, bright and pure"— for the fine linen is the righteous deeds of the saints. And the angel said to me, "Write this: Blessed are

those who are invited to the marriage supper of the Lamb." And he said to me, "These are the true words of God." (Revelation 19:6–9)

The bride, the church, has made herself ready. The groom is Jesus Christ, and there are guests who are invited to the wedding feast. We can see that this is a great celebration and the focus of a great deal of attention. History is coming together in one amazing ceremony and feast. And both the bride and the groom are eagerly looking forward to that day.

Jesus Christ, the bridegroom, will be given a kingdom, and his people will reign with him.

> Then the seventh angel blew his trumpet, and there were loud voices in heaven, saying, "The kingdom of the world has become the kingdom of our Lord and of his Christ, and he shall reign forever and ever." (Revelation 11:15)

Christ is the king, and on that day, the kingdoms of this world will come under his direct rule and reign. He is counted worthy of reigning because he gave his blood to ransom people to himself. These people will come from every tribe and language and people and nation. There are no words to describe the glorious culmination of history portrayed in this scene. And the amazing thing is that his bride is going to reign with him!

> And they sang a new song, saying, "Worthy are you to take the scroll and to open its seals, for you were slain, and by your blood you ransomed people for God from every tribe and language and people and nation, and you have made them a kingdom and priests to our God, and they shall reign on the earth." (Revelation 5:9–10)

> Then I saw thrones, and seated on them were those to whom the authority to judge was committed. Also I saw the souls of those who had been beheaded for the testimony of Jesus and for the word of God, and those who had not worshiped the beast or its image and had not received its mark on their

foreheads or their hands. They came to life and reigned with
Christ for a thousand years. (Revelation 20:4)

Blessed and holy is the one who shares in the first resurrection!
Over such the second death has no power, but they will be
priests of God and of Christ, and they will reign with him for a
thousand years. (Revelation 20:6)

As the bride of Christ, the church will have the blessed privilege
of being with Christ and ruling and reigning with him. Christ will
rule over the kingdom which God has been planning for him down
through the centuries. God promised a seed to Abraham that
would bless the entire world. God promised a descendant to David
who would sit on his throne, and would rule from that throne
forever. This is the one who was promised by Isaiah the prophet
when he said:

For to us a child is born, to us a son is given; and the
government shall be upon his shoulder, and his name shall be
called Wonderful Counselor, Mighty God, Everlasting Father,
Prince of Peace. Of the increase of his government and of
peace there will be no end, on the throne of David and over his
kingdom, to establish it and to uphold it with justice and with
righteousness from this time forth and forevermore. (Isaiah
9:6–7)

The wise men, who came to see Jesus after his birth, knew he
would be a king. Even King Herod knew. The prophets of the day
were even able to tell where this king would be born. The kingdom
belongs to him. And, before he is officially granted the kingdom
and installed as king, he will take his bride. All history has been
targeted toward this one event, and all the principalities and powers
will see the glory of the mercy and grace of God who took fallen
sinners and turned them into a bride for Christ.

There will be a new heaven and a new earth.

Peter says, *"But according to his promise we are waiting for new heavens
and a new earth in which righteousness dwells"* (2 Peter 3:13). There is

coming a day when the present order of things will be overthrown. Those who have maintained their rebellion against God will be thrown into the lake of fire to suffer forever. *"And if anyone's name was not found written in the book of life, he was thrown into the lake of fire"* (Revelation 20:15). But as Peter said, we are looking forward to a new heaven and a new earth.

John says this about the new heaven and the new earth:

> Then I saw a new heaven and a new earth, for the first heaven and the first earth had passed away, and the sea was no more. And I saw the holy city, new Jerusalem, coming down out of heaven from God, prepared as a bride adorned for her husband. And I heard a loud voice from the throne saying, "Behold, the dwelling place of God is with man. He will dwell with them, and they will be his people, and God himself will be with them as their God." (Revelation 21:1–3)

Those whom God has called will live in the new heaven and the new earth, there to enjoy the presence of God, and to glorify him forever. God will wipe away every tear. There will be no more sorrow or death. There will be abundant joy and exuberant life. And the Bible tells us that the tabernacle of God will be with men, and he will dwell with them. God wants to dwell with his people. He has had this for his goal from creation onward. He wanted to be with Adam in the garden. He lived among the Israelites as they traveled through the wilderness. He lived in the temple in Jerusalem for a time. Then Christ came and now dwells in his people. And finally, forever he will live and reign with the people he has called to himself from every people, tongue, tribe, and nation. Forever they will glorify him who rescued them and will testify of his goodness and grace to the amazement of all onlookers. There is a purpose to it all. Where will it all end? It won't! Will you be a part of it?

What in the World is God Doing?

Worthy is the Lamb who was slain,
to receive power and wealth and wisdom and might
and honor and glory and blessing!

And they sang a new song, saying,
"Worthy are you ... for you were slain,
and by your blood you ransomed people for God
from every tribe and language and people and nation,
and you have made them a kingdom
and priests to our God,
and they shall reign on the earth."

The kingdom of the world has become
the kingdom of our Lord and of his Christ,
and he shall reign forever and ever.

We give thanks to you, Lord God Almighty,
who is and who was,
for you have taken your great power
and begun to reign.

Hallelujah!
for the Lord our God the Almighty reigns.

Let us rejoice and exult and give him the glory,
for the marriage of the Lamb has come,
and his Bride has made herself ready.

Behold, the dwelling place of God
is with man.
He will dwell with them,
and they will be his people,
and God himself will be with them as their God.

Where Will it All End?

He will wipe away every tear
from their eyes,
and death shall be no more,
neither shall there be mourning,
nor crying, nor pain anymore,
for the former things have passed away.

"I am the Alpha and the Omega,"
says the Lord God,
"who is and who was and who is to come,
The Almighty."

"It is done!"

(Scripture quotes taken from Revelation 1:8; Revelation 5:9-12;
Revelation 11:15, 17; Revelation 19:6-8; Revelation 21:3-6;
Revelation 22:13)

Made in the USA
Monee, IL
19 February 2022